THE

PROGRESS AND PRESENT STATE OF

BRITISH INDIA

THE

PROGRESS AND PRESENT STATE OF BRITISH INDIA.

A MANUAL FOR GENERAL USE,

BASED ON OFFICIAL DOCUMENTS, FURNISHED UNDER THE AUTHORITY OF HER MAJESTY'S SECRETARY OF STATE FOR INDIA.

BY

MONTGOMERY MARTIN

GYAN

Published by

Gyan Publishing House
5, Ansari Road
Daryaganj, New Delhi-110002
Phone: 011-47034999, 9811692060
E-mail: books@gyanbooks.com

Distribution Network
gyanbooks.com
India, USA, Canada, UK, Australia, France

ISBN: 978-81-212-8246-8 (PB)
First Published, 1862

2nd Impression 2023

Printed at: Gyan Press, Delhi.

THE PROGRESS AND PRESENT STATE OF BRITISH INDIA
Author: MONTGOMERY MARTIN

BRITISH INDIA;

ITS

RECENT PROGRESS AND PRESENT STATE.

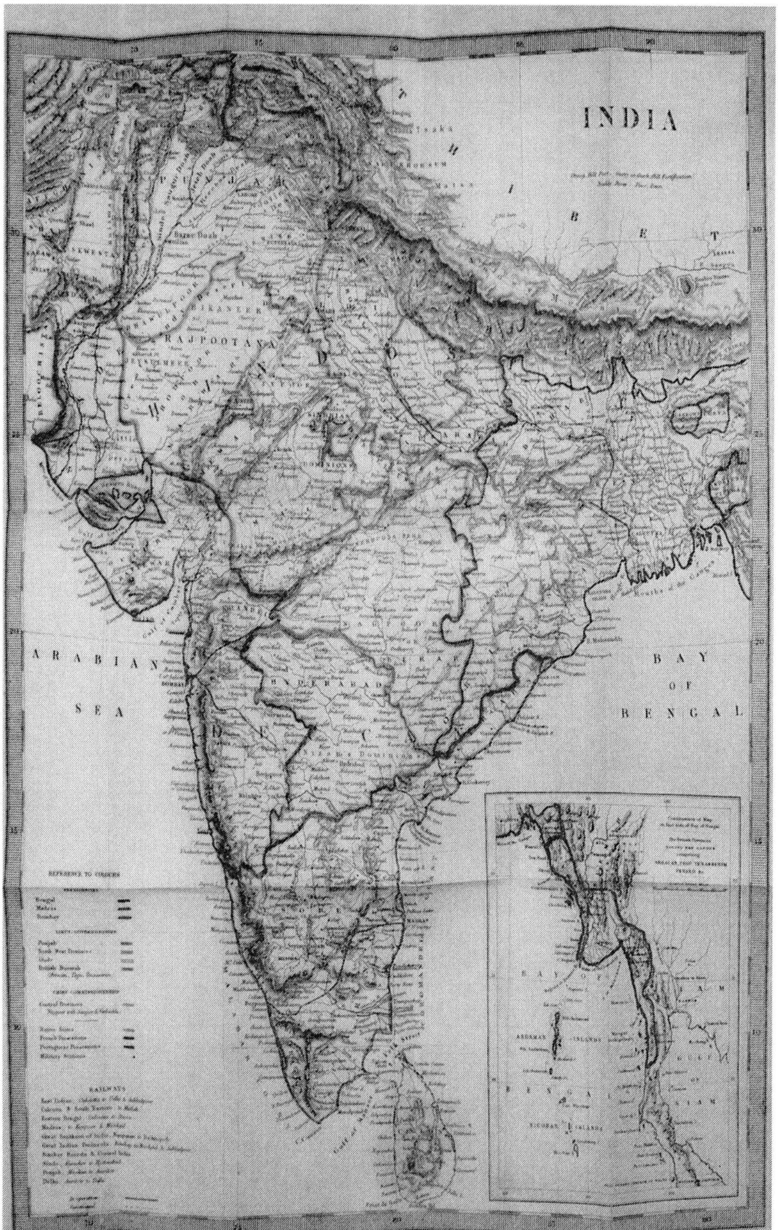
INDIA
T H I B E T
PUNJAB
RAJPOOTANA
BIKANEER
HYDERABAD
ARABIAN
SEA
BAY
OF
BENGAL
REFERENCE TO COLOURS
RAILWAYS
ANDAMAN ISLANDS
NICOBAR ISLANDS
SIAM
Mouths of the Ganges

THE

PROGRESS AND PRESENT STATE

OF

BRITISH INDIA.

A MANUAL FOR GENERAL USE,

BASED ON OFFICIAL DOCUMENTS, FURNISHED UNDER THE AUTHORITY OF HER MAJESTY'S SECRETARY OF STATE FOR INDIA.

BY

MONTGOMERY MARTIN,

AUTHOR OF 'HISTORY OF THE BRITISH COLONIES,' 'INDIAN EMPIRE,' 'CHINA,' ETC.

LONDON:

SAMPSON LOW, SON, & CO., 47, LUDGATE HILL.

1862.

CONTENTS.

TABLES.

ERRATA.

Chap. I. p. 3, *read* "The Khiljis *and House of Toghlak*—A.D. 1288 to 1412."
,, p. 7, *read* "Fort St. David," *not* "St. David's."
,, p. 16, *read* "the Carnatic, *half of Oude*, and the city of Surat."
,, p. 30, *read* "*Sattara*," *not* "Cattara."
,, III. p. 161, *read* "Jhansi," *not* "Jhansie."
,, IV. p. 203, *read* "Sudder Mofussil (or Country) Courts."

INTRODUCTION.

THE present state of India is a question which materially affects every class of the British community; the statesman, the merchant, the artisan, the Christian philanthropist, have each distinctive points of view from which the subject is one of deep interest. The political standing of Britain among the kingdoms of Europe will be strengthened by the successful administration of India, and general and individual wealth increased thereby; while failure must lower her military and maritime position and depress her trade and manufactures; in either case there remains the same solemn responsibility to the Source of all Power, to whom nations and individuals are alike accountable for their measures and their motives. Moreover, there exists a general desire to obtain authentic information on the actual condition of India, now that the ship of the State has righted after the calamitous tempest of 1857-58. Sufficient time has elapsed since then to show the manner in which the Ministers of the Crown are exercising the powers formerly delegated to the East India Company, and to enable their chief measures to take effect, or produce at least some result. The following pages are intended to offer a digest of the principal facts that mark the present condition of India, and which, possibly, the reader may be the better enabled to appreciate, for being heralded by a brief chronological summary of the chief events in the long roll of centuries which have passed since Hindoostan was first noticed by European writers.

The records of history afford no parallel to the British dominion in the East. The subjection of one hundred and sixty million of people to the British Crown, and the dependence of forty million on its protection, is a fact calculated to astonish the most unthinking minds, and awaken serious considerations in those who look beyond the present moment, and speculate on the future position of Great Britain among the nations of the earth. So long as India with its swarming myriads was viewed as the property of a mercantile corporation, and termed in parliamentary documents "the dominions of the East India Company," the people of England took little interest in the subject; they viewed it as a distant land with an unhealthy climate, where men went to acquire fortunes in a few years by some means or another, and then returned home to purchase estates, live in splendour, and send their sons and nephews forth to gather fresh fruit from the "pagoda-tree." But that train of thought has had its day; the fiction of the "E. I. Company's dominions" has been roughly swept away. We have been brought face to face with the truth, that for weal or for woe England has become identified with Hindoostan. The public debt of

India of one hundred and twenty-five million sterling was borrowed chiefly from English capitalists; also the fifty million invested in Indian railways, on a guaranteed interest at the rate of five per cent. per annum, secured on the Indian revenues: besides which twenty million sterling have been embarked by Englishmen in banks and joint-stock mercantile associations. Thus, the forcible separation of Hindoostan from Britain would involve the loss of about two hundred million pounds sterling.

Irrespective of political and financial considerations, there are other bonds of union. The large Anglo-Indian commerce is increasing yearly, and admits of almost indefinite extension. The two countries stand in the advantageous relation of cultivator of the raw materials, and consumer of the manufactured articles; and the markets of the world are open for their joint productions. There is another question for reflection: India is a tributary to England, into which she has poured vast wealth for a century. There is scarcely a county in which Indian gold has not been invested. For a long period the drain on India was never less than three million sterling per annum; for more than a quarter of a century it ranged from four to six million, and it is now estimated at ten million pounds per annum. This large addition to the fructifying capital of Britain is obtained without any cost or sacrifice. India defrays all the charges of her government at home and abroad, including the heavy item of military protection; on which account two hundred thousand well-trained troops are maintained, and are available for service in any part of the East.

It is no small advantage to England that her educated middle classes, whose numbers are rapidly increasing, find in India scope for honourable ambition and personal enterprise, with remunerative employment for skill and industry.

Another point remains to be noticed: a large fund accrues annually in Great Britain and Ireland from the unspent surplus of private incomes. This has been variously estimated at from twenty to thirty million sterling, and is ever seeking a fair rate of interest. Millions of these savings have been lost in South American, Spanish and other loans, and in bubble or fraudulent enterprises. It is of the highest importance that safe investment be available for this capital, which is otherwise wasted and lost, to the injury of the national resources. India for many years would absorb all the spare money of England, which would be safe under good government, and yield a fair return. But on the question of good government everything hinges. We must not again forget that if the possession of India be fraught with many benefits, it is also attended with peril and responsibility. While accepting the one we cannot escape the other.

Circumstances have at length led (or driven) us into the right path; just principles are being brought into action; and the old system of oppression and exaction appears to be doomed. Never had a nation a clearer opportunity than is now presented to England, in which all the interest lies in doing that which is right, and where nothing but injury can result from doing wrong.

I have faith in the reality of Christian doctrines; that their practice brings wisdom unto rulers; and that without such teaching all human policy and statecraft is folly. There has been much talk of evangelising India; but the justice, the mercy, the charity, the unselfishness which lies at the base, and is the very core of a Christian government, have until recently been wanting. Happily the exercise of these qualities is being understood as not antagonistic to, but inseparable from, successful administration; and there is reason to hope that Parliament and public opinion are learning to recognise the primary duty and even the political expediency of *Justice to India.*

BRITISH INDIA.

CHAPTER I.

HISTORICAL SKETCH.*

THE earliest information obtained in Europe of the condition of India was derived from the narratives of Greek historians regarding—

The Macedonian Invasion.—B.C. 327 to 325.

Alexander crossed the Indus, at Attock, by a bridge of boats. After overcoming the resistance offered by a Hindoo prince, bearing the family name of Porus, whose capital was Canouj, on the Ganges, the Macedonian monarch penetrated as far as the junction of the Beas with the Sutlej. His army would proceed no further, and he was compelled to retire. A fleet under Nearchus sailed from the Indus on a voyage of discovery to the Persian Gulf, while Alexander marched homewards through Beloochistan, along the coast where, according to tradition, the Assyrian invaders of India under Semiramis, and the Persians under Cyrus, had perished almost to a man.

This expedition was followed by a rapid increase of commerce, the products and manufactures of India being exchanged for the coined gold and silver of Europe, but of

* The authorities for this Historical Sketch will be found in the History of India, from the Invasion of Alexander to the Close of the Mutiny and Rebellion in 1859, given in the 'Indian Empire,' vols. i. and ii., by the author of the present work.

the internal history of the country little is known until Moslem writers recount the

Conquests of the Arab Empire.—A.D. 664 to 750.

The first Mohammedan invaders appeared at Mooltan in 664. In 711, Sinde was occupied by the troops of the Caliph Walid; but the Arabs made no further conquests, and were expelled from Sinde in 750 by the Rajpoot tribe of Sumera. No incursions were made into India by the Mohammedans for the next two hundred and fifty years, and very little is known of the history of India during that period.

House of Ghuznee.—A.D. 1001 to 1167.

The first permanent establishment of Mohammedan power in India was made by Sultan Mahmood, the ruler of a small, newly-founded state, called Ghuznee, after its capital, situated in the heart of the Suliman mountains. Mahmood made numerous expeditions into India in the years 1001 to 1025, captured Delhi, Canouj, and other chief cities, and in his character of an iconoclast destroyed many Hindoo temples, carrying off among his booty the famous sandal-wood gates of the temple of Somnauth in Guzerat, which eight hundred years later were taken by British troops from Ghuznee, and replaced at Somnauth by order of the Governor-General, Lord Ellenborough.

The Punjab, from its vicinity to Ghuznee, was placed under a regular Mohammedan administration; and about the commencement of the eleventh century the seat of government was changed from Ghuznee to Lahore, the capital of the Punjab. The House of Ghuznee became extinct in 1186; but another Mohammedan dynasty (the House of Ghor) took possession of the Punjab, and from that period Mohammedan power marched on in India with steady aggression, the Hindoo principalities falling one by one, each after a desperate struggle, until only a few preserved their independence either in Hindoostan Proper—that is, India north of the Vindhya mountains and the Nerbudda; or in the Deccan—the country south of that range and river.

It was not, however, a single dynasty, but many different and co-existent sovereignties, which effected, in the course of centuries, the Mohammedan conquest of India.

Slave Kings of Delhi.—A.D. 1206 to 1288.

Shahab-oo-deen, the last of the Ghor princes, conquered Delhi, and placed it in charge of Kootb-oo-Deen a Turki slave, who, when his patron was slain by the Gukkurs, assumed sovereign power.

Altamsh succeeded to the throne in 1211, and reduced the greater part of Hindoostan Proper. During his reign Sinde and Mooltan were ravaged by the fierce Mogul, Ghengis Khan.

The Khiljis.—A.D. 1288 to 1412.

A Tartar tribe, long settled among the Afghans, gave kings to Delhi from 1288 to 1321, when the *House of Toghlak* was founded by the governor of the Punjab, who was the son of a Turki slave by an Indian mother. The reign of the last of the Toghlak kings was marked by the invasion of Timur the Tartar or Tamerlane, who sacked and 'looted' Delhi, in 1397, massacred an immense number of its inhabitants, and carried off a multitude of men and women into slavery. Timur caused himself to be proclaimed Emperor of India, but took permanent possession of the Punjab only.

The House of Lodi.—A.D. 1412 to 1526.

A Patan dynasty ruled Delhi from 1412 to 1421, when the succession was interrupted by three brothers, Seyeds (or descendants of Mohammed), but reverted to Behlol Lodi in 1450, and remained in his family until it was seized by Baber, the virtual founder of the long and brilliant line of Padshahs or Emperors, the last of whom, expelled from Delhi in 1858, yet lingers in exile in Tonghoo.

The Great Moguls or House of Timur.—A.D. 1526 to 1707.

Baber, after ruling Cabool for twenty-two years, invaded Hindoostan, of which he claimed possession in right of his ancestor Timur; and, having seized on Delhi, Agra, and other cities, employed himself in consolidating his usurped dominions until his death in 1530. Humayun, his son and successor, was driven into exile, in 1542, by Patan or Afghan chiefs. After a series of vicissitudes and romantic adventures Humayun regained possession of the throne in 1555; but died from a fall on the terrace of the Delhi palace, in 1556, and was succeeded by his only child, the famous Akber, who reigned for nearly half a century, being nearly the whole time contemporary with Queen Elizabeth.

Jehangeer, the son of Akber by a Rajpoot princess, ascended the throne in 1605, and was succeeded in 1627 by his son Shah Jehan, who was also of Hindoo descent by his mother's side.

Aurungzebe usurped the imperial authority in 1658, imprisoning his father, and slaying his brothers. During his long reign the Mogul empire reached and passed its culminating point of greatness and prosperity. He destroyed the last of the independent Mohammedan kingdoms in the Deccan, and alienated the affections of the Hindoos, by a spirit of bigotry which contrasted forcibly with the tolerance which characterised the other Indian princes of his house. The Rajpoots, Seiks and Jâts revolted against him in Hindoostan. In Southern India the Mahrattas, under their chief Sevajee, formed themselves into a powerful state; and Aurungzebe, in his last campaign against them, in extreme old age, narrowly escaped dying their prisoner.

From this period, 1707, the empire rapidly fell to decay, and the various provinces were erected into independent states by usurping governors, or fought for by Hindoo or Mohammedan adventurers, whose claims, however founded,

State of British India, in the Year 1859-60.*

To face p. v.

Presidencies or Provinces under British Administration.	Area in Square Miles.	Population.	Number to each Square Mile.	Gross Revenues.	Taxation per Head.	Military Strength.		Police Force.	Maritime Commerce with all Foreign or External Ports.			Shipping and Tonnage with all Foreign or External Ports.			
									Merchandise and Treasure.			Arrivals.		Departures.	
						Europeans.	Natives.		Imports.	Exports.	Total.	Number of Ships.	Tonnage.	Number of Ships.	Tonnage.
				£.	s. d.	Number.	Number.	Number.	£.	£.	£.				
Bengal, Behar, &c. ..	280,200	41,498,608	148	12,803,214	6 2	7,977	9,379	23,468	20,251,377	12,516,429	32,767,806	751	534,862	870	631,963
North-West Provinces ..	116,493	30,110,097	258	5,705,691	3 9	13,568	13,085	24,616							
Punjab, including Delhi	100,406	14,794,611	147	3,064,733	4 1	18,296	22,113	24,991			Inland Provinces				
Madras	128,551	23,127,855	180	6,550,980	5 8	6,157	22,869	22,500	3,000,846	2,492,156	5,493,002	2,011	310,090	2,889	412,166
Bombay	83,340	10,141,918	121	6,821,964	13 5	11,749	23,519	18,200	9,534,781	13,388,013	22,922,794†	882	393,972	830	423,218
Sinde	54,403	1,795,594	33	455,700	5 0	1,524	3,978	4,244	368,878	105,261	474,139	223	41,159	182	28,872
Territories under the immediate control of the government of India;—															
Oude	27,890	8,071,075	289	1,255,978	3 1	5,518	2,722	8,640							
Berar or Nagpoor ..	71,834	4,343,163	60	417,866	1 11	1,659	3,407	6,561			Inland Provinces				
Hydrabad assigned Districts	16,566	1,100,328	66	296,172	5 4	3,989	4,077	2,256							
Pegu	32,451	1,024,885	31	497,532	9 8	2,231	6,824	5,111	395,936	118,389	514,325	93	34,830	113	40,019
Tenasserim and Martaban	34,838	333,833	9	109,217	6 6	238	3,052	1,100	70,285	268,960	339,245	130	37,289	143	51,149
Coorg	2,116	118,464	56	26,368	4 5	..		no returns							
Bairseah	456	not known	..	8,875	..	..		no returns			Inland Provinces				
Mysore	27,000	3,822,053	141	958,460	5 0	2,507	4,795	not given							
Total	976,547	140,282,484	144	38,972,750	5 6	75,413	119,820	‡141,687	33,622,103	28,889,208	62,511,311	4,090	1,352,202	5,027	1,587,387
Other Native States under the government of India	190,135	16,173,209	85												
Total	1,166,682	156,455,693	134												
Add to gross revenues, receipts from other sources, against which area and population cannot be shown				607,176		1,673	9,011	Military in other parts of India.							
Total revenues of India .. .. £				39,579,926		77,086	128,831	Total Military in India.							

* No complete returns in England of a later date.

† Commerce of Bombay for the Year 1860-61: imports, 18,626,301*l.*; exports, 19,480,039*l.*; total, 38,106,340*l.*

‡ The figures under column of Police show an approximate of what the force was in 1859. At present the Police system in India is being thoroughly and completely reorganised.

were usually decided by the sword. Such was the state of India when the East India Company took those first steps, which have ended in placing the sceptre of a mightier empire than any Mogul ever ruled in the hand of the Queen of England.

Portuguese and Dutch Settlements in India.
A.D. 1497 to 1600.

Previous to the discovery of the mariner's compass in 1497, the Venetians and Genoese were the most extensive traders with the East of the European nations. The Portuguese monopolised the commerce for the greater part of the next hundred years, and employed the Dutch as carriers; but when war broke out between the two nations the Dutch proved the stronger, and supplanted the Portuguese in their Indian trade and chief settlements.

Origin and Proceedings of English East India Company.
A.D. 1600 to 1698.

On the closing day of the sixteenth century Queen Elizabeth signed the original charter of the East India Company, and in 1602 their first ships appeared in the Indian seas.

In 1615 Sir Thomas Roe arrived at the court of Jehangeer, and after long delay obtained certain trading privileges for the Company. An independent Hindoo prince, the Zamorin of Calicut, had already protected them in the formation of factories on the Malabar coast, and these were all placed under the control of the Presidency established at Surat.

In 1625 a piece of ground was obtained at Armegaun, from the Naig or local chief, and a factory built thereon, which in 1628 was described as being defended by twelve pieces of cannon, and twenty-eight factors and soldiers. In 1640 the factory was removed to Madras, where Fort St. George was erected by permission of the Hindoo sovereign of the country, a petty prince of ancient descent, the Rajah of Chandragiri. In 1653 Madras was raised to the rank of a Presidency. About the same time a licence to trade throughout the Mogul Empire, without payment of custom dues except at Surat, was granted to the Company by Shah Jehan, at the request of Mr. Boughton a surgeon of one of the East Indiamen, in return for medical service rendered to the Emperor's favourite daughter. Factories were immediately established at Hooghly and other places in Bengal.

In 1668 the Island of Bombay, which had been given to Charles the Second as the dowry of the Infanta of Portugal, was transferred by the King to the Company, and in 1684 the seat of government was removed there from Surat. In 1698 the English obtained leave from Prince Azim, one of the grandsons of Aurungzebe, who commanded the Mogul army in Bengal, to purchase the territory on which Calcutta now stands, and to exercise justiciary authority over the English and Native inhabitants.

The Persian Invasion.—A.D. 1738.

The Persian invasion under Nadir Shah hastened the ruin of the Mogul Empire. He sacked Delhi, and is said to have slaughtered thirty thousand of its inhabitants and carried off thirty millions in money, besides bullion and jewels, wrung from the people by torture. Cabool and Sinde were annexed to Persia. The ravages of the Persians were confined to Hindoostan, and their departure was hastened by fear of the Mahrattas then ably ruled by Bajee Rao, the second of the usurping Peishwas or First Ministers who governed at Poona in the name of the descendants of Sevajee, who lived as titular sovereigns at Sattara. At this time Bajee Rao and his commanders, Puar, Holcar and Sindia, who after his death founded principalities, exacted a part of the revenues under the name of Chout or Surdeshmooki (a fourth or a tenth) from almost every state in India. Ali Verdi Khan, the Mogul governor of Bengal, resisted their demands, and as a means of defence against the common enemy, permitted the English to form a trench round Calcutta, seven miles in extent, which still bears the name of the Mahratta ditch.

General History.—A.D. 1745 to 1761.

The declaration of war between England and France gave rise to hostilities in the Madras Presidency; but tranquillity was preserved in Bengal by the determination of Ali Verdi Khan.

The Peace of Aix-la-Chapelle, in 1748, took away the pretext for war between the rival Companies in India; but the quarrels of native princes offered remunerative employment for their troops, and by taking part with different candidates for the sovereignty of the Carnatic, the French and English were brought into hostility with each other. The French first raised native levies and disciplined them at Pondicherry in the European manner. The English followed their example, and in the successful defence of Arcot by Clive in 1751, the sepoys manifested extraordinary courage and devotion. Up to this time the French had been in the ascendant, but thenceforward the English gained increasing advantage, until in 1754 Dupleix, the French Governor-General, was recalled in disgrace, and a treaty of peace concluded, which left Mohammed Ali, the English candidate, Nabob of the Carnatic.

The war which ruined Dupleix made the fortune of Clive, who had come to India as a "writer" or clerk, and had, in common with other factors and agents, been compelled to lay down the pen and handle the musket in defence of the Company's goods. The military abilities of Clive gained him a commission and rapid promotion. He was governor of Fort St. David's (Madras) when Surajah Dowlah, having succeeded his grandfather Ali Verdi Khan, as governor or Subahdar of Bengal, besieged and took Calcutta on the 20th June, 1756. In obedience to a hasty general order for their safe keeping, the whole of the captives, one hundred and forty-six in number, were thrust by the guards into the small garrison prison, known as the Black Hole, and in the morning, when an order for their removal came from Surajah Dowlah, only twenty-three survivors crept forth from amid heaps of festering corpses.

The tidings of the fall of Calcutta and the tragedy by which it had been followed, excited the fiercest resentment at Madras. An expedition was fitted out, with Clive in command of the land forces, and Admiral Watson of the naval portion. Calcutta was recovered; Hooghly, the chief port of Surajah Dowlah stormed and sacked, and the war was being carried on by Clive and Watson with great vigour, when tidings of the renewal of hostilities between England and France made it advisable to come to terms with the Subahdar, to prevent his forming an alliance with the French. A large sum was paid by the Subahdar in compensation for the outrages committed at Calcutta, and the correspondence between him and Clive assumed a most confidential tone. Admiral Watson captured Chandernagore, and Clive strove to persuade Surajah Dowlah to co-operate with him in expelling the French from India. But the attempt was fruitless. The Subahdar remembered his grandfather's policy of keeping European rivals in check by using one against the other, and he now strove to temporize in his own feeble fashion by intriguing with both parties.

Clive, who was as complete a master of the art of dissimulation as of war, retaliated by conspiring with Meer Jaffier, the Subahdar's commander-in-chief. The last of a long series of deceptions was played at Plassy, where Clive and the Nabob met in hostile array on the 23rd of June, 1757.

It was for some time doubtful which side Meer Jaffier meant to betray; at length he decided against his master, who seeing himself abandoned by half his army, fled from the field of battle, but was captured and slain by order of Meer Jaffier's son Meeran, who perished shortly afterwards by a stroke of lightning. Meer Jaffier was placed on the musnud of

Bengal by the English, but they were from this time the actual rulers of that province, as well as of Behar and Orissa.

After the downfall of Surajah Dowlah, the French commander, Count Lally, formed an alliance against the English with Hyder Ali, a Mohammedan adventurer, who had usurped the chief authority in the Hindoo state of Mysoor, but the co-operation of Hyder Ali was broken off at a critical moment by occurrences which obliged him to return in all haste to Mysoor. Pondicherry was besieged by Colonel Eyre Coote, captured in January 1761, and its fortifications razed to the ground. Lally returned to France to die on the scaffold; the French Company was soon afterwards abolished, and that nation never acquired territorial importance in India.

While the French and English were struggling for ascendancy in the Carnatic, the Afghans and Mahrattas were fighting for supremacy in Hindoostan. In 1754, Delhi was sacked by the Doorani and other Afghan tribes, under Ahmed the Doorani chief who founded the kingdom of Candahar. In 1759, Ahmed Shah invaded India for the fourth time. The Mahrattas met him on the plains of Paniput, and were defeated with such heavy slaughter that they were unable to regain their previous height of prosperity and power. The conquerors, worn out by a long and harassing campaign, quitted India without attempting to follow up their victory.

Progress of East India Company.—A.D. 1764 to 1773.

The battle of Buxar was fought in 1764 with Shuja Dowlah, the usurping Vizier of Oude. Shuja Dowlah was defeated, and the Mogul Emperor Shah Alum, who had been nominally the master but really the prisoner of the Vizier, placed himself under British protection, and subsequently confirmed the Company in their possession of Bengal, Behar, and Orissa, by conferring on them the Collectorate or perpetual Dewannee of those provinces with a stipulation for the payment by the Company to the Emperor of two hundred and sixty thousand pounds per annum, as a first charge on the revenues of Bengal. The reverence felt throughout India for imperial grants made this arrangement of importance to the East India Company, and the manner in which they repudiated this and other conditions guaranteed to the unfortunate Shah Alum, was quite unjustifiable. The only extenuation is to be found in the financial difficulties which attended the Company throughout its entire career.

The expectations raised by Clive of the prosperity which would follow the territorial acquisitions of the Company, were so far from being fulfilled, that it was found on this and subsequent occasions, that increase of revenue was almost invariably attended with more than commensurate increase of expenditure; the cost of government by Europeans, the growth of a standing army in each Presidency, and other sources of legitimate or illegitimate expense, swallowing up all the anticipated surplus, and leaving nothing for the development of the resources of the country or even for the maintenance of roads, canals, and other public works constructed by Native rulers.

The terrible famine of 1769-70, by which, according to Warren Hastings, Bengal, Behar, and Orissa lost half their inhabitants, created much excitement in England, and the Company were blamed for the misgovernment and extortion which had aggravated if not caused the calamity, and especially for the oppressive measures by which they strove to keep up the revenues. Notwithstanding their involvments, the yearly dividends of the Company from 1766 to 1772 averaged eleven per cent., in the latter year they reached twelve and a half per cent., while the bonded debt of Bengal had increased to one million seven hundred thousand pounds. The Company appealed to Parliament to save them from bankruptcy. The result of a prolonged inquiry was the first direct connexion of the English Government with the management of Indian affairs. By the Regulating Act passed in 1773, a Governor-

General was appointed to preside over Bengal, and exercise a certain control over the Presidencies of Madras and Bombay, which were maintained by the revenues of the Bengal Presidency. The servants of the Crown and of the Company were prohibited, under heavy penalties, from private trading, or receiving gifts from the Natives, and the maximum of the legal rate of interest was fixed at twelve per cent. per annum.

Administration of Warren Hastings.—A.D. 1773 to 1785.

Warren Hastings, the first Governor-General, was already at the head of the Bengal administration when the Regulating Act came into operation, and with it a council of four members, the majority of whom (including Philip Francis, the supposed author of 'Junius') strongly denounced the past measures of Hastings, and especially the Benares Treaty concluded with Shuja Dowlah.

By one article in this treaty, Hastings sold to the Vizier of Oude the provinces of Corah and Allahabad, which rightfully belonged to the Emperor Shah Alum, who was at this time helpless at Delhi in the hands of the Mahrattas; and by another, he hired out British troops for the expulsion of the Rohillas from Rohilcund, of which country Shuja Dowlah coveted possession. The excuse offered for these proceedings was the emptiness of the Company's coffers, but the council did not scruple to accuse Hastings of having replenished his own by the same arrangement. The charge of private interest was also brought against Hastings in connexion with proceedings subsequently adopted by him for relieving the financial embarrassments of the Company, particularly with regard to the tyranny by which the Rajah of Benares was driven to rebellion by the demand of an enormous contribution, and then deposed; and the cruel means adopted to extort money from the Begums of Oude.

But though few attempted to justify Hastings' mode of

obtaining supplies, none could withhold their admiration of the energy with which he overcame some of the greatest dangers, both internal and external, which ever menaced the existence of British power in India. In 1782, he described the Indian administration as burdened with an exhausted treasury; an accumulating debt; a system charged with expensive establishments, and precluded by the multitude of dependents and the curse of patronage from reformation; a government debilitated by the various habits of inveterate licentiousness; a country oppressed by private rapacity; and deprived of its vital resources by the enormous quantities of current specie annually exported in the remittance of private fortunes; by an impoverished commerce and by the entire maintenance of the Presidencies of Madras and Bombay. As the last or greatest of his difficulties, Hastings named "a war actual or depending in every quarter, and with every power of Hindoostan." In fact, the intestine strife, aggression and cupidity of the Madras and Bombay authorities, had led to the formation of a confederacy of Native states, whose sole point of union was enmity to the English.

Hyder Ali and another powerful Mussulman sovereign of the south of India known as the Nizam of the Deccan, had united for the first time with each other and with their mutual foes the Mahrattas. There were many French officers in the Mysoor army, and the renewal of European war opened up to France an opportunity of regaining her power in India at the moment when England had least means of guarding her distant possessions. A French fleet was known to have sailed for the Indian seas. The prospect of the onslaught of Hyder Ali, thus reinforced by Native and European allies, turned the torpor of the Madras authorities into panic. They appealed to Hastings, who acted with equal energy and judgment. He suspended the incapable and venal Governor of Madras, placed the conduct of the war in the hands of the veteran Sir Eyre Coote, drew off the Mahrattas from the confederacy with Hyder Ali, and dispatched troops and treasure with such promptitude that they reached the seat of war before the expected French squadron. The victory of Porto Novo, won by Coote, in 1781, was a severe check to Hyder Ali, who died in the following year; and his son and successor Tippoo Sultan was restrained in his proceedings against the English by the withdrawal of the French troops who had come to his aid, but were recalled by their government on the restoration of peace with England.

Many officers, however, took service with Tippoo Sultan and the Nizam, and afterwards exercised a dangerous influence against the English, though, for the time, the peril was overcome. Hastings was everywhere triumphant, in the council as well as in the field. The councillors who had opposed and denounced him were gone, General Clavering was dead; and Francis, who had been wounded by Hastings in a duel, had returned to England, where he employed himself in preparing the way for the impeachment, which was brought forward against the ex-Governor-General on his arrival in 1785. The trial lasted seven years. It ended, as might have been expected from its length, in an acquittal; but the expenses it involved, together with his extravagance, left Hastings an absolute pauper until the Company came to his relief with a pension and afterwards with donations to meet his frequently recurring difficulties.

In 1784 the Board of Control was formed by Mr. Pitt as a further check on the East India Company.

Marquis Cornwallis.—A.D. 1786 to 1793.

Lord Cornwallis united in his own person the powers of Governor-General and Commander-in-Chief, and was successful in both capacities. His internal administration was marked first by the establishment of a fixed land-rent throughout Bengal, on the sound principle of ensuring to the Natives the fee-simple of the soil; and secondly, by the formation of a judicial system to protect life and property.

Tippoo Sultan's invasion of Travancore, a state under British protection, occasioned the renewal of war with Mysoor. Lord Cornwallis in co-operation with the Nizam and the Mahrattas, with the Rajah of Coorg and other minor princes, marched against Seringapatam the capital of Mysoor in 1792, and there dictated terms to the Sultan, who was compelled to purchase peace by the cession of half his kingdom.

Sir John Shore.—A.D. 1793 to 1798.

Sir John Shore, afterwards Lord Teignmouth, was selected to succeed Lord Cornwallis, on account of his pacific disposition, rectitude, and financial ability. The continuance of peace was, however, of brief duration. It was evident that Tippoo Sultan was only waiting an opportunity for renewing hostility with the English; preparations were therefore made for another war with Mysoor, and these, together with other causes, compelled the Governor-General to open the Treasury for a loan bearing twelve per cent. interest. Notwithstanding the high character of the administrator, his four years' rule ended with an exhausted treasury, an increasing debt, and an impending war.

Marquis Wellesley.—A.D. 1798 to 1805.

Lord Mornington, better known as Marquis Wellesley, arrived in India in 1798, accompanied by his younger brother Henry (afterwards Lord Cowley), as his private secretary. Colonel Wellesley (afterwards Duke of Wellington) had been above a year in India with the 33rd regiment, and thus the remarkable talents of the three brothers were brought to bear on the intricate questions of Indian policy.*

The immediate danger arose from the hostility of Tippoo Sultan, who was entering into various alliances, offensive and defensive, against the English. Tippoo, besides intriguing

* See 'Wellesley Despatches,' in five vols., edited by the author of the present work.

with native Indian powers, had expressed his desire to co-operate with Zemaun Shah of Afghanistan (the successor of the fierce Doorani conqueror of Paniput), for the invasion of Hindoostan. The French expedition to Egypt was viewed as a preparatory step to the invasion of India; and Tippoo had violated his treaty with England by sending an embassy to the French Governor of the Mauritius, and receiving such auxiliaries as that island could furnish. The Governor-General vainly remonstrated with the Sultan on his breach of faith, but could get nothing from him but false or prevaricating replies. The result was the renewal of war with Mysoor. Seringapatam was taken in May 1799, and Tippoo Sultan slain. The Hindoo dynasty, displaced by Hyder Ali, was restored to their capital of Mysoor, with a revenue exceeding that of the ancient Hindoo kingdom. The family of Tippoo was munificently provided for. The fortress, city, and island of Seringapatam remained in the hands of the English. The chief authority was vested in Colonel Wellesley, who was also appointed commander of the army above the Ghauts. No English functionary ever worked more cordially and effectively with a Native coadjutor than Arthur Wellesley with Poorneah, the minister of the boy-Rajah of Mysoor, and their success was evidenced by the rapid extension of public works and the unexampled prosperity which prevailed throughout the country. It was in the six years spent in the arduous civil and military duties of this position that the abilities for rule of Colonel Wellesley were manifested and trained. His justice and accuracy (which was a part of his justice), his untiring industry and singular power of attending to detail without losing sight of leading principles, were as useful in establishing a new administration as in organising an army.* To govern men was his natural vocation, but his strongest

* See 'Wellington Despatches,' first edition, by Colonel Gurwood, vols. i. ii. iii., and 'Supplementary Despatches of the Duke of Wellington, edited by his Son,' vols. i. to iv.

efforts were always and everywhere for peace; and even in actual war he maintained a consideration for the welfare of the people of the country and a respect for their chiefs, which enabled him to be at once a subjugator and a pacificator.

His Indian campaigns were fit forerunners of his Peninsular career. The principal of them were undertaken against the Mahratta chieftains, Sindia, Holcar, and the Rajah of Berar; and the battle of Assaye in 1803 was one of the most remarkable of the victories by which the enemy was reduced to sue for peace. The Bengal army, under the command of Lord Lake, was brilliantly successful in Northern India. The battle of Laswaree gave to England the command of Agra and Delhi, and the unfortunate emperor who had been blinded by a Rohilla chief and re-captured by Sindia, now gladly placed himself under British protection.

The fortress of Bhurtpoor alone resisted repeated attacks, and its Rajah was allowed to purchase peace by the payment of two hundred thousand pounds.

The other chief events during the administration of Lord Wellesley were the assumption of Tanjore, the Carnatic, and the city of Surat; and the extension of what was termed the Subsidiary system, namely, the subsidising of British troops for the protection of Native states. This measure the Governor-General believed would prolong the existence of the protected Native states and regulate the balance of power, while it established the supremacy of England over the chief part of the Indian Peninsula. Under his rule it would probably have done all this, but unfortunately his whole policy was for a time misunderstood. He returned to England to find himself threatened with impeachment, and his pledges of protective alliance were violated by the adoption of a non-intervention policy, which, though fair sounding, involved the abandonment of the weaker powers to the will of the stronger, especially in the case of the Rajpoot princes, whose adherence to the British had drawn on them the anger of the Mahrattas.

Marquis Cornwallis.—A.D. 1805 to 1806.

Lord Cornwallis returned to India in failing health. By his decease the chief authority devolved upon the senior member of council, Sir George Barlow, who had promptly seconded Lord Wellesley's system as conducive to the peace of India; but who now readily embraced the new theory of the East India Directors in the avowed expectation that the Native states would, in consequence of the peace policy, engage in intestine strife which would prevent them from interfering with the English. The Rajah of Jeypoor and others remonstrated forcibly against the faithlessness of leaving them unprotected against Sindia, and Lord Lake was so disgusted by the breach of treaties which he had been instrumental in forming, that he resigned his command and returned to England.

In 1806 a sepoy mutiny took place at Vellore, where the sons of Tippoo Sultan resided as state prisoners, caused partly by the machinations of the princes and their adherents, and partly by some most ill-advised regulations requiring the Native soldiers to shave their chins and lips, remove the mark of caste from their foreheads, and wear what they termed a hat-shaped turban.

The mutiny was put down, the obnoxious orders repealed, and Sir John Cradock recalled for having issued them. The sons of Tippoo were removed from Vellore to Bengal with diminished allowances, and the Native troops became again cheerful and obedient.

Earl of Minto.—A.D. 1806 to 1813.

Lord Minto arrived in India strongly inpressed in favour of the non-intervention policy, but he soon saw reason to revert to the more generous system of Lord Wellesley. Sir George Barlow's withdrawal of protection from the petty chiefs south of the Sutlej had tempted Runjeet Sing the Rajah of Lahore, to extend his conquests on the left bank of that river. The menaced chiefs were, therefore, again taken under British protection and a permanent military station formed at Loodiana.

In 1809 an adventurer named Ameer Khan, at the head of large numbers of armed banditti called Pindarries, invaded the territories of the Rajah of Berar, and Lord Minto was compelled to interfere for his defence.

In 1810, permanent possession was taken of the Mauritius, as a means of securing the fleets of the East India Company against French aggression. The Goorkalese, a tribe who had gained possession of the valley of Nepaul, had committed serious aggressions on chiefs who as British feudatories were clearly entitled to protection. Lord Minto, immediately before his return to England, demanded from Nepaul the surrender of Bhootwal, a border district of Oude.

Marquis of Hastings.—A.D. 1813 to 1823.

Lord Moira, afterwards Marquis of Hastings, received an unsatisfactory reply from the court of Katmandoo to the demand of his predecessor, and after much fruitless negotiation commenced a war which terminated in the complete defeat of the Goorkas; the restoration of the usurped districts, and the cession of the province of Kumaon, with the chief part of the Terai, a fertile but unhealthy tract situated at the base of the Himalaya.

The suppression of the Pindarries was Lord Hastings' next and greatest work. Ameer Khan was bought off with other leaders; and the remainder were hunted down separately, till Cheetoo, the most famous of them, was devoured by a tiger in a jungle in 1818; after which catastrophe the remainder of these once formidable and ferocious bands dispersed, and were no longer distinguishable from the general population. The deposition of the Peishwa Bajee Rao, the nominal head of the Mahratta confederacy, was the result of a series of proceedings in which he strove to cope by diplomacy against overwhelming force. By the treaty of Poona in 1816, he was reduced from an independent position to a state of vassalage. In 1817 he went to war with the English, but was defeated, and compelled to resign every remaining political right, and retire into private life, with an allowance of eighty thousand pounds a-year. Bithoor, near Cawnpoor, was the place appointed for his residence. The Rajah of Sattara, being set free by the downfall of the Peishwa, threw himself upon British protection and was placed on the gadi or Hindoo throne of Sattara, the capital of his ancestor Sevajee.

The year 1817 was memorable for the famine and cholera by which India was ravaged. In ten days the army under Lord Hastings on the banks of the Nerbudda was decimated.

Earl Amherst.—A.D. 1823 to 1827.

The administration of Lord Amherst commenced, in 1823, with a Burmese war, which had been long impending. The struggle was fierce, costly, and protracted; but at its close the King of Ava agreed to pay the English a million sterling, and to receive a British resident at his court. He likewise ceded Arracan and Tenasserim, and renounced all claim upon Assam, Jynteea, Cachar, and Munnipoor.

In 1826 the famous Jât fortress of Bhurtpoor was captured by Lord Combermere, from the hands of a usurping chief.

In 1827, Lord Amherst repaired to Simla, on the lower range of the Himalaya, which from that time became the favourite retreat of the chief military and civil officers from the heat and insalubrity of Calcutta and other places.

Lord William Bentinck.—A.D. 1825 to 1828.

Lord William Bentinck's administration was marked by many measures of internal reform. The extirpation of the Thugs and Phansigars, gangs of murderers and thieves, was ably carried through; Suttee or the suicide of widows, was forbidden; the ban was removed which had rendered Native converts to Christianity outlaws; and Natives were employed in offices from which they had been previously debarred.

The establishment of the "overland route," by way of the Red Sea, Egypt, and the Mediterranean, shortened the transit between England and India; and the navigation of the Ganges by steam-vessels was proved practicable. Double batta allowances were abolished in the Bengal army.

The deposition of the Rajah of Coorg and the annexation of the principality were caused by vague allegations brought against him by his sister and her husband. The brave mountaineers rallied round their hereditary chief, and were ready to die in his cause; but the Rajah refused to fight against the powerful allies of his ancestors, and surrendered with his family, unconditionally. He came to England in 1850 in the hope of obtaining the restitution of 85,000*l.*, invested by the Coorg family in the Government funds, and died, while still a state prisoner, in London, 1859, worn out by the delays and disappointments which attended the prosecution of a suit on the success of which the comfortable maintenance of his wives, children, and numerous relatives depended.

Earl of Auckland.—A.D. 1835 to 1842.

The chief event in the administration of Lord Auckland was the Afghan war, which originated in the unjustifiable interference of the Calcutta government with the affairs of Afghanistan. The siege of Herat by the Shah of Persia aided by Russian officers, was viewed with great uneasiness, that fortress being regarded as the key of Afghanistan. Dost Mohammed, the ruler of Cabool, was desired to form no connexion with Russia. His reply was deemed unsatisfactory; whereupon, without waiting for the termination of the siege (which being unsuccessful left Herat independent), Lord Auckland formed a treaty with Runjeet Sing to depose the Dost, and replace an exile named Shah Soojah in the country which twenty years before had witnessed his expulsion.

This project was carried into effect after the occupation of several fortresses. Shah Soojah was triumphantly installed by British troops in the Balla Hissar, or palace-citadel of Cabool, in 1839. Dost Mohammed surrendered in the following year; but the temper of the people, and especially of the haughty chiefs of the various Afghan tribes, continued so refractory that it was found needful to support Shah Soojah by the presence of a body of European and Native troops, and to aid by large contributions the scanty revenues of Cabool, which, small as they were, had to be collected by force of arms.

Sir William Macnaghten, the British envoy, knew that the East India Directors would not long choose to pay a million and a quarter per annum to preserve their nominee at Cabool; and he strove to diminish the expenditure by withdrawing or lessening the allowances paid to certain Khilji leaders for guarding the passes against marauding tribes. The experiment was hazardous. Shah Soojah pointed out the excitement thus created; but Macnaghten exultingly declared that the noses of the chiefs had been brought to the grindstone, and that all was still from Dan to Beersheba.

The murder of Sir Alexander Burnes, with his brother and another officer, although accounted for by the provocation given by the profligate conduct of the chief victim,* was also a warning of the state of public feeling. It soon became evident even to Macnaghten that, as the reinforcements of men and money, asked for by him from Lord Auckland, did not arrive, no course remained but to obtain honourable terms and evacuate Afghanistan. Unfortunately Macnaghten and the military leaders, old General Elphinstone and Brigadier Shelton, differed in their views of the policy to be pursued, and the sixteen thousand troops (European and Native) frittered away their resources in the straggling cantonments, till the murder of Macnaghten, in the course of the negotiations,

* Kaye's 'War in Afghanistan,' i. 615.

brought matters to a crisis, and a treaty was concluded, by which the English pledged themselves to surrender the forts still held by them, including Ghuznee and Jellalabad; to replace Dost Mohammed on the throne; and pay a ransom of one hundred and forty thousand pounds in return for the beasts of burden necessary for their retreat to Hindoostan.

On the 6th of January, 1842, with deep snow on the ground, the fatal retreat commenced. It was from the first too irregular to be called a march. The predatory tribes swarmed forth to harass the invaders. The Khiljis crowned the heights of the Koord Cabool pass, and three thousand fugitives perished there. The Englishwomen who accompanied the troops traversed the pass uninjured, except Lady Sale who received a bullet in her arm; but it was so evident that they could not long endure the perils and privations of the retreat, that the ladies with their husbands and children were given over to the protection of Akber Khan, the favourite son of Dost Mohammed, by whom they were honourably treated and finally surrendered to the British Government. On the 10th of January the ill-fated force was intercepted in a narrow gorge on the road to Jellalabad, and large numbers, including a mass of sepoys and camp-followers, were hewn down by Afghan knives. On the 12th, the remainder of the troops having forced their way with the bayonet to the Jugdulluck Pass, found their passage obstructed by a barricade of trees and bushes, and themselves a prey to the "jezails," or long rifles, of the foe. A single European, Dr. Brydon, succeeded in escaping to Jellalabad, and announced to Sir Robert Sale and his small garrison the total destruction of the British army. Lord Auckland quitted India in the following month, leaving on record a minute which showed that the Afghan war had already necessitated an expenditure of eight million sterling. At its conclusion, the war is said to have cost three times that sum,* and to have occasioned

* Arnold's 'Administration of Marquis of Dalhousie,' i. 13.

a far more irreparable damage by destroying the prestige of invincibility which had attended the British army.

Earl of Ellenborough.—A.D. 1842 to 1844.

Soon after the Earl of Ellenborough succeeded to the Indian administration the fortress of Ghuznee was surrendered by Colonel Palmer to the Afghans, but Candahar and Jellalabad were held by Nott and Sale until they were relieved by British reinforcements. Ghuznee was retaken by the British and destroyed by fire. Jellalabad, Candahar, Khelat-i-Khilji (between Candahar and Ghuznee), Ali Musjid, and other fortresses were destroyed, and the "army of retribution" proceeded to Cabool, where the city was sacked, the Grand Bazaar and the Mosque razed to the ground, and even the famous "Hundred gardens" fell before the fury of those whom Lord Brougham denounced as our "incendiary Generals." The barbarism of these proceedings was rendered the more remarkable by the manifesto issued by Lord Ellenborough, in which he ordered the evacuation of Afghanistan, and acknowledged the error committed in its invasion. Shah Soojah had been murdered at Cabool after the departure and massacre of the British force, and Dost Mohammed was now suffered to return and occupy the vacant throne.

The conquest of Sinde, which was effected in 1843, has been termed "the tail of the Afghan war." Some connection existed between these events, inasmuch as the navigation of the river Indus was insisted upon by the English, as a means of reaching the Cabool valley, and latent hostility arose in consequence with the Ameers or rulers of Sinde. But a comparison of the contradictory accounts given by Sir Charles Napier and Sir James (then Colonel) Outram,* the British resident, shows that the quarrel was forced upon the Ameers. The Sinde war, by which the East India Company gained a fertile province and the Indus for a boundary, entailed a

* See Napier's 'Sinde,' and Outram's 'Commentary.'

heavy expenditure, which their finances could ill bear. The booty taken by the army at Hyderabad after the battle of Meanee was enormous. Sir Charles Napier, who had come out to India with an empty purse, obtained 70,000*l.* prize-money; a circumstance which manifestly influenced his opinion regarding what he styled that "very advantageous, useful, and humane piece of rascality,"* the seizure of Sinde.

Sir Henry Hardinge.—A.D. 1844 to 1848.

Lord Ellenborough was superseded by Sir Henry Hardinge, whose attention was diverted from the promotion of public works by the outbreak of war on the north-western frontier. The murder of Kurruck Sing the son and successor of Runjeet Sing, had been followed by a state of disorganization throughout the Punjab, and the only point on which the Seik factions agreed was in enmity to the English. Preparations were made at Lahore for the passage of the Sutlej by a Seik army. The Governor-General hastened to meet the foe, and, when the Seiks crossed the river, the Commander-in-Chief, Sir Hugh Gough marched against them, and in December 1845 defeated them at Moodkee. Sir Harry Smith gained a victory at Aliwal in January 1845. The Seik entrenchments at Ferozepoor were carried in February, after a battle in which the Governor-General and the Commander-in-Chief fought side by side, and the Seiks were driven over their bridge of boats across the Sutlej by the British, who dictated terms of peace beneath the walls of Lahore. The independence of the Punjab ceased, although the boy-prince Dhuleep Sing was recognised as Maharajah. A British resident and British troops were stationed at Lahore. The protected or cis-Sutlej states were annexed, as well as the Jullundur Doab, including the Himalayan valleys of the Spitee and Peenee, which brought Tartars for the first time under direct British rule. The Alpine region between the Beas and the Sutlej was also

* 'Life of Sir Charles Napier, by Sir William Napier,' ii. 155.

taken, and a fine was levied to meet the expenditure of the war. But the Lahore treasury was exhausted, and Golab Sing, an adventurer who had become governor of Cashmeer and the Jummoo territory, was permitted to assume sovereignty on payment of the deficient sum. Lord Hardinge's motive in making this arrangement was probably the exhausted state of the European troops, whom four pitched battles had reduced to three thousand men; otherwise, remembering the antecedents of the lovely and salubrious valley which had formed the favourite retreat of the Great Moguls, and the importance of its position at the entrance to Hindoostan, it would hardly have been left in the hands of a man who had few pretensions to its possession except his friendly attitude and power of becoming a troublesome foe.

Marquis of Dalhousie.—A.D. 1848 to 1855.

The Marquis of Dalhousie became Governor-General of India in 1848. The Seik treaty was not carried out, and appeared to have been agreed to by the Lahore durbar (or government) as a means of gaining time. Ranee Chunda the mother of Dhuleep Sing conspired with the chief Seik sirdars or nobles against the English; but before her plans were matured circumstances occurred which renewed the war before either party was able to carry it on with vigour.

Mooltan, the capital of the province of that name, occupies a position of great commercial importance. The strength of its fortress and the wealth of its bazaars attracted foreign invaders from the time of Alexander the Macedonian to that of Runjeet the Seik. At the death of Runjeet the fortress and province were ruled by a chief whose subordination to the Lahore court was almost nominal. Upon his death his son the Dewan Moolraj was recognised as his successor, and a nuzzurana or present demanded in return. Moolraj promised to pay eighteen lacs of rupees (one hundred and eighty thousand pounds) just before the outbreak of the first Seik war. He came to Lahore in 1846 under the guarantee of Sir John Lawrence, and, after paying the stipulated sum, was compelled to assent to the surrender of a part of his province, and to pledge himself to the payment of nineteen lacs yearly on account of the remainder. The Dewan was besides alarmed at the intended introduction of English courts of justice into Mooltan, which, by their costly and tedious proceedings, inspired the natives with aversion. He spoke of resigning Mooltan on condition of receiving a jagheer in exchange, but was told that his resignation must be unconditional, and his accounts for ten years would be called for. "How can I produce my father's papers?" was the reply; "the ants have eaten them, or if the ants have left any, they are useless for your purpose. I am in your hands." The answer was natural enough in the son of a man who had exercised an almost irresponsible despotism under Runjeet Sing—a ruler who, like Hyder Ali, found a notched stick sufficient for his accounts. But the British resident (Currie), who acted on behalf of the Seik council, construed the despair of Moolraj into resignation,* and informed him that a Seik sirdar and an English political agent would be sent to relieve him from the charge of Mooltan. Moolraj returned to his fortress a ruined man; inquisition into the past as well as insignificance for the future was before him. He was in failing health, and harassed by domestic as well as political trials.

In April 1848 a new governor, Khan Sing, was sent by the British authority at Lahore to Mooltan, with two young Englishmen, Vans Agnew and Lieutenant Anderson, and a Goorka escort of five hundred horse. On entering the fortress a sepoy rushed at Vans Agnew, and wounded him, and Lieutenant Anderson was cut down by some troopers; but Khan Sing and the Goorka escort took up the wounded

* Arnold's 'Administration of Marquis of Dalhousie,' i. 66.

men and carried them to the Eedgah, a Mohammedan place of worship, where, in the evening, they were deserted by the chief part of their guards, broken in upon by a city mob, and beheaded by a Muzubbee—or member of a caste of sweepers and executioners. "We are not the last of the English," said Vans Agnew, as he sat by the couch of Anderson, holding his hand, and waiting for death.

The murderers took the heads of the officers and flung them at the feet of Moolraj. The die was cast, and, with hesitation and disgust, he accepted the crime and its consequences. Khan Sing was bidden by the infuriated people to carry back to Lahore the boy (Vans Agnew) he had brought to govern Mooltan men. When the bodies were flung aside by the rabble, they were taken up by some Afghan merchants, who, acting with the concurrence of Moolraj, wrapped the remains in silken shawls, and buried them at the Eedgah, after the custom, as they said, of England.

The first intelligence of the catastrophe was conveyed in a pencilled note, written by poor Agnew when lying wounded in the Eedgah, to General Cortlandt, once in the service of Runjeet Sing, but subsequently a most able and faithful commander in the British army. The note was received by Lieutenant Edwardes on the 22nd of April. By his promptitude and the exertions of Cortlandt, backed by two thousand men, levies were raised, and the spread of revolt to some extent checked. But the delay in sending troops from headquarters gave time for Moolraj to strengthen his position. The war became general; many of the Seik sirdars declared against us, and the views of Ranee Chunda were so evident that, to avoid the excitement of a public trial, she was privately conveyed to Benares. Mooltan was ineffectually besieged by General Whish at intervals from September 1818 to the end of the year. In November a stratagem was resorted to (of a letter written as from General Whish), which deprived Moolraj of the co-operation of Shere Sing, (the reputed son of Runjeet Sing), who quitted Mooltan at the head of five thousand men and twenty guns. The weakened garrison still held out, and on the last day of December made a sortie against the besiegers which was repelled with great loss by the new levies headed by Sir Henry Lawrence, who had returned from England and just joined the camp. The town was captured early in January, and on the 22nd of that month the garrison surrendered unconditionally. Moolraj—who was, in fact, the head of the Seik cause, and by far the ablest man engaged in it—tore himself away from his chiefs and adherents, who clung to him and fell at his feet with expressions of passionate devotion. Nor were the European troops unmoved when the chief, with his spare figure and dignified bearing, issued alone from the fortress he had held so bravely, and rode on his splendidly-caparisoned Arab to the British camp, where he learned his probable (and eventual) sentence of transportation, the idea of which unnerved him for the first time, and drew from him an entreaty for any other doom, even immediate and disgraceful death.

Ten days before the fall of Mooltan a fierce battle was fought at Chillianwallah between the British under Lord Gough and a powerful Seik force under Shere Sing. The valour and still more the popularity of the Commander-in-Chief partially atoned for the defective plan on which he acted, but the doubtful victory was attended with heavy loss of life, and with a disastrous panic among the cavalry. The battle of Goojerat was, however, admirably planned and fought out by Lord Gough, who, on the 21st of February, ranged his force of twenty-five thousand men against about forty thousand of the enemy (including one thousand five hundred Afghan horse from Cabool), and by a decisive victory brought the second Seik war to a triumphant conclusion. The chief sirdars surrendered, and the Punjab was annexed to British India, a pension of large amount being granted to Dhuleep Sing, his mother, and other members of the ex-royal family.

The "Koh-i-Noor" diamond, of which Runjeet Sing had despoiled the unfortunate Shah Soojah, fell into the hands of the conquerors, and was sent to England, where it forms a portion of the British regalia. This famous gem is asserted to be the identical diamond possessed by Karna, King of Anga, one of the heroes of the Maha Bharat, or great war, which took place in the fourteenth century B.C. Mr. Arnold states that a baneful influence is attached to the jewel by Hindoo tradition, and he cites instances of the misfortunes of its alleged wearers, including Vicramaditya, rajah of Malwa, the Emperor Humayun, and Nadir Shah, who, on the surrender of Delhi, saw the "Mountain of Light" gleaming on the head of the conquered Mogul Mohammed Shah, and immediately changed turbans with him in pledge of friendship. No authority is quoted by Mr. Arnold for his account of the descent of the gem, and many important links are wanting in his statement. For instance, Humayun, when in exile in Persia, was compelled by Shah Tahmasp to surrender to him a diamond of incalculable value, which was probably the one captured at Agra (see 'Memoirs of Humayun'), and there were other famous gems taken by different invaders from Delhi. The possession of the British "Koh-i-Noor" can be clearly traced from Nadir Shah and his ill-fated successors until the exiled Shah Soojah reluctantly surrendered the jewel to Runjeet Sing, by whom it was worn without any ill effects. Its next wearers were the three successors of Runjeet, of whom one died of poison, the second was shot on the throne with the "Koh-i-Noor" on his arm, and the third (Dhuleep Sing) was deposed. Still, as violent deaths are the rule rather than the exception with Eastern princes, the tradition which connects the retention of sovereign power with this imperial gem is far more in accordance with its adventures than any supposition of inherent ill-luck; for the list of its possessors (if Mr. Arnold's account be correct) must have included Akber, Shah Jehan, Aurungzebe, and "the crowned Dacoit" Runjeet Sing.

In 1852 a second Burmese war, occasioned by the unauthorised proceedings of the Burmese and British subordinates, resulted in the capture of Rangoon, the capital of Pegu, and the permanent occupation of that province.

The numerous annexations of Lord Dalhousie were for the most part carried out in violation of the rights conferred by the law of adoption, an ancient and venerated Hindoo ordinance. Cattara had been the scene of a cruel injustice on the part of the Bombay authorities, who in 1839 deposed the excellent reigning prince, and placed his intriguing and dissolute half-brother on the throne, under rigid supervision. On the death of this man in 1848 without male heirs, the principality was annexed on the plea of lapse, and great excitement and dissatisfaction were caused by this step towards the suppression of the remaining Native states.

In May 1853 the Nizam of Hyderabad was forced to surrender to the East India Company about a third of his territories in payment of arrears due for the compulsory maintenance of a British contingent.

The Rajah of Jhansi (a small Mahratta state in Bundelcund) died in November 1853, having written on his deathbed a letter to the Governor-General, entreating that his adopted child might be accepted as his successor, and that the Ranee Lakshmi Bye might officiate as regent, according to the custom of the country. The British agent, in forwarding this appeal, bore witness to the fidelity of the Jhansi Government to the English, as having been maintained under circumstances of considerable temptation; and he described the Ranee as being "highly respected and esteemed," and "fully capable of doing justice to such a charge." It was no new thing among the Hindoos for a woman to bear rule, and no sovereign ever governed more successfully than the excellent Mahratta princess, Ahaliya Bye, of Indore.* Lord Dalhousie did not, however, listen to these arguments, but acted in this case as he had done in others. The disappointed Ranee, a young, beautiful, and resolute woman, made a vow of vengeance, and kept it.

The kingdom of Nagpoor or Berar was annexed on the ground of failure of legal heirs, as were other minor States; but the greatest of Lord Dalhousie's appropriations was performed just before he left India, by the deposition of the King of Oude, and the annexation of that country on the plea of its misgoverned and disorganised condition.

The East India Company entirely concurred in the policy of the Governor-General, and congratulated themselves on the acquisition of twenty-five thousand square miles of territory, containing five million of inhabitants, "without the expenditure of a drop of blood, and almost without a murmur." † The Company did not then foresee the torrents of English and Indian blood which were to be poured forth before the supremacy of England should be established in Oude; and they did not choose to hear the murmurs which gave warning of the coming struggle.

The cardinal error of Lord Dalhousie was that he governed India for the Company, and looked at every question from the Leadenhall Street point of view. Overworked,—writing, as was said of him at Lahore, sixty minutes to the hour, in furtherance or vindication of his policy,—he thought only of the judgment the Directors and the British public would pronounce on his conduct, and entirely overlooked the accumulation of grievances pent up in the Native mind, and the consequences which would ensue should the immense Bengal army, itself little more than a local militia, turn

* See Sir John Malcolm's 'Central India,' vol. i.

† 'Oude Blue Book for 1856,' p. 288. The annexations of Lord Dalhousie are described at length in the introductory chapter to the Mutiny, given in the 'Indian Empire,' vol. ii.

against the British Government, and the sepoys fraternize with their countrymen and co-religionists. In the absorption of Native states Lord Dalhousie acted with the full concurrence of the Directors, but in the arbitrary extinction of hereditary titles, and in crushing the Native aristocracy, he went further and faster than his employers cared to follow him.

His treatment of the aged representative of the Great Moguls was inexcusable, and excited in the breasts of the Mohammedans of Delhi vindictive feelings, which bore fruit during the Mutiny in the massacre of the Europeans. All real power, except in the narrow limits of the city and district of Delhi, had been taken from the Mogul, but he was still prayed for under the title of Emperor in the mosques of India; and although the Calcutta government styled him "King of Delhi," the relics of his original position as suzerain of the East India Company remained in so far that he would receive the Governor-General only as an inferior, and the last English captain of the palace-guard, when summoned to the royal presence, approached barefoot, and with other signs of extreme respect, up to May 1857.

On the death of the heir-apparent in 1849, Lord Dalhousie recommended "the suppression of the House of Timur whenever the old king should die." The Directors consented, but so unwillingly, that another heir-apparent was recognised at Calcutta, on the hard condition that on his accession to the titular sovereignty he should quit the palace at Delhi, and receive the Governor-General on terms of equality.

In 1856 the heir-apparent died of cholera, and great excitement arose on the re-opened question of succession. The position of the royal family was one of poverty and mortification. Within the palace walls there was a population of above five thousand persons, of whom three thousand were of the blood royal. Their numbers had increased until the pension allotted for their sustenance was insufficient to procure them regular food. The Calcutta Government, acting as their trustees, hedged them in with restrictions, forbade their entering the service of the army or the state, and made no effort whatever either for their moral or physical welfare. The ignorance and sensuality of the "Sullateen," as the younger members of the family were called, became a bye-word with the English; but the reproach came badly from the mouth of those who were open to a countercharge of selfish neglect for having taken no pains to educate or uphold a family, the care of which was in fact accepted by the Company with the Sunnuds or Charter which conferred on them the large revenues of Bengal.

The most powerful representative of the East India Company put the finishing stroke to a long series of injuries when he decreed the expulsion of the Moguls from their hereditary home, and waited for the death of the old king, to sweep away the few prerogatives which remained, without holding out one gleam of hope to cheer and encourage the princes to lead a better life, or even making a useful career possible to them. Yet Lord Dalhousie had so little fear of their treachery as to leave Delhi garrisoned with only Native troops, stored with a capacious magazine, and abundant munitions of war, in charge of a few officers, who with their families were unsupported by a single British soldier. There can be no doubt that among the despised "Sullateen" there were men, Prince Feroze Shah for instance, who, had they been treated with generosity or even justice, trained in the English service, and educated in the knowledge of British resources, would have held Delhi for us and fought on our side as zealously as any of the rajahs whose states had happily not been merged in the whirlpool of annexation.

In his internal proceedings Lord Dalhousie proved an admirable administrator. The force of his intellect, his remarkable aptitude for business, energy, and unflagging industry had given a powerful stimulus to progress in India. In the famous Minute in which he summed up the leading events of his eight years' rule, he adverted to his labours for the establishment of railways at the Three Presidencies and in Sinde, of telegraphic communications between the chief cities, of cheap and uniform postage, improved means of transit, and reduced import duties. Lord Dalhousie deserves great credit for what he accomplished, because, fettered by the Directors, it was next to impossible to get anything at all done for or in India. The fatigue and anxiety he there underwent probably contributed to the sudden prostration which followed his return to England, and ended in his death, at the very time when his counsel was most desired on Indian politics even by those who strongly disapproved his annexation proceedings. Had he been spared in physical and mental vigour, none would have appreciated more thoroughly the wonderful change made in our entire India system, or watched more approvingly the operations of a fostering and liberal government, than the late gifted Marquis of Dalhousie.

Viscount Canning.—A.D. 1856 to 1862.

When Viscount Canning became Governor-General India was considered to be profoundly tranquil. A small minority saw reason for anxiety in the disorganisation and discontent caused by the recent rapid series of annexations, in the numbers of aristocratic families reduced to poverty by the breaking up of Native courts, and the masses of armed men dispersed over the country by the disbandment of Native armies. The excessive poverty of the labouring class everywhere, and the terrible famines which periodically recurred, were the direct consequences of the want of proper means of transit and irrigation, and of the scanty encouragement which any Governor-General could give to commerce and agriculture while burdened with the charge of numerous new provinces, the revenue of which could not (under the old system) be made to defray their own expenditure, and which were maintained from the surplus income of Bengal, with some help from Bombay and Madras. The Punjab, at the time of its acquisition, was justly viewed as a province requiring the greatest care for its retention. Picked men were sent to govern it, entrusted with extraordinary powers, and funds to an extent never provided in any other case were spent in its settlement. The two Lawrences were at first associated in its rule, but it was impossible that they should long work together. The stern civilian, John Lawrence, was supported in his views by Lord Dalhousie; and Sir Henry left a province where, it is affirmed, people were occasionally hanged on no[*] better authority than an open note from an assistant-commissioner to a deputy expressing his opinion that they were guilty.

The subjugation of the Punjab was carried out with quiet but unflinching severity, and notwithstanding the dissent implied by the resignation of some leading officials and the unsatisfactory nature of the financial results, it was resolved to put the same system in operation in Oude. The experiment was made with means, both in soldiers, civilians, and money, very inferior to those employed in the Punjab. Utterly incompetent functionaries were appointed to pronounce judgment upon the landed rights of the talookdars or chief proprietors in Oude, and Lord Canning has subsequently admitted the injustice of their decisions. The financial commissioner (Martin Gubbins) testifies to the neglect of British officials as having aggravated the sufferings of the nobility and gentry, and he describes ladies and children never before seen outside the zenana, as having become used "to go out at night and beg their bread."[†]

The princesses of Oude were treated with cruel indignity. Though it is "a far cry" to Downing Street, their complaint reached the ear of Lord Stanley, who demanded an explanation of the assertion that they had been rudely

* 'Non-Regulation Provinces of India,' Fraser's Magazine, March, 1862.
† Martin Gubbins, 'Mutinies in Oudh,' p. 70.

driven from their recognised home. The Indian government tardily acknowledged* that the Chief Commissioner, Mr. Coverley Jackson, had expelled the royal inmates of the Chutter Munzil palace and taken possession of it himself, for which act he had been censured by the Governor-General in council, and the palace restored to the ladies. This admitted grievance is probably one of many others which may account for the bitter hatred afterwards shown by the adherents and domestic servants of the Oude family, as well as by the mass of the Lucknow citizens, to the English at the Residency.

Sir Henry Lawrence pointed out, at an early stage of proceedings in Oude, the numerous jungle forts and guns of the chiefs as a special source of danger in the event of revolt. His remonstrances were unheeded until the peril could no longer be overlooked; then, at the end of March 1857, when about to seek in England the restoration of a frame breaking down under hard work, anxiety of mind, and grief of heart for the loss of a beloved wife, he stayed his steps, at the urgent request of Lord Canning, and went to Lucknow, there to find himself too late to avert the calamity of which he had vainly given warning, and to die its victim.

THE MUTINY.

In January, 1857, the little cloud which heralded the mighty storm was clearly visible. It appeared in an unexpected quarter. Since the days of Clive the Native army had been increasing until it numbered nearly three hundred thousand men, while the European force was about forty-five thousand. The faith of the English community, both civil and military, in the loyalty of the sepoys was unbounded; only one thing, it was believed, could drive them to even passive mutiny—namely, interference with Moslem custom or Hindoo caste. A solitary instance, perhaps, of

* Despatch of Lord Stanley, 13th October, 1858, and Reply of Lord Canning, 25th November, 1859. Parl. Papers, Commons, 12 July, 1861.

personal vengeance might occur, but organized, active revolt was out of the question. That women and children should be deemed in danger from the Natives was unheard of. European ladies were in the habit of travelling hundreds of miles, guarded by Natives only, and no instance was on record of their having sustained any injury. Caste, however, had been much talked of during late years; it was considered to impede the efficiency of the Bengal troops; and among many attempts made to check its influence, the most important was an order issued by the commander-in-chief, General Anson, in 1856, by which all recruits were required to swear that they would go by sea or land wherever their services might be desired. This at once excluded the conscientious Brahminist from the army. A sea voyage is in itself forbidden by his creed; and he can only preserve caste by enduring severe privations in his food, while both Hindoos and Mussulmans must abstain from the frequent ablutions to which creed, custom, and climate alike impel them.

General Anson was a man of active habits, strong prejudices, and no military experience either European or Indian. He introduced several minor measures which the Bengal troops viewed as intended to pave the way for the abolition of their religious privileges and even vested rights.

Affairs were in this state of growing intolerance of caste on the part of the officers, and timid distrust on the part of the sepoys, when orders were given to instruct the army in the use of the Minié rifle. Three years before, when the change of musket was first proposed, and some rifle ammunition sent to India, Adjutant-General Tucker had warned the Government, that "in the greasing composition nothing should be used which could possibly offend the caste or religious prejudices of the natives." *

No such precaution was taken: the grease was supplied by

* Letter of Major-General Tucker to the 'Times,' 1857.

a contractor, without any special orders as to the materials to be used; and the filthy cartridges were offered to Mohammedans, many of whom actually chose death rather than pollute their lips with them; and to Brahminists, who could not do so without irrevocably losing caste—that is, being outlawed and excommunicated in this life and the next.

The first greased cartridges made in India were prepared with tallow. One of the Native workmen employed at the Dum Dum arsenal taunted a sepoy with the impending disgrace. "You will soon lose your caste," he said; "you are to be made to bite cartridges covered with the fat of pigs and cows." This speech made a deep impression. As early as January 1857, the commanding officer at Barrackpoor, Major-General Hearsey, represented to Government the extreme excitement of the sepoys, and repeatedly urged that they should be allowed to prepare their own bullet-patches. Finding his remonstrances unheeded, he became only the more urgent that no further time should be lost; for he added, "We are dwelling on a mine ready for explosion."

At length the Governor-General in Council wrote to General Anson, who was enjoying the cool breezes of Simla, for new instructions regarding the rifle practice; but the General could not be made to see the danger, and persisted in refusing any concession, to what he termed the "beastly prejudices" * of the natives, until the time for conciliation was over. Before the formal withdrawal of the cartridges and the recantation of his past system were promulgated, the mine had exploded, the Bengal army was for the most part disbanded or in revolt, and many British stations besieged or in ruins.

The first outbreak occurred at Berhampoor, on the Ganges, on the 26th February, upon the refusal of the 19th Bengal Infantry to receive the suspected ammunition.

* 'Crisis in the Punjab,' by Frederick Cooper, Deputy Commissioner of Umritsur, p. 37.

The colonel strove to compel the men, telling them that if they persevered in their refusal, he would take them to Burmah or China, where, through hardship, they would all die. It was known that Lord Dalhousie had punished the refusal of the 38th Bengal Infantry to march to Burmah by sending the regiment by land to Dacca, where the cantonments were very bad, and the loss of life proportionately heavy. Still the 19th refused the cartridges. Their sentence was very severe. The corps was disbanded; and when the men, after strong appeals for mercy, could obtain no remission of their sentence, they dispersed sadly, but quietly, and never appear to have taken any part in the subsequent rebellion. The men of the 34th Bengal Infantry had been the instigators of the resolve of the 19th. They were at Barrackpoor; and incendiary fires and night meetings gave, as in almost every later instance, warning of discontent. The first blood was shed on the 29th March, 1857, on the Barrackpoor parade, by a fanatic named Mungul Pandy, who, after wounding his adjutant, strove to commit suicide, and succeeded in inflicting upon himself a severe injury. He was executed in April.

Meanwhile the cartridge question was discussed throughout the Bengal army; and a vague fear gained ground daily in the native mind, which verged upon the madness of panic. In Oude it was believed that the British government had resolved, not only on depriving the sepoys but the Natives in general of their caste, by mixing immense quantities of bone-dust with the flour sold in the bazaars; and it needed all the influence of Sir Henry Lawrence to gain a hearing in contradiction of these rumours. But he laboured strenuously, and succeeded in so far as to prevent an outbreak in Oude long after other localities, where much less cause for revolt existed, had become scenes of bloodshed and desolation.

Meerut.

The crisis came at Meerut, a large cantonment, thirty-two miles from Delhi. The proportion of European troops here was very large. There were one thousand eight hundred and sixty-three men, exclusive of sappers and miners, to two thousand nine hundred and twelve Natives; the reason for this large number of Europeans being to keep in check the garrison at Delhi, which was exclusively composed of Native troops, under European and Native officers.

The skirmishers of the 3rd Native Cavalry were ordered to use the new cartridges. Five consented. Eighty-five refused, were tried by court-martial for mutiny, found guilty, and sentenced to work in gangs on the roads as felons for a term of years.

Major Harriott, Deputy Judge-Advocate at the trial, would hear no testimony in favour of the accused; he wrote to a friend that night, "The court is over, and those fellows have got ten years apiece. You will hear of no more mutinies."

On the 9th May a memorable punishment parade was held, and the mutineers, who were all Mohammedans of high family, were heavily ironed and shackled. These proceedings occupied three hours. That night and the following day, Sunday, were spent by the Native troops in discussing the miserable condition of their comrades and their own fears and grievances. Many drugged themselves with bhang, and towards the time of evening service the excitement became very great, when a rumour got abroad that the 60th Rifles (Europeans), then parading for church, were about to seize the arms and horses of the 3rd Native Cavalry, and turn the men adrift, as the 19th Native Infantry had been treated.

The panic soon became general. The majority of the Native troops rose in open mutiny; the imprisoned troopers were released and their fetters broken off. A body of the 3rd Cavalry flung themselves on their horses, galloped to the gaol, released the captive troopers, struck off their fetters, and bore them away in triumph. At the same time twelve hundred other prisoners were set at liberty. It was now the turn of the Europeans to be panic-struck, and in this single instance throughout the mutiny they were, with few exceptions, paralysed with terror and amazement. There was no fighting at all. With every reason to be on their guard against a probable outbreak, the military authorities suffered themselves to be surprised by the unpremeditated and sudden rising of the Native troops, and then no commanding officer was found to head the eighteen hundred Europeans, with such Natives as remained faithful, and lead them at once against the mutineers. No resistance was offered: sepoys, city rabble, and released convicts were left to their own devices. A general rush was made by the Europeans to the artillery school, a large and easily defensible enclosure, with lines of barracks. Colonel Finnis was shot dead while trying to reason with the mutineers; and his own men, who had been staunch up to that moment, placed their other officers in safety and then joined the mutineers. The bazaar people and camp followers swarmed forth. Bands of thieves began murdering and plundering in all directions: the Native cantonments were set on fire and the houses of the officers rifled and burned. Some officers behaved admirably. Captain Craigie, for instance, succeeded in keeping together his troop of the 3rd Native Cavalry during nearly the entire night, leaving his wife in her home in the Native lines under the protection of four Native troopers. In all about forty Europeans were sacrificed at Meerut, through the incapacity of the officials.

It does not appear at what hour the telegraphic communication with Delhi was broken off; but the news was conveyed to Agra as late as nine in the evening by a private message from the postmaster's sister, to prevent her aunt from starting for Meerut. When it became known that the mutineers had taken the road to Delhi, Captain Rosser, of the Carabineers, asked permission to follow them with cavalry and guns,* or at least to ride to Delhi and warn the unprotected Europeans; but his offers were refused, and there is no evidence that either Hewitt, Archdale Wilson, or any leader made so so much as a suggestion on behalf of the city, which the Meerut station had been specially formed to protect. Remembering what was done elsewhere by a handful of troops, and even by single civilians, it is marvellous to read of the Meerut people gazing at the moon and wondering what would befall "our Christian brethren in Delhi on the coming morn, who, less happy than ourselves, had no faithful and friendly European battalions to shield them from the bloodthirsty rage of the sepoys." † One of those battalions might have saved Delhi, by forestalling the thirty troopers who are said to have revolutionized India; but the blundering severity which provoked the outbreak was paralleled by the selfish apathy which made no effort to put it down, or to stretch out a hand to warn or succour a neighbouring community. The fall of Delhi, with all its miserable consequences, political and social, was the immediate result of the misconduct at Meerut.

Delhi.

At daybreak on Monday, May 11th, no one in Delhi, European or Native, appears to have had any idea of what had occurred at Meerut. Shortly after the morning parade, about thirty of the 3rd Cavalry crossed the river Jumna by the bridge of boats, entered Delhi unopposed, by one of its seven gates, and murdered a European connected with the telegraph office. The troopers, reinforced by about a hundred other Meerut mutineers, marched to the palace. The guards offered no opposition, and several Europeans were massacred in the court-yard. The King wrote a letter immediately to Agra, narrating the mutiny and massacre, and describing himself as powerless in the hands of the sepoys; and his com-

* Raikes' 'Revolt,' p. 13. † Rev. Mr. Rotton's 'Siege of Delhi,' p. 6.

munication was the first account received from Delhi either at Agra or Calcutta.

The Delhi sepoys for many hours kept aloof from the Meerut mutineers. Neither party had a plan or a leader. The first thing they did, after throwing off the authority of their English officers, was to quarrel among themselves and set fire to the cantonments. Very few regiments injured their officers; but the leading mutineers, here and elsewhere, killed the most popular Europeans, because of the influence they exercised in keeping back their men. The English families took refuge in the Flag-staff tower, a circular brick building from which the daily gun was fired; but several persons were killed on the way. Lieutenant Willoughby, eight Europeans and some Native assistants, took up their station in the magazine, resolving to defend it to the last. One strong hope cheered the Europeans. Every eye turned eagerly towards the road to Meerut, from whence a rescue was momentarily expected: of course they looked in vain; none was even contemplated by the Meerut authorities. At three o'clock Lieutenant Willoughby and his companions, after holding out to the last anticipating succour, found the arsenal no longer defensible, and fired the trains laid in readiness. Two of the Europeans perished; the others crept through the smoking ruins and escaped by the sally-port on the river face. Lieutenant Willoughby did not reach Meerut, and is supposed to have been killed near the river Hindun. Nearly a thousand of the Natives who surrounded the magazine or lived in the adjacent streets are said to have been killed by the explosion; but the destruction of arms was far more partial than was at first hoped.

The Europeans in the tower fled from Delhi at about six o'clock, some in carriages or carts, and others on foot. The majority made their way to Meerut, Agra, or Kurnoul; but several were killed on the road. Those who remained hidden in Delhi were nearly all dragged forth and slain: men, women, and children, even those who had taken refuge in the palace, were indiscriminately massacred.

While the great change from "passive and respectful" mutiny to active, defiant, revolt was taking place, General Anson was absent on a shooting excursion out of reach of the telegraph among the hills near Simla.

He had erred grievously, but he was a brave man, and met the danger in a spirit, which, if shown at Meerut, might have saved Delhi. Convinced at last of the fatal impolicy of his past proceedings, the General issued an immediate order for the public withdrawal of the offensive cartridges, couched in language intended to soothe and conciliate the Native troops; but, as has been stated, before this proclamation could be circulated, the greater part of the Bengal army had ceased to exist. He held a council of war, and desired to press forward instantly for the re-capture of Delhi; but there was no commissariat, there were no camels, no provisions, not a single medicine chest available. Yet Anson rightly judged that every day, nay every hour, that the Imperial city remained in the power of the mutineers, was multiplying their resources; they were besides gaining confidence, and learning the value of the munitions of war with which Delhi was abundantly stored.

Of the Umballah council, not one man lived to see the capture of the city. General Anson died of cholera at Kurnoul on the 27th June; his successor General Barnard, Brigadier Halifax, and Colonel Mowatt fell victims to the same disease; and Colonel Chester was killed in action.

The British army encamped before Delhi on the 8th of June. Strengthened by reinforcements of men and money, raised in the Punjab by Sir John Lawrence, from the hereditary foes of the Delhi Mohammedans, and aided by the devoted fidelity of several Native princes, the British held their ground for many weary months. Their numbers were quite insufficient to blockade the city, into which mutinous regiments from different stations were constantly flocking, and bringing supplies of all descriptions, including the contents of the numerous military and civil treasuries of the stations plundered in various parts of Hindoostan. The King made repeated overtures to the British, and the Queen Zeenat Mahal was extremely anxious to obtain terms for the life of the King, and for their young son; but her proposals were rejected, it having been well ascertained, at an early period of the siege, from the reports of spies and in other ways, that the King and Queen had really no power to procure the surrender of the city.

Early in September the last British reinforcements arrived, and the Delhi sepoys, among whom the want of leaders had long been manifest, began to abandon the city in large numbers. By the 12th September, two practicable breaches had been effected, and the storm of the outworks commenced on the following morning. The British loss in killed, wounded, and missing, was two thousand one hundred and fifty-seven Europeans, and one thousand six hundred and eighty-six Natives. Among the lives lost was that of Brigadier-General Nicholson, the "first soldier in India." *

Lord Dalhousie, impressed by Nicholson's conduct in the Punjab, called him a "tower of strength," and so he proved at Delhi. He led the storm of the city, conducted the first critical movements to a successful issue, and then fell near the Lahore gate, shot through the body. He lingered for ten days, and, during intervals of mortal agony, was still able to counsel General Wilson on the course to be pursued. Notwithstanding his reserved and silent habit, his warm Irish heart won the affections of those who served with and under him, as completely as his talents and modesty secured their esteem. On the 23rd it was whispered throughout the camp "Nicholson is dead!" and Europeans and Natives, soldiers

* Russell, 'Times,' 20th August, 1858.

and civilians, lamented their common loss. The leading officials lowered into a grave, near the Lahore gate, the stalwart frame which had been a little while before described as "fit for an army or a people to behold." Some personal friends had previously cut from his head two or three of the curls which climate and a life of hardship had already turned from black to grey, although he was but five-and-thirty years old; and the Seiks, as they bent over his grave, mourned in characteristic manner for the chief, "the tramp of whose war-horse could be heard a mile off."

The King with Zeenat Mahal, and their son, fled to the mausoleum of the Emperor Humayun, called the Kootb Minar, several miles from Delhi, a strong and defensible structure; but they gave themselves up to Captain Hodson on receiving a pledge of personal safety. Three of the other Delhi princes subsequently surrendered from the same place, after two hours' negotiation, carried on through a member of the royal family, whose intervention was procured by the promise of his life. What assurances were given to the princes to induce them to surrender does not appear in the account given by Hodson and his sole European companion, Lieutenant Macdowell. But that some promise, direct or indirect, must have been made, is evident from the fact of these princes (whose family and creed were sufficient vouchers for their personal courage) being persuaded into separating themselves from three thousand armed adherents, and giving themselves up to the custody of two English officers and one hundred Seik troopers, instead of massacring the Hodson party, and then joining the Begum of Oude, Khan Bahadur of Bareilly, or other insurgent leaders.

On leaving the tomb the princes saluted Hodson, and remarked that their conduct would of course be investigated in the proper court. He bowed assent. Then, notwithstanding the vehement opposition of the faithful Mohammedans, the princes went away with Hodson and the Seiks in a "ruth" or covered vehicle drawn by bullocks. The Mohammedan soldiers, in obedience to the orders of their unfortunate masters, did not attempt to follow them; but when the ruth reached within a mile of Delhi, a mob gathered round the guard, and seemed disposed to attempt a rescue. Whereupon (according to Lieutenant Macdowell) Hodson made the princes descend, and after seizing their arms, compelled them to "strip and get into the cart; he then shot them with his own hand." *

Captain Hodson's vexation at being compelled by General Wilson to make over to the prize agents a considerable portion of the property taken by him from the persons of the King and princes, was forcibly expressed. His passion for "loot" was notorious. In Europe his conduct was stigmatized in terms rarely applicable to a British officer, as that of an executioner who looked sharply after his perquisites, and stripped his victims before slaughtering them—"pour ne pas gâter le butin." †

Besides the princes slain by Hodson, many others surrendered or were captured by the British. Among the prisoners were seven sons or grandsons of the King, who all escaped. The majority of them were retaken, summarily tried, hung, and thrown into the Jumna; but others remained at large, including Prince Feroze Shah, who became a noted general.

During the siege of Delhi, mutiny and massacre, and death in all its worst forms stalked over India. Many British stations were scenes of murder, pillage, and fire. Native towns and villages were, in retaliation, burnt to the ground, sepoys in appalling numbers blown from guns, and peasants hung from trees, for actual or alleged revolt. Scattered posts were held by resolute Englishmen, supported by a few devoted Natives, and almost everywhere the domestic servants were true, often even to the laying down

* Hodson's 'Twelve Years in India,' p. 315.

† Colonel Seaton's Letter; Hodson's 'Twelve Years in India,' p. 317.

of their lives for the families they served. Insurrection, partial insurrection that is, had been added to revolt, but the crisis at the worst never approached a war between Europeans and Natives as such. Had it done so, had all India merged its various antagonisms in hatred of the Feringhee, the English (unless preserved by miracle) must, in the words of a Mohammedan proclamation, have been swept into the sea, or at least shut up in their fortresses on the sea-coast. In some instances the fierce and deadly struggle resembled a war of race and creed; but, without exception, in every case of offensive and defensive strife the English had Natives of India for auxiliaries as well as for foes. The sharpest contests took place where the leadership of the mutineers fell into the hands of individuals embittered by personal grievances. Thus one spot became the scene of horrors unapproached elsewhere, and English lips shudder, and an English pen falters at the word—

Cawnpoor.

This place had been selected in 1775, as the station for the subsidiary British troops maintained at the expense of the Oude Government. General Sir Hugh Wheeler was an old, experienced, and popular commander. For the defalcation of the Native troops he was prepared, but their active hostility he thought out of the question. Still on the 22nd May, he wrote to Lord Canning, expressing a confident hope that the arrival of the promised British reinforcement from Calcutta would place Cawnpoor beyond danger. He mentioned also that he had been strengthened in men and guns by the Maharajah of Bithoor. This chief, Nana Sahib, was the adopted son of the late Peishwa, and by right of adoption, had claimed the continuance of the pension of Bajee Rao, or at least that some provision should be made for the family. He himself inherited the large savings of his adopted father, which furnished him with the means of sending emissaries to England to plead his cause; and one of these, named

Azim Oollah, a showy, wily, vengeful Mahommedan, found favour in Belgravian drawing-rooms, and spent money as freely as a Russian prince; but returned to Bithoor at last (*viâ* the Crimea, where war was then raging) exasperated by the failure of his undertaking. It was this man who was the incitor of the treacherous cruelty practised at Cawnpoor. The Nana himself was a handsome, sensual, ill-educated, common-place Hindoo, but decidedly popular among the English for the lavish hospitality exercised towards them. Such was the confidence placed in him, that when the outbreak became imminent, the whole of the treasure, upwards of one hundred thousand pounds, was given into his charge.

On the 6th June, the Native troops mutinied, and seized the Treasury, which the Nana's guard did not attempt to defend. Then the mutineers marched off towards Delhi, but were persuaded by Azim Oollah to return and attack their officers and families, who had taken refuge in two long barracks standing in the centre of an extensive plain, and unhappily, commanded on all sides. The only defence was a trench bounded by an earth bank, five feet high. About nine hundred persons, of whom seven hundred and fifty were Europeans, were blockaded in the intrenchment, and of these very few had secured a single change of raiment, and some were only partially dressed. The shirts of the men were used to bandage the wounded, or supply swaddling clothes for the three or four children born during the twenty-one days of siege. The dastardly assailants were kept at bay, although the heat was so intense that muskets exploded untouched. Owing to the exposed position of the well, not even a pint of water for washing was obtained during the whole time. It was at the cost of many lives that a few buckets were drawn to appease the maddening cravings of thirst, or to prepare the daily half-pint of split peas and flour into the porridge on which strong men and delicate women, the old general and the dying children supported existence, varied at rare intervals with some horse or dog broth, the animals being procured by sallies of the garrison. The destruction of one of the bungalows by fire drove two hundred women and children into the trenches for shelter, where they passed twelve days and nights on the open ground. Many were killed by the missiles of the foe, others cruelly wounded; some went mad; several became idiotic; and every night corpses were lowered into a dry well. At length when human endurance was nearly worn out, and the hope of succour from Calcutta or Allahabad (where mutiny had also occurred) had given place to despair, Nana Sahib prevailed upon General Wheeler to surrender, under the promise of being safely conveyed by way of the Ganges to Allahabad.

On the morning of the 27th of June the beleaguered community, reduced to half their original number, emaciated and in rags, entered the fatal boats, where smouldering charcoal was hidden under the hatches for their destruction. No sooner was the embarkation complete than the boatmen sprang into the river; firing from the banks commenced, the majority of the boats were swamped, and the Europeans brought to shore. The men were then all shot or cut to pieces, having first by their own request prayed together; the women were carried off to prison, except one lady, who clung with desperate force to her husband, and avoided protracted suffering by dying with him. Only four Englishmen escaped. The 'Story of Cawnpoor,' written by one of these (Lieutenant Thomson), contains a most touching account of the siege.* The Christian heroism displayed by the men and the fortitude and delicate feeling of the women were so wonderful that perhaps the strength of the English character was never manifested more clearly than during the prolonged agony undergone at Cawnpoor. The misery of the widowed ladies and children

* 'Story of Cawnpoor,' by Lieutenant (now Captain) Mowbray Thomson.

lasted three weeks longer, and their lives ended even more horribly than those of their husbands and fathers.

The troops, tardily dispatched from Calcutta, under General Havelock, advanced from Allahabad on the 7th of July; and after defeating the rebels on their line of march, reached Cawnpoor on the 17th. The Nana had fallen back upon Bithoor (nine miles distant), but before retreating, Azim Oollah had persuaded him to order the massacre of the English women and children; on the ground that, if carried off, their countrymen would certainly follow to rescue them; and, if left alive at Cawnpoor, their testimony would be fatal to many who would otherwise escape identification; whereas, if they were slain, the Nana might retreat unmolested, and his accomplices be undetected. The diabolical cunning of Azim Oollah prevailed. In addition to the hundred and sixty-three women and children, of Cawnpoor, there were forty-seven other captives, who had been seized with their husbands and fathers in the flight from mutiny and massacre at Futtehghur. The men had been killed, their wives and children saved and honourably treated, at least in the sense of being spared any personal indignity. Some Native nurses (ayahs) had remained faithful, and are believed to have shared with their mistresses the agonies, which, various as they were, did not include the wrongs which to virtuous women and tender mothers would have been worse than death. It has been established, after the most sifting inquiry, that no woman was dishonoured at Cawnpoor, nor was any child injured until the whole hapless, helpless multitude was doomed to death. Their place of confinement was the Sevada Kothee; the guards were sepoys of the 6th Native Infantry, and these men, under threats of extermination, were commanded to go in and shoot the women and children. They opened the door, fired once wildly at the ceiling, and then rushed away, determinedly refusing to have anything more to do with such devilish work. Upon this, two abandoned women—Adla, a professed courtesan, who exercised great influence over the Nana, and her servant, a slave-girl—found five men (two of whom were butchers and two villagers); these wretches being armed with swords, entered the prison, hacked and hewed down their wretched victims for many hours, and yet left the slaughter incomplete.* The groans continued all night, and shortly after daybreak on the 16th the dead and dying were flung promiscuously into a dry well, which, on the following morning, Englishmen looked upon and shuddered. The floor of the Sevada Kothee was ankle-deep in blood, the plaster on the walls was scored with sword-cuts; "not high up, as if men had fought, but low down, and about the corners where the poor crouching creatures had been cut to pieces." Tresses of long hair, children's shoes, and Bibles were found scattered about, and afterwards the excited soldiery traced wild words on the walls. But the gentle victims themselves left no appeal for vengeance on their foes, no reproach for neglect to their friends. The sight of the choked-up well, from whence the mangled limbs of his countrywomen protruded in ghastly disorder, drew from Major North the exclamation, "The blood of those innocents cries out from the earth in reprobation of a system which, from its slothfulness, led to this catastrophe."† The removal of the bodies would have been a horrible task for the living, and a fresh desecration to the dead. The well was therefore bricked over. Twenty men of Her Majesty's 32nd, marching through Cawnpoor in the following November, erected a stone tablet to the murdered women of their regiment, inscribed with the words, "I believe in the resurrection of the dead." These brave fellows chose their motto wisely. No words could afford a more consoling view of the suffering endured by the helpless multitude who were led through so terrible a path to the better life unto which we trust they have attained.

* Results of Official Inquiry.

† 'Journal,' p. 92.

Bithoor.

General Havelock did not proceed to Bithoor until the 19th, when he found the palace fort evacuated. The plunder both here and at Cawnpoor was very great, and the intoxication of the troops with the liquor which Azim Oollah was said to have left in readiness on purpose, fully answered the expectations of that arch schemer.

Lucknow.

Lucknow extends along the right bank of the Goomtee for four miles, and its buildings cover an area of seven miles. Its population exceeded one million persons, of whom two hundred thousand were fighting men, and as many more armed citizens. By both these classes the British were hated, for having deposed the King, degraded and insulted the Royal family, abolished the Court (on the expenditure connected with which the tradespeople had depended for a livelihood), and imposed heavy taxes on all classes.

In the middle of May Sir Henry Lawrence considered the defection of the Native troops inevitable, but he refused to anticipate it by disarming them, because this measure might precipitate an outbreak at Cawnpoor and the sub-stations of Oude, besides which every disbanded regiment helped to replenish the Delhi garrison. He took active measures for strengthening and provisioning Lucknow, and the European troops, in all about nine hundred and twenty-seven in number with seven hundred and sixty-five Natives, cheerfully did his bidding and prepared for the worst.

A partial mutiny took place on the 30th May, and in the first ten days of June, mutiny and disorganization spread over every station in Oude, and fugitives from Seetapoor, Mohumdee, Mullaon, Secrora, Gondah, Bahraech, Mullapoor, Fyzabad, Sultanpoor, Salone, Pershadipoor, and Duriapoor came thronging into Lucknow. The fate of those who fell into the hands of Nana Sahib after escaping from Futtehghur, has been stated.

On the 30th of June, Sir Henry Lawrence (probably influenced by the accounts given by Sir Hugh Wheeler of the cowardice and disorganisation of the rebels) marched to Chinhut, about eight miles from Lucknow, with a force of three hundred and fifty Europeans, and as many Natives, to meet what was reported to be a detachment from a large body of mutineers, about to advance on Lucknow. The enemy proved to be in much greater force than had been expected, the Native artillery joined them, and seventy-eight out of eighty Seik troopers galloped back to Lucknow, leaving the Europeans to charge alone. A deadly fire was poured by the mutineers from the loopholed walls of the village of Ishmaelpoor. The order for retreat was given by Sir Henry Lawrence, who was seen wherever the fire was hottest, issuing directions and encouraging the men, who were struck down by his side at every step. At length, about half the original number of the force re-entered Lucknow. The foe followed close at their heels, and the siege commenced.

The two main posts to be defended were the Residency and the Muchee Bawn. There were also several private dwellings which their occupants had done what they could to render defensible. Most of them had Tye Khanas or spacious cellars, built to secure the householders a refuge from the heat of the sun, and capable of affording shelter from the round shot of the enemy. Two batteries were in process of erection, one by the gallant Captain Fulton, the dauntless miner and counter-miner (whose loss at a late period of the siege was so bitterly lamented), the other by the equally brave Lieutenant Anderson. The retention of the Muchee Bawn was found to be inadvisable. All the smaller posts lay round the Residency; they were in fact little more than a number of buildings of various kinds scattered over a large garden; and formed a group on which it was resolved to concentrate the troops. There was no protecting wall, but the least defended spots were believed by the enemy to be mined, and were avoided accordingly. On the 1st of July, by means of a semaphore on the top of the Residency, Sir Henry Lawrence directed Colonel Palmer to "spike the guns well, blow up the fort, and retire at midnight," from the Muchee Bawn.

The order was obeyed. The two hundred and twenty-five Europeans traversed unnoticed the three-quarters of a mile between the fortress and the Residency, which they reached with the treasure and two nine-pounder guns. Half an hour afterwards, the explosion took place, to the astonishment of the Natives, and also of a drunken Irishman left sound asleep in the fortress; who, coming to his senses at daybreak, and finding himself in the midst of ruins, harnessed two bullocks, and made his way unmolested, with a cart full of ammunition, to the gates of the Residency.

On the same day, Sir Henry Lawrence had a narrow escape of his life. He occupied a small room in the most exposed angle of the Residency, which gave shelter to a hundred ladies and children, as well as to the sick soldiers, and the families of the men of the 32nd Regiment. A shell (from the howitzer lost at Chinhut) entered the window and burst at his feet. Sir Henry was entreated to quit the house, as it was evident from the incessant firing that the rebels knew where he was, but he refused, and would not even change his room, urging the improbability of another missile being pitched into that small chamber. The next morning a second shell flew in through the window, and in exploding struck Sir Henry with such force as nearly to separate his left leg from the thigh. He was removed to Dr. Fayrer's house, which speedily became the target for the rebel marksmen, and he lingered in great agony till the 4th, when he died, calmly speaking to those around him of the life beyond the grave. The fact of his death was withheld for many days. His body was lowered into a pit with that of several other companions in arms. But when his loss could no longer be concealed, an outburst of grief followed, and the besieged English mourned for him as a friend and a leader, whose like they would never see again. Brigadier Inglis, the next Commandant of Lucknow, declared that but for the foresight and precaution of Henry Lawrence, every European in Lucknow might have slept in a bloody shroud. Throughout India, by Europeans and Natives, soldiers and civilians, from Calcutta to the army before Delhi, Sir Henry Lawrence was lamented as a statesman, whose experience had increased the value of his talents and integrity; and, better far, whose Christian character had exercised an ennobling influence on those around him, and rendered him, unconsciously to himself, the most generally beloved man in India.

At midnight, on the 25th, Ungud, a faithful native messenger, stole through the besieging force with a communication from General Havelock, stating his confident expectation of being in Lucknow in five or six days. The hopes thus raised were not realized. Havelock equally overrated his victories and his resources.

He was a good and popular colonel, but a bad general; narrow and prejudiced in his views, with the leaning to favouritism, which is so fatal a weakness in the commander of a mixed force. He commanded admirably in the field, but his arrangements for the shelter and commissariat of the troops were ineffective, and the men under his command were exposed to needless hardships. Notwithstanding his energy and conscientiousness, those who have investigated his campaigns in Oude are not surprised to find that his attempts to march the fifty miles between Cawnpoor and Lucknow were twice defeated; and that the troops with which he had on the 23rd of July talked of "relieving Lucknow, and reconquering and pacificating Oude," were on the 15th of August represented by him as in "process of absorption by disease." Colonel Neil, who held command at Allahabad, and had been of great assistance to Havelock, was evidently dissatisfied with his proceedings, and described the troops as "much used up," and "not equal to a few miles' march."

Bitter disappointment was expressed at Lucknow at the delay of the relieving force, and Brigadier Inglis wrote to General Havelock on the 5th of August, that if he hoped to save the Europeans at Lucknow no time must be lost in pushing forward. The garrison was diminishing rapidly under the fire of the besiegers; even slight wounds often proved mortal, and in every instance amputation was followed by death. There remained two hundred and fifty women, two hundred and thirty children, and one hundred and twenty sick and wounded, to be defended by three hundred and fifty European and three hundred Native troops.*

General Proceedings.

Happily the month of August was marked by a great change in the conduct of the war. Sir Colin Campbell started from England at a day's notice to assume the chief military command. He reached Calcutta on the 15th of August, and learned the then precarious position of the army before Delhi; that Oude was becoming more disorganised daily, and that the talookdars who had protected the European fugitives were now inclined to side with the mutineers, whose hopes were high for the fall of Lucknow. The Doab was in the hands of the mutineers, communication with the Punjab cut off, and the Gwalior contingent (a remarkably well-trained body of troops), after being long held in check by the Maharajah Sindia and his able minister, Dinkur Rao, had at length broken out into mutiny and massacre, and threatened Agra with siege. Many of the Native princes, especially Holcar the Maharajah of the Mahratta principality of Indore, the Nizam of Hyderabad (the suc-

* Despatch of Brigadier Inglis, August 16th, 1857. 'Parliamentary Papers on the Mutinies,' No. iv. p. 157.

cessor of the prince, half of whose dominions had been annexed by Lord Dalhousie) with his able minister Salar Jung, and his venerable uncle Shums-ool-Omrah, were faithful to the English, and incurred personal peril and heavy expense by their firmness. The representatives of many of the ex-royal families exerted themselves strenuously to prevent an outbreak among their late subjects, but some took a different course. Among these was the Ranee of Jhansi, who, when the troops mutinied there and at the neighbouring station of Nowgong, consented to become their leader, and is believed to have sanctioned, if not ordered, the massacre of the officers and their families, in all thirty-seven Europeans.

The Ranee levied troops, caused guns to be taken from the places (in pits or wells, or behind brick walls) where they had been hidden by her late husband, seated herself on the Gadi or royal cushion of Jhansi, and surrounded by her kinsfolk and people, prepared for a death-struggle.

The ex-King of Oude and his minister were among the numerous persons whom the panic-stricken people of Calcutta pointed at as conspirators. They were seized at an early period of the mutiny, and kept in captivity until its conclusion, but after the most rigid investigation no tittle of evidence was proved against them.

The worst evil with which Sir Colin Campbell had to contend was the dilatoriness of the Calcutta officials. Their proceedings, it was said, all bore one or other of the post-office stamps—"insufficient" or "too late." Their neglect of the suggestions and entreaties of Sir H. Lawrence regarding the transit of troops had caused the fall of Cawnpoor. Now all the energy and dogged perseverance of the veteran General were directed to developing the arrangements initiated by Sir Patrick Grant. He gained his first and best victory at Calcutta, in establishing a system by which two hundred men were regularly forwarded along the Great Trunk Road to Allahabad in covered carts drawn by bullocks, and their meals prepared in readiness for their arrival at each halting-place.

Troops began to pour into India. The first help came from the colonies. Sir Henry Ward sent to Calcutta almost every British soldier from Ceylon; Sir James Higginson did the same from the Mauritius; Sir George Grey despatched four seasoned regiments from the Cape; and, to crown all, the Earl of Elgin, recognising the emergency, instead of proceeding to China, landed at Calcutta and placed seventeen hundred troops at the command of his early friend the harassed Governor-General of India. The Chinese expedition included in its ranks Captain William Peel, a first-rate artillery officer and a dashing, dauntless sailor. He rapidly organised a Naval brigade, and on the 18th of August with four hundred blue-jackets and ten 68-pounders, left Calcutta for Allahabad.

Lieutenant-General Sir James Outram returned from the Persian expedition in August, and was appointed Chief Commissioner in Oude. He was prevented from immediately proceeding to the relief of Lucknow by the outbreak of mutiny and insurrection in the province of Behar, where Kooer Sing and other Rajpoot chiefs had been driven to revolt by the impolitic severity of certain civil and military authorities, whose only system of dealing with the Natives, whether sepoys or peasants, chiefs or priests, Moslems or Hindoos, was by village burning and "unlimited hanging." This was especially the case in Patna, where a reign of terror was commenced by the Commissioner Mr. Taylor (in defiance of the instructions of Mr. Halliday the experienced and temperate Lieutenant-Governor of Bengal), which was happily ended by Mr. Taylor's removal, not on account of his severity, but because of an "ill-judged and faint-hearted order" * issued by him for the abandonment of several stations in Behar,

* 'Times,' (Sir C. Trevelyan), Oct. 24th, 1857.

which the local authorities took upon themselves the responsibility of disobeying.

The influence of Sir James Outram was successfully exerted in checking the sanguinary proceedings of the Special Commissioners, whose conduct at length attracted the attention of the Governor-General in Council, and caused the withdrawal or limitation of their commissions. Outram likewise recommended that there should be tribunals instituted for the trial of sepoys who should surrender and had not been guilty of murder. "It was," he said, "high time to show that we did not intend to wage a war of extermination against all Hindoos, or against all sepoys because they were sepoys." *

This seems strong language now; but then extermination was the leading idea of the "Hanging Commissioners," who, though civilians, far exceeded the military in the Draconian character of their code. The Non-Regulation Provinces had always been remarkable for the frequency and arbitrary manner in which capital punishments were inflicted, and now the wholesale executions were carried on to such an extent that the amazed authorities at Calcutta could not even procure accurate lists of the numbers and crimes of the slaughtered multitudes. Whole regiments were destroyed for no other reason than the alarm which the tendency to panic, shown by the sepoys, excited in the Europeans. A remarkable specimen of this state of feeling is given by Mr. Cooper, in his 'Crisis in the Punjab.' He there relates the manner in which the entire 26th Native Infantry were exterminated; their sole crime being running away in a panic on seeing their major killed by a fanatic, one of their number. Cooper details his pursuit of the sepoys for forty miles; the mobbing and drowning of great numbers in a river which they were too exhausted with fatigue and fasting

* Letter to Mr. J. P. Grant, 'Times,' June 7th, 1858.

to swim; and the surrender of some hundreds on perceiving what they construed as a leaning to mercy in their pursuers, followed by their execution in parties of ten by the Seik troopers (one of whom swooned under the prolonged horrors of the scene). He concludes by describing the suffocation of forty-five sepoys in a bastion, where they were confined without food or water during the whole night which preceded the execution, as being "unconsciously the tragedy of Holwell's Black Hole re-enacted." The dead bodies were flung by the village sweepers into a deep dry well, and Mr. Cooper triumphantly points to the well at Ujnalla as a pendant to the well at Cawnpoor. The Begum of Oude and other Native leaders denounced the massacre at Cawnpoor as having brought a curse on their cause. Some at least of the English chiefs thought differently of Mr. Cooper's "pendant;" for Mr. (now Sir Robert) Montgomery, who next to Sir John Lawrence was the most influential and possibly the ablest administrator in the Punjab, congratulated his subordinate in a demi-official letter, dated [Lahore] Sunday, 9 A.M., in the warmest terms on a deed which would be a feather in his cap as long as he lived, and added, "Three other regiments here were very shaky yesterday, but I hardly think they will now go. I wish they would, as they are a nuisance, and not a man would escape if they do."* This rejoicing over the extermination of a thousand men, and eagerness to find a pretext for the destruction of three thousand more, reads strangely from the pen of one of the most prominent advocates for the propagation of Christianity in India, but it tends to explain why our success as subjugators has been attended by failure as evangelists.

It is greatly to the credit of Lord Canning that he never gave way to the frenzy which prevailed at this epoch; never wavered in the example of calm courage and confidence in the

* Cooper's 'Crisis in the Punjab,' p. 168.

mass of the population, which he and his lamented lady gave to the panic-stricken community at Calcutta, and never failed to deprecate the mad cry for vengeance which the utterly false statements of violated women and mutilated children raised in England. After searching investigation, made on the spots where the worst excesses of mutiny and massacre had been committed, not a single case of violation or mutilation was proved. The wildest tales were narrated at the public meetings held for the purpose of raising a fund for the relief of the European sufferers by the mutiny, for which about half a million sterling was eventually subscribed. On the 7th of October, 1857, the day set apart by the nation for fasting and prayer on the occasion of this great calamity, some pulpits were disgraced by the utterance of vengeful sentiments excited by the whispered rumours which got abroad during the panic in India, and the wrongs darkly hinted at in letters to England by writers whose judgment was for the time unhinged by terror. But the most circumstantial stories of imaginary horrors did not originate in India, but emanated, in the form of alleged extracts from family correspondence, from London garrets. After circulating first in the lower and then in the higher class of English newspapers, these *canards* went to India, where, though everybody allowed such things had not come under their personal observation, it was said they might have happened in remote stations. So the snowball grew the faster the farther it rolled, and, in reckless hands, proved a weapon by means of which bitter humiliation was added to the desolation brought by the mutiny to many English homes, and a vindictive spirit roused towards the Natives which now, from its recognized injustice, is giving place to a partial reaction in their favour.

Lucknow.

The original plan of General Outram was to march from Benares to Lucknow, and thereby avoid the numerous river-courses between Cawnpoor and that city. But Havelock's force was by this time so enfeebled that he could hardly hold Cawnpoor, and General Outram was therefore obliged to march to his assistance. Cawnpoor was reached on the 15th of September. On the 19th, the army, consisting of three thousand one hundred and seventy-nine troops, of whom two thousand seven hundred and seventy-nine were Europeans and four hundred Natives, crossed the Ganges under the command of General Havelock; for Outram refused to supersede Havelock in the military command, and accompanied the expedition in his civil capacity as Commissioner of Oude. He ought, however, to have assumed the responsibility as leader, for his intimate knowledge of Lucknow and the whole surrounding country peculiarly fitted him for the task. The delegation of authority was generous rather than just. The result was that Havelock erred in the conduct of the expedition by acting in opposition to Outram's better judgment, and many lives were needlessly sacrificed.

On the 23rd of September the troops reached the Alumbagh or World's Garden, the summer palace of the late Queen-Mother of Oude, about three miles from Lucknow, which they occupied after expelling a rebel force. Leaving the European sick and wounded there with the baggage and tents, under a guard of two hundred and fifty men, the main body marched to Lucknow on the 25th of September. The Charbagh bridge was carried, but with heavy loss; and then General Outram, who had by this time taken the command of the first brigade, pressed on by a circuitous by-way towards the Residency, thus avoiding the main road, which was two miles long and had been cut through and strongly barricaded. Darkness was coming on, and Outram suggested to Havelock that the troops should halt within the courts of the Fureed Buksh Palace, so as to afford the rear-guard and the wounded time to close up.

But Havelock was of opinion that he would be exposed to

more severe loss by halting than by pressing forward. The men were impatient, and "young Havelock, nephew to the general, unable to resist the excitement, suddenly exclaimed, 'For God's sake, let us go on, sir!'"* whereupon the order to advance was given, and Outram, with a handkerchief bound round his arm, which had been wounded by a musket-ball, resumed his place at the head of the column, and was the first to enter the English entrenchments by the Baillie Guard gate. But the loss on the way was fearful even to the main body, who had to force their way through the narrow streets where every house was tenanted by foes and every window bristled with fire-arms. Brigadier-General Neil and other leaders were picked out by the rebel marksmen and mortally wounded. It was of course simply impossible for the rear-guard and baggage to pass unsupported through this strait of fire; they were sacrificed by Havelock; the dhoolies were burnt; seventy-seven of the wounded and sick were massacred, and sixty-one men of the rear-guard killed. The total loss of Europeans and Natives in killed, wounded, and missing was five hundred and thirty-five.

The Lucknow garrison dared not leave their post to welcome their countrymen. A few officers and men, off duty, came to the Baillie Guard, and helped to pull in the relieving force, as Europeans and Seiks clambered through the narrow doorway half blocked up with a mud-wall, while the balls of the enemy whistled round them. Many of the newly-arrived Europeans did not know where the hostile positions ended and the Residency line began, and a cruel mistake occurred in consequence. The Baillie Guard had been held from the commencement of the siege by a European officer, "burly Jack Aitken," and a band of the 13th Native Infantry. Some of the 78th Highlanders seeing the sepoys, bayoneted three of them; who made no resistance; but one of them, in falling, cried,

* Major North's 'Journal of an English Officer in India,' p. 199.

"Never mind! it is all for the good cause; welcome friends!" as he expired. No truer hero died that day.

General Outram now assumed the command. The heavy cost at which the reinforcement had been effected, and the weakened state of the garrison, rendered it out of the question to attempt conveying the sick and wounded, the women and children—in all, fifteen hundred helpless persons—through five miles of disputed suburb. He therefore contented himself with extending and strengthening the position by locating British troops in three of the adjacent palaces, which stretched along the Goomtee river from the Residency to the Kaiserbagh, and instituting a vigorous defence.*

General Proceedings.

Sir Colin Campbell completed his arrangements at Calcutta on the 27th of October, and travelled night and day to the seat of war. On the road he narrowly escaped falling into the hands of a body of the mutinous 32nd Native Infantry, and arrived at Futtehpoor (half-way between Allahabad and Cawnpoor), just as a British column (including Captain Peel's brigade) had defeated a body of Dinapoor mutineers. The struggle had been severe, and the mutineers had retreated to Calpee, to join a rebel force, commanded by Tantia Topee, a Brahmin, who had been from boyhood in the immediate service of the Nana, but who was now heard of for the first time. From his character and conduct there is every reason to believe that Tantia spoke the truth in denying that he had any share in the Cawnpoor massacres. He rose to power subsequent to the perpetration of that last horrible crime, which even the sepoys repudiated with horror. As to the Nana

* According to General Outram the original defenders of the Residency (in which list he apparently includes civilians as well as soldiers) numbered 1692 persons, of whom 927 were Europeans, and 765 Natives. Of these there remained on the 25th September only 577 Europeans and 402 Natives, including the sick and wounded.—Despatch, September 30th, 1857; 'London Gazette,' February 17th, 1858.

and Azim Oollah, they never seem to have held their heads up afterwards, or to have had a thought or a care beyond that of preserving their necks from the halter.

The mutineers in general rallied round Tantia Topee with a confidence they never evinced in any other leader. The Gwalior contingent, after breaking away from Sindia, and carrying off their siege-train, on the 13th of October, placed themselves under the orders of Tantia Topee, and joined his head-quarters at Calpee, on the Jumna, towards the end of November. They were expected to have arrived some weeks earlier, and the uncertainty of their movements increased the difficulty experienced by the Commander-in-Chief in providing for the defence of Cawnpoor.

Lucknow.

Sir Colin's whole force only numbered four thousand two hundred men; and he had to decide whether the rescue of the Lucknow garrison from their sixty thousand besiegers was to be attempted by hazarding the safety of the intrenched camp at Cawnpoor, which protected the communication across the Ganges and with Allahabad. A letter from Lucknow, dated October 28th, probably settled the question. Outram felt strongly the difficulty in which Sir Colin was placed, and urged him to make the relief of Lucknow a secondary consideration, as the garrison "could manage to screw on, if absolutely necessary, till near the end of November, on further reduced rations." The truth was that the amount of grain in store was greatly underrated; and Outram, while meaning to take the most cheerful view of his position, unconsciously exaggerated its danger.

Sir Colin marched from Cawnpoor on the 9th of November, and on the 12th encamped at the Alumbagh, and communicated the news of his arrival to Outram by means of a semaphore telegraph. The march to the Residency was facilitated by a brave act on the part of one of the garrison, an uncovenanted civilian, named Kavanagh, who, accompanied by a faithful Hindoo guide, Kanoujee Lal—made his way in disguise from Lucknow, and brought the Commander-in-Chief plans of the city, and advice from Outram as to the best mode of effecting an entrance.

Sir Colin changed his intended route, in compliance with these suggestions, and on the following morning (the 14th), with about four thousand men, including seven hundred cavalry, and a siege-train manned by Peel and his sailors, he made a flank march across the country, and advanced by the Dilkoosha Palace, the Martinière College, and the line of palaces leading towards the Residency. The Dilkoosha and the Martinière were taken after a running fight of about two hours; a bridge over the canal which joins the river Goomtee near the Martinière was seized, and a lodgment effected in a suburb on the further side: then the army bivouacked for two nights without tents, with their arms by their sides, being detained by a misapprehension of orders regarding the provisions and small arms to be forwarded from the Alumbagh. On the morning of the 16th, Sir Colin, leaving detachments at the Dilkoosha and Martinière, marched with a force reduced to three thousand bayonets to the Secunderbagh, a palace approached by a lane through a wood, and surrounded by a solid loopholed wall. After an hour and a half's fighting the only gate was stormed, and the garrison, numbering two thousand men, were put to the sword.

When the Secunderbagh had been stormed, the Naval Brigade went to the front and advanced upon the Shah Nujeef, a domed mosque, inclosed in a loopholed wall. Here Captain Peel led up his guns within a few yards of the building, to batter the massive stone defences. "It was an action almost unexampled in war. Captain Peel behaved very much as if he had been laying the 'Shannon' alongside an enemy's frigate."* For three hours a heavy cannonade was main-

* 'Despatch of Sir Colin Campbell,' Nov. 18th, 1857. Parl. Papers.

tained; but at the end of that time the British were losing ground. Even Peel's bright face became anxious (writes Colonel Alison) and Sir Colin sat on his white horse, exposed to the whole storm of shot, the men falling fast round him, watching in vain for any impression to be made on the mosque, which "sparkled all over with the bright flash of small arms." *

At length Sir Colin, who never expended a man where a bullet would serve his turn, saw that bullets were useless here. Addressing the 93rd Highlanders, he said that he had not intended to have employed them again that day, but that the Shah Nujeef must be taken with the bayonet, and —he would go with them himself. Whether he was justified, as Commander-in-Chief, in placing his person in such imminent peril, is a delicate question. Perhaps he could not resist sharing the danger of that terrible charge, could not bear to hurl his men at the stone walls without being himself in the ranks; perhaps he considered the risk to the army of his death, worth running for the sake of the confidence and enthusiasm which would be inspired by his presence; but whatever his motive may have been, he never hinted in his despatches that he had taken the head of the troops, or alluded to the slight wound he had previously received. The Royal Artillery dashed forward at the word of command, unlimbered the guns in the teeth of a deadly fire, and poured in round after round of grape. Peel worked his guns with redoubled energy. Under cover of this iron storm Sir Colin rode forward at the head of the 93rd, and the column advanced till they reached the foot of the loopholed wall. They had no scaling-ladders, and Peel's guns could make no breach. The muskets of the garrison were fast picking off the officers; Sir Colin's staff gathered round him; Lieut.-Colonel Alison, riding a little in advance, had his left arm shattered by two balls; and his younger brother was struck off his horse by a bullet in

* Colonel Alison's article in 'Blackwood's Magazine,' October, 1858.

the breast. Baird, Metcalfe, and Foster, Brigadier Hope, the gallant volunteer Lord Seymour, and Kavanagh the brave messenger from Lucknow, all had their horses hit in two or three places. At length, by Sir Colin's order, some rockets were thrown with admirable precision into the building. Shortly after this Brigadier Adrian Hope, with about fifty men, crept through the jungle, and perceived a narrow fissure in the wall, through which a man was pushed. His companions followed, and found that the garrison, terrified by the rockets, had evacuated the fortress by a back entrance, which, happily for the British, afforded the foe a means of escape.

That night the troops again bivouacked in the open air. Next day the joint operations of Sir Colin, from the Shah Nujeef, and of Outram, from the Residency, expelled the enemy from the intervening buildings; and long and loud was the hurrah of the troops as Outram and Havelock rode out (though the road was within musket-shot of the enemy) to grasp the hand of Sir Colin Campbell, and to welcome Mansfield, Hope Grant, Adrian Hope, Peel, and all the noble band. The total British casualties were one hundred and twenty-two killed, and four hundred and fourteen wounded.

The relief of the Residency was speedily followed by its evacuation; for Sir Colin considered that to leave another small garrison in Lucknow would be to repeat a military error; he therefore resolved on placing a strong movable division at the Alumbagh, as the best means of holding the city in check, and exercising an influence over the surrounding country.

The Kaiserbagh, or King's Palace, was strongly garrisoned by the enemy. It was bombarded by Sir Colin, in order to divert attention from the preparations for evacuating the Residency. These were so well made, and the movement itself so admirably carried out, that the women and children, the sick and wounded, the treasure, jewels, and money were carried off, through "a narrow, tortuous lane, the only line of retreat open, in the face of fifty thousand enemies, without molestation." *

General Havelock died of dysentery on the 24th, and was buried at the Alumbagh, where General Outram remained with four thousand men, while Sir Colin started for Cawnpoor with about three thousand, and the whole of the wounded, as well as the women, children, and treasure rescued from Lucknow, making in all two thousand persons to be protected.

Cawnpoor.

While the Commander-in-Chief was marching to Cawnpoor, that ill-omened spot again became the scene of a series of disasters. General Windham was in command there, with seventeen hundred effective men; and, mainly by the exertions of Captain Mowbray Thomson (the survivor and historian of the first siege), a small fort had been erected, which protected the bridge across the Ganges. The horrors he had so recently witnessed and shared had not altered his kindly view of the natives in general, and his conduct had secured a degree of influence which enabled him to procure abundant labour and to hurry on the work, on which four thousand persons were employed; the men digging for twopence a-day, from sunrise to sunset; the women and children carrying away the earth in their hands, and earning each a penny. The fort was just finished, when the Nana's troops and the Gwalior contingent marched upon Cawnpoor, led by Tantia Topee.

General Windham had no experience in Indian warfare. Probably he had heard of the repeated assertions made by the force previously besieged in Cawnpoor, that two hundred British troops might have saved them, and he did not understand the widely different character of the present foe. Tantia Topee and the siege-train of the Gwalior contingent were new elements, the importance of which General Windham could not have understood, or he would hardly have disobeyed

* Sir Colin Campbell's 'Despatch,' Nov. 23rd, 1857.

the instructions of the Commander-in-Chief, by leaving his intrenchments on the 26th of November to meet the enemy. After marching several miles, General Windham came upon the advanced guard of the rebels, and chased them until the main body was seen approaching in such strength that he gave the order for a retreat, and falling back upon Cawnpoor, bivouacked on a plain outside the city. The next morning he was suddenly attacked by Tantia Topee; and after five hours' fighting in the front, he found that his flank had been turned by the enemy, who had penetrated the town, and assailed the fort. An order was given for a general retirement within the intrenchment. A panic ensued. The field-stores and baggage of the Commander-in-Chief's army, including five hundred tents and valuable private property of all descriptions, left behind on the march to Lucknow, were not removed into the fort; and on the evening of the 28th, when Sir Colin Campbell crossed the bridge (having ridden on in advance of the column), he found the native town in possession of the foe; heard that the loss in three days had amounted to three hundred men (including Brigadier Wilson and Major Stirling killed); and that an immense amount of ammunition and camp requisites had fallen into the hands of Tantia Topee, who was at that moment engaged in appropriating the useful portion of the spoil and making a bonfire within sight of the fort, of the greatcoats and spare clothing which Sir Colin had with so much urgency obtained at Calcutta for the troops.

It must have sorely chafed the old Highlander to be compelled to stand still and witness the conflagration. But he felt that the protection of the women and children must be his first consideration, and that nothing could be undertaken which would compromise the safety of those by whom so much had been borne, and for whom so much had been sacrificed. When all the families and the wounded were despatched to Allahabad or elsewhere, Sir Colin breathed freely, and his despatches attest his relief at being rid of these "incumbrances." On the morning of the 6th December he issued from the cantonments. Captain Peel and his sailors, with their twenty-four pounder guns, advanced with the first line of skirmishers. The enemy was defeated, and pursued for many miles with great slaughter. The camp of the Gwalior contingent was taken, and thirty-two guns captured. The total casualties among the victors were only ninety-nine. The remains of the Gwalior contingent found their way to Calpee, where Tantia Topee employed himself in re-assembling his scattered forces.

The next step taken by the Commander-in-Chief was to re-establish the communication between Delhi and Agra, by sweeping the Central Doab with several British columns, and driving the mutineers across the Ganges into Oude and Rohilcund. This was successfully accomplished. Futtehghur was re-occupied January 2nd, 1858, and Sir Colin desired to march into Rohilcund and destroy the rebel government established there by Khan Bahadur Khan, a Rohilla chief, the representative of the family driven out by British troops in the time of Warren Hastings. Lord Canning, however, differed from Sir Colin, and overruled his plan, by compelling him to proceed to Lucknow instead, and also by delaying the attack on that city until Jung Bahadur, the Nepaulese leader, should arrive with nine thousand Goorkas to take part in the siege. Sir Colin waited until the end of February, and then obtained the reluctant assent of the Governor-General to march on Lucknow, without any longer waiting the tardy arrival of the Goorkas.

Great excitement was caused in Lucknow by the news of the coming force. Huzrut Mahal, the Begum of Oude, besought the chiefs to drive Outram from the Alumbagh before the main body should be able to join him. Flinging aside her veil, she addressed her council face to face, and in one of the repeated attacks made on the Alumbagh she was seen encouraging the troops from her elephant. But all in vain, there was no longer a chance of success. Sir Colin Campbell, with twenty thousand men and one hundred and twenty guns, was coming calmly on, resolved to make the artillery do the work, however slowly, and to risk no street fighting, no forcing a way through lanes, where his men might be shot down from houses as from batteries, or slaughtered from behind barricades.

The assault on Lucknow commenced on the 2nd of March; the River Goomtee was bridged over on the 5th, and on the 16th the city was completely in the possession of the British. The Secunderbagh and the Shah Nujeef were easily gained. The Chuckerwallah, or Yellow Bungalow, a building occupying a leading position on the race-course, was gallantly defended by a few sepoys, the last of whom was taken alive, and most horribly tortured by some Seiks, abetted by a few Englishmen.* The chief stand was made at the Kaiserbagh, and at a palace named the Begum's Kothee. Sir Colin was not present at the capture of the latter building, being compelled to await the arrival of Jung Bahadur, to whose dignity an official reception was deemed necessary. The Kaiserbagh was evacuated on the 14th, and the Begum and the other rebel leaders fled from Lucknow with a large body of adherents. The loss of the enemy could be only conjectured, but it must have been very large. Three thousand bodies were buried by the conquerors, who had one hundred and twenty-seven killed, and five hundred and five wounded. Captain Hodson received his death-wound while searching a dark room in which sepoys were concealed.† Captain Peel was shot through

* 'Up among the Pandies,' by Lieutenant Majendie, pp. 180-188.

† In a note written by Mr. Robert Montgomery to congratulate Hodson "on catching the king and slaying his sons," he added, "I hope you will bag many more." "Making a bag" was the phrase used in the Punjab for slaying a large number of sepoys, just as "disposed of" or "accounted for," when applied to a regiment, meant "exterminated." The phrase used by Mr. Montgomery is remarkable, considering the manner in which Hodson was killed

the thigh while laying his guns before the Dilkoosha, but, to the joy of the whole force, the wound did not prove mortal, and he was slowly recovering, when, being placed in an infected hospital litter, he contracted the small-pox, of which he died April 27th, 1858.

It was a sad drawback on the triumphs of this period to lose the man whose skill and valour had led his gallant sailors to perform feats hitherto unparalleled, and quite as useful as they were extraordinary. As a public man, the first naval officer of his day—in private life, social, genial, unselfish; the son of a prime minister, yet simple, hardworking, and thorough in every professional and extra-professional duty—England might well be proud of William Peel.

After the occupation of Lucknow, two ladies and a child were discovered in the city. The husband of one lady, Captain Orr, and the brother of another, Sir Mountstuart Jackson (the nephew of the Commissioner by whom the Oude princesses had been ejected from their palace), had been put to death, with several other prisoners, upon the refusal of Sir James Outram (acting upon instructions from Calcutta) to negotiate for their lives on any other terms than a money ransom, which the rebels refused to accept.

The booty taken at Lucknow was enormous. A million and a quarter was received by the prize-agents, and many individuals must have realized fortunes on the day that the Kaiserbagh was given up to plunder. One casket, which disappeared, contained one hundred thousand pounds' worth of jewels. The Seiks were better "looters" than the British, and the Goorkas, though late for the fighting, were in time for the sack and the plunder. In fact they were so active that it became necessary to request the Nepaulese chief to quit Lucknow before anything like tranquillity could be restored. When they took their departure the whole force

by the chance shot of a fugitive sepoy, and the numberless perils which the dashing dragoon had previously escaped.

was a mere baggage-guard, and it was even necessary to detach a British column to escort them safely on their homeward route. Their chief, Jung Bahadur, was made a Knight Grand Cross of the Bath.

Reduction of Central India.—Jhansi, Calpee, and Gwalior.

While the operations above related were conducted by the Commander-in-Chief, the reduction of Central India was effected under his directions by two columns furnished from Bombay, under Generals Rose and Roberts, in co-operation with a brigade sent from Madras under General Whitlock. The force under Sir Hugh Rose, consisting of five thousand men, in two brigades, took Ratghur Fort, and on the 3rd of February relieved Saugor Fort, in which one hundred and fifty European women and children had been shut up since the previous June. Sir Hugh Rose then forced his way through the passes on the road to Jhansi, and on the 23rd of March commenced the blockade of the city, which included within its walls a granite fort standing on a rock.

The defence was desperate. The shells of the assailants caused an extensive conflagration on the first day of the siege, but the garrison repaired their shattered defences, re-opened their repeatedly-silenced batteries, and struggled on against an overwhelming force. The women were seen working in the batteries and carrying ammunition. The garden battery was fought under the black flag of the fakirs. Everything indicated a general and determined resistance.

Tantia Topee came to the assistance of the Ranee with the Rajah of Banpore, a chief who, like many others, had protected European fugitives, but had been reluctantly drawn within the vortex of mutiny. Sir Hugh Rose met the advancing force; dispersed and drove them across the Betwa with great loss.

The Ranee, Lakshmi Bye, defended Jhansi to the last, and on the 3rd of April, when a breach had been effected and the

British entered the town, the hand to hand fighting did not cease. The garrison, instead of fleeing into the fort, maintained their posts to the last. Forty of the Ranee's body-guard defended the royal stables, and strove, even when dying on the ground, to strike again; while the troops at the palace, seeing further defence impossible, set fire to trains of gunpowder laid in readiness, and perished in the explosion.

The Ranee and a party of the garrison quitted the fort during the night. She was hotly pursued, and would, it was thought, have been captured, but that the ever-vigilant Tantia Topee sent an escort, or probably came himself, to meet her. On the 4th of April the fort and remainder of the city were taken possession of by the troops; who, infuriated by the recollection of the massacre perpetrated there, revenged it by fearful excesses. No less than five thousand persons perished at Jhansi; the men in many cases flinging themselves down wells, after first killing their wives, sooner than fall alive into the hands of the conquerors. The executions were very numerous, and included the father of the Ranee. Of the British there were thirty-eight killed, and two hundred and fifteen wounded. The plunder was very great.

From Jhansi Sir Hugh Rose marched to Calpee, which was held by the Gwalior contingent. Tantia Topee and the Ranee of Jhansi strove to stop the advance of the General by entrenching themselves at Koonch, but they were driven out, and pursued with horse-artillery and cavalry for more than eight miles. It was expected that a desperate stand would be made at Calpee, the more so because a letter had been intercepted addressed to the mutineers at that stronghold, written by the Ranee of Jhansi, urging them to defend with vigour their only arsenal. But Calpee, though strong in its maze of ravines, was unprovided with the stone walls in which the Natives (the Mahrattas excepted) place their chief confidence. The mutineers had lost heart from repeated defeats; and, on the appearance of the

British force, they fired a few shots and fled, leaving their chiefs no alternative but to accompany them.

Tantia Topee, however, had not yet played his last card. Disguising himself, he went to Gwalior, and there sounded the temper of the people and soldiers. Then returning to the Calpee fugitives, who had been re-assembled by the Ranee of Jhansi, and were posted on the Gwalior road, he wrote to Sindia and his grandmother (by adoption), a lady who exercised considerable political influence under the title of the Baiza Bye, repeated assurances that no harm was intended them, but that opposition was useless, as their troops and people were on the revolutionary side. Sindia, in an impulse of impatience, and in opposition to the counsels of his able minister Dinkur Rao, marched forth, on the 1st of June, to attack Tantia Topee; the assertion of Tantia was justified by the event, and the Maharajah, deserted by his troops, fled to Agra.

The rebel force took possession of Gwalior. General Rose lost not a day in marching thither. The cantonments outside the city were captured by the British on the 16th of June. On the following day a squadron of the 8th Hussars made a brilliant charge through the enemy's camp, and, notwithstanding their previous fatigue and the intense heat, the Dragoons did much execution with their revolvers. The Ranee was sitting in the camp when it was surprised by the troopers, with another lady, a Brahminee concubine of the late Rajah's, who never left her; but, being in military attire, their sex was not observed. They mounted their horses and fled. The Ranee received a shot in the side, and a sabre-cut on the head, but rode on till she fell dead from her saddle. Her guards surrounded the body, and, raising a funeral pyre, burnt her remains, according to the Hindoo custom. The faithful Brahminee was also mortally wounded.

The loss of the Ranee was a crushing blow to the rebel cause. Even after Jhansi had fallen, Sir Hugh Rose declared, that the high descent of Lakshmi Bye, her unbounded liberality to her troops and retainers, and her fortitude, which no reverses could shake, rendered her an influential and dangerous adversary; and he announced her death to the Government as that of the bravest and best military leader of the rebels.

The Maharajah re-entered his capital on the 20th of June, after little further opposition. Tantia Topee having given his followers the well-understood order of "total dispersion"—that is to say, to fly in small numbers and reunite at a given point, there was a temporary cessation of field operations. Sir Hugh Rose resigned his command, and retired to Poona to recruit his wasted strength, and the men were placed in cantonments for the remainder of the hot season.

Rohilcund Campaign. Reduction of Oude. Fate of leading Rebels.

The Begum of Oude, when driven from Lucknow, fled to Bareilly, the capital of Rohilcund, where Prince Feroze Shah (one of the sons of the captive Emperor of Delhi, who, warned by the fate of his brothers, had preferred flight to surrender), and other rebel leaders with their followers, had taken refuge with Khan Bahadur, the old but brave and able Rohilla chief.

The calm, well-organized advance of Sir Colin Campbell, and the admirable arrangements of the chief of the staff, General Mansfield, rendered the prolonged defence of Bareilly almost impossible. On the 5th of May the British marched on a suburb of Bareilly, where a fierce onslaught was made by a hundred and thirty-three Mohammedan fanatics called Ghazis, or holy warriors—grey-bearded men, who, waving their curved swords above their heads, and crying "Glory to God! the faith, the faith!" rushed on the bayonets of the 42nd Highlanders, of whom about twenty were wounded. Every Ghazi was killed.

The suburbs were cleared and the cantonments secured,

after which, Sir Colin, true to his policy of not exposing his men to street fighting, bivouacked on the open plain. On the next morning the city was attacked on the north side by a body of troops under Brigadier Jones, the last of three columns which the Commander-in-Chief had caused to be concentrated on Bareilly. This great city, though without walls, was held by many thousand men of desperate fortunes; but they forsook it, and fled before the overwhelming force brought to bear upon them by Sir Colin, which moved with a sort of mechanical accuracy unparalleled in an Indian army.

The occupation of Bareilly was rapidly followed by the proclamation of an amnesty to all but notorious rebels; and by this means tranquillity was speedily restored in Rohilcund, where indeed the people, having been left since the mutiny of the East India Company's sepoys utterly ungoverned, could not be blamed for having fallen under the rule of Khan Bahadur, the representative of their ancient chiefs.

Thus, in June 1858, not a city or fortress of any magnitude remained in the hands of the rebels. The reduction of Oude, which Sir Colin Campbell commenced in July, was slowly but surely accomplished; and, by a mixture of firmness and conciliation, the Commander-in-Chief was enabled to report to Government, at the beginning of the year 1859, that there was no longer a vestige of rebellion in Oude.

The Begum retired upon Nepaul with her son Birjis Kuddr. Prince Feroze Shah, of Delhi, proved a skilful leader, but he had taken the field too late for any prospect of success. After making many efforts to rally the disheartened sepoys under repeated defeats, he also was driven into the Terai, where altogether about twenty-five thousand persons were assembled. Of these many fell victims to jungle fever, others were killed in encounters with our forces, and about two thousand, including several chiefs, were captured by the Goorkas and made over to the British authorities. Khan

Bahadur of Bareilly was one of these. He was tried and executed; so also was Jowalla Pershaud, one of the council which decreed the final massacre at Cawnpoor. Yet though that crime was denounced by the rebel leaders in general, and by the majority of the mutineers, as having brought a curse on their cause, neither the unpopularity of the Nana Sahib, nor the fifteen thousand pounds offered for his apprehension, could induce the Natives to betray him; and some chiefs, like the Rajah of Churda, sheltered him in his extreme need, and were also driven into the jungle, where it is believed that the Nana and his counsellor Azim Oollah both died of fever. Mummoo Khan, the commander of the Begum's forces at Lucknow, being dismissed by her, surrendered himself to the British Government; was tried and found guilty of having (though reluctantly) consented to the execution of the English prisoners at Lucknow, and was sentenced to transportation for life. Lonee Sing, the aged Rajah of Mithowlee, had kindly received and sheltered these same fugitives when they escaped from Segowlie; but the peremptory demand of the Oude durbar had at length procured their being sent to Lucknow. Lonee Sing was tried for having surrendered them, and sentenced to transportation for life. He died while the decree was being carried into execution.

Tantia Topee fought to the last. He was entrapped by Maun Sing, one of the most powerful of a class of talookdars or landholders of Oude, who, as farmers of the revenue, had risen to power and amassed enormous wealth, to the injury of the old aristocracy and the peasantry. Maun Sing fought against the British at Lucknow, but he subsequently forsook his Native allies; and, by his information, Tantia Topee was captured while sleeping in the jungle near Sepree. This able general, whose movements Russell's graphic pen compared to forked lightning, and who led our troops so many weary marches—crossing the Nerbudda to and fro, passing between our columns, behind them, and before them, traversing mountains, ravines, valleys, swamps, and marching for weeks together thirty and forty miles a-day—was a comely, well-made Brahmin, fifty years of age, with a large, finely-shaped head, piercing black eyes, sharply-arched grey eyebrows, and an abundant head of grey hair, with whiskers, beard, and moustache of the same colour. When apprehended and heavily ironed, he was quite calm—said he wanted no trial, and expected nothing but death; only he wished that it might be speedy, and that his captive family might not be made to suffer on his account. He was tried by court-martial and hanged. The Rajah of Gonda, Bainie Madhoo of Shunkerpoor, and the gallant old cripple Nirput Sing of Royea, were among the Rajpoot chiefs who joined the Begum of Oude, the wife of their deposed and captive sovereign, when her cause was desperate; they died in the jungle—the first of fever, the other two in battle with the Goorkas. Several Rajpoot chiefs surrendered to Sir Colin Campbell (or rather to Lord Clyde, his great services having been acknowledged by the grant of a peerage). One of the bravest, Mehndie Hussein, as he entered the British camp, said, "I was twenty-five years in the service of the King of Oude." The cordial greeting of the Commander-in-Chief showed how well he understood the force of these words in the mouth of an honourable foe.

Exile of the King and Queen of Delhi.

Of all the notable persons who had rebellion and its short-lived "greatness thrust upon them," none paid a heavier penalty than the octogenarian King of Delhi and his beautiful Queen Zeenat Mahal.

After the capture of the city, judicial measures of extreme severity followed the military excesses committed there. The Commissioner (Mr. Greathed), a just and temperate man, whose mind had not been soured by personal losses or humiliations, died of cholera immediately after the occupation of the city. Had he lived, he would doubtless have restrained the disgraceful proceedings of certain civilians, who, having fled in terror, returned in triumph, and inflicted capital punishment with such indiscriminate fury, that the first act of Sir John Lawrence on receiving charge of Delhi and Meerut, "was to put a stop to civilians hanging from their own will and pleasure, and to establish a judicial commission to try offenders."*

The pledge given by Captain Hodson to the King and Queen of Delhi for "freedom from personal indignity," † did not suffice to preserve them from being imprisoned in a mean and dirty chamber over one of the archways of the palace, where they were constantly intruded upon by Europeans; nor did it save the aged King from the misery of a public trial,‡ which lasted twenty-one days and ended in his being pronounced "a false traitor to the British Government, and an accessory to the massacre in the palace." In reply to the first charge, he pleaded that he was helpless in the hands of the mutineers; with regard to the massacre, he declared that he and Zeenat Mahal had thrice interfered to save the Europeans at the risk of their own lives; and there is reason to believe this was really the case, for the Queen and one of the princes had been rendered exceedingly unpopular in Delhi by their efforts on behalf of the English and Native Christians.

The defence of the King did not prevent the infliction of the severest penalty which the primary condition of his surrender permitted. The connexion between the E. I. Company and the House of Timur ended in the last of the Company's representatives sentencing the last Great Mogul "to be transported across the seas as a felon." On the 4th

* Speech of Capt. Eastwick, Deputy-Chairman of E.I.C., Aug. 25th, 1858.

† Hodson's 'Twelve Years in India,' p. 305.

‡ The trial was conducted by Major Harriott in a similiar spirit to that evinced at the Meerut court-martial (see p. 40). Harriott died suddenly on landing from India at Southampton in March, 1859, with 30,000*l.* in his portmanteau, and bequeathing 100,000*l.* to a nephew.

of December, 1858, the King, Queen, and Prince Jumma Bukht, with his half-brother (a mere child), and some of the ladies of the zenana were conveyed in H.M.S. *Megæra* to Rangoon, and thence to Tonghoo, an inland station in British Burmah.

Annexation of the Sovereignty of the East India Company.

The same storm which drove Mohammed Shah from his hereditary palace, to die in exile, terminated the so-called double government exercised by the East India Company, in co-operation with the ministers of the Crown. The financial difficulties caused by the Mutiny, and the generally unsatisfactory state of India, became the subject of anxious inquiry in the House of Commons; and after some discussion, decisions were formed, in accordance with which all political power was taken from the Directors and transferred to the Crown. The Company was left an incorporated body, with no concern in India beyond the receipt of dividends on their capital stock. The sovereign power so long exercised by the East India magnates, and the monopoly of patronage which had made the government of a great Empire almost like a close borough in the hands of a powerful family, passed away with the last glories of the House of Timur. The Palace at Delhi, and the great offices in Leadenhall Street, had had their day; and while the Dewani Khas (the imperial hall inlaid with jewelled legends which compared that favoured spot to Elysium), was given over to pillage, the huge building in the City of London was thrown open to public view previous to its being offered for sale by auction and bought for its site and materials. It was with strange feelings that men who had served the Company from boyhood, coming home after the mutiny, fresh from scenes of war and fire, razed forts and pillaged palaces,—visited the East India House and wandered through the gloomy corridors and deserted rooms which they remembered to have seen thronged with soldiers and civilians, clerks and messengers, anxious and earnest on their several errands. And few could help lingering in the council chamber, and thinking of the men of bygone generations, who by the sword or by the pen had been instrumental in conquering India, and whose marble statues stood in their lofty niches with the dingy gilt ceiling above, and the old-fashioned armchairs below, once occupied by successive generations of potentates, who, under the plain names of Chairman and Directors of a London Company, had exercised a degree of authority over millions of people, to which that of the Doge and Council of Venice in its palmy days was poor beyond comparison. Here the fate of emperors, kings, and governors-general had been decided upon; here the career of Clive and Warren Hastings had been watched and criticised step by step; here the subsidiary system of Lord Wellesley and the social reforms of Lord William Bentinck were discussed; and lastly, here the annexations of Lord Dalhousie were suggested and applauded. Another turn of the wheel, and the armchairs of the Directors were left as vacant as the Peacock throne of Delhi, and scores of other ivory thrones or jewelled cushions, the lumber of extinct power. The sovereignty of the "Honourable Masters" of the most powerful body of men ever ruled by their fellow-subjects, was annexed by their supreme government in a manner not unlike that in which the Directors had appropriated Oude, with the difference of the utmost possible regard being shown to the claims of the deposed English rulers, and their retainers. In both cases the plea for annexation was the same, that of misgovernment. The shortcomings of the East India Company were brought to light by the blazing fires of mutiny and insurrection. There is no need to dwell further on this point, and even while protesting against their many sins of omission and commission, none can examine the proceedings of the "Merchant Adventurers," without being amazed by the difficulties they surmounted and the greatness they achieved.

Change of Government.

The decree by which the Crown and Parliament of Great Britain assumed the sole responsibility of governing India, was enacted on the 2nd of August, 1858, under the name of an Act for the better Government of India. Much fear was entertained by the advocates of Indian reform that there would be no radical change in the administration; that the Natives would be still jealously excluded from all positions of rank and emolument; that the fee-simple of the land would in most parts of India be withheld; that pretexts would be seized for annexing the few remaining Native states and pauperising their aristocracy; that public works would be neglected as heretofore, and the enterprise of British settlers discouraged.

These apprehensions were increased by the arbitrary procedure adopted in Oude towards the ancient Rajpoot chieftains, and towards the wealthy but newly-risen class, who together constituted the landed proprietors of the new province. The first step taken by the Indian Government after the reoccupation of Lucknow indicated, that however generously disposed Lord Clyde and Sir James Outram might be towards the now submissive talookdars, their opinions would have no influence at Calcutta. A proclamation was sent by the Governor-General in Council to be issued by Outram as Commissioner in Oude, by which the whole territory in that province was declared to be confiscated, excepting the estates of five or six chiefs. Outram remonstrated in forcible language against this proceeding, but Lord Canning persisted in considering that "any proclamation put forth in Oude in a liberal and forgiving spirit would be open to misconstruction." * The result was, that Outram was compelled to leave Oude for the same reason which had driven Henry Lawrence from the Punjab. He was superseded by Mr. (now Sir Robert)

* Lord Canning's 'Despatch,' March 31st, 1858.

Montgomery, who came from the Punjab for the purpose, with a staff ready to carry out the policy which an unprejudiced witness declares that "every man, civil and military, in the British camp, considered too harsh and despotic." *

Outram exerted his influence with the chiefs to prevent their being driven to despair by the new decree; assuring them they would be treated with leniency and consideration. The expectations he held out were fully realised; the "confiscation proclamation" was disapproved in England, and Lord Ellenborough, then President of the India Board, on his own responsibility wrote to Calcutta a strong repudiation of the whole proceeding. His Lordship's despatch was taken up as a party question, and caused his resignation; but though he and Outram were sacrificed, the talookdars of Oude were saved from ruin, and the Government probably from another insurrection.

The Proclamation of the Sovereignty of Queen Victoria was published throughout India on the 1st of November, 1858; it was graciously worded and followed by measures calculated to inspire the people with hope that a new era had commenced, and that they would be dealt with for the future in a spirit of just and uniform liberality, almost impossible under the complicated system of double government and divided responsibility. The sacrifices exacted in the newly recovered provinces were unavoidably severe. In Oude, for instance, the razing of fortifications, the surrender of cannon by the chiefs, and the disarming of the population, were measures no Native rulers had ever the power of enforcing; but the British Government were willing at the same time to make concessions which the East India Company had resolutely withheld. In defiance even of the articles of an Act of Parliament passed in 1832, the Company had refused to appoint Natives to offices of trust or emolument. No

* Russell's 'Diary in India,' vol. i. p. 356.

public employment was given to the higher class of Natives in any degree proportionate to their social position; and this deprivation was the more bitterly felt, because, under the House of Timur, the Hindoos had shared with the conquering Mohammedans the honours and emoluments of the imperial service; Brahmins had been faithful and most able chancellors, and Rajpoots commanders-in-chief. But the class-interests and prejudices of the Company prevented the employment of Natives in any but the lowest positions, and this narrow policy might have been inherited by the British Government, but for the convictions of Lord Stanley, whose visit to India, and intercourse with Sir Henry Lawrence, led him, in his subsequent position as Secretary of State for India, to take a decided course, and exercise a most happy influence at a very critical period.

By his reiterated orders the little state of Dhar was restored to the boy prince from whom it had been taken by the Governor-General in Council in November 1857, because the troops of the young Rajah had revolted against his Government and joined the mutineers. This righteous act has given satisfaction in India. It is much to be regretted that Lord Stanley should have ceased to fill the important office for which he was so well suited; but there is reason to hope that his successor, Sir Charles Wood, has undertaken its arduous duties in an equally just and resolute spirit. The work to be done is very heavy. Reform is needed throughout India. Even in our oldest provinces, the tenure of land, the proceedings of the courts of judicature, and the system of taxation calls for revision; but, in the more recently acquired Non-Regulation provinces, as they are termed, the duty is most imperative that a less arbitrary mode of administration should be adopted, and the laws so simplified and digested, as to render the welfare of the people as little as possible dependent on the happy accident of a gifted ruler, or liable to be experimented upon by inexperience, or what, though improbable, is still possible, oppressed by wilful tyranny or corruption.

A strong tie was formed between the English and the chiefs who fought for their government and shielded their fugitives. The bond has been strengthened by the honours and rewards bestowed upon Sindia the Maharajah of Gwalior, and his able minister Dinkur Rao; upon Holkar the Maharajah of Indore; on the Nizam of Hyderabad, his minister Salar Jung, and his uncle Shums-ool-Omrah; on the Rajahs of Kaporthulla, Puttiala, Bhurtpoor, Jheend, Rewah, Bulrampore, and Punnah; upon the Rana of Dholpoor, the Ranee of Bhopal (who had controlled her people with remarkable sagacity), the Rao of Cutch, the Nawabs of Kurnoul, Rampoor, and many others; not forgetting that model of patriarchal rulers, of good landlords, and kind hosts, the old Rajpoot Rajah of Byswarrah, the protector of the Cawnpoor fugitives, Thomson and Delafosse.

But the most important measure enacted since the change of government, and which contrasts forcibly with the old system of timidity and distrust, is the nomination of Natives to seats in Council at each Presidency, and the establishment of a Native magistracy. In Oude it has been officially stated that the "administration is conducted on the great principle of recognizing a powerful landed aristocracy as an important element of political prosperity."* In that province therefore, the attempt made before the mutiny of crushing all classes, as if under an iron roller, to the same dead level of insignificance, has been abandoned, and the result already attained is that "the relations between the Native aristocracy and the servants of government are on a freer and kindlier footing in Oude than in most parts of India."†

The ex-King Wajid Ali, has accepted the pension of twelve lacs per annum, which he refused at the time of his depo-

* 'Report on Administration of British India,' Calcutta, 1861, p. 35.

† Idem, p. 33.

sition, and it has been officially intimated that provision will be made for the King's wife the Begum Huzrut Mahal, and his son Birjis Kuddr, in the event of their surrender.

This is one indication among many others that the Indian Government, secure in its strength, can afford to deal generously with its defeated foes. In Great Britain the last echoes of the Vengeance cry were silenced by reports of the misery and actual starvation caused by the famine in the North-West Provinces, and the subscriptions raised for the relief of the sufferers amounted to above one hundred thousand pounds. The largeness of the sum, and still more the general sympathy expressed by all classes in England and the Colonies for their Indian fellow-subjects, showed that the breach made by the mutiny was healing more rapidly than could have been expected. The manner in which the relief was distributed was very creditable to the Commissioners employed in the arduous duty; and Colonel Baird Smith, the able engineering officer, who so materially assisted in the capture of Delhi, died, worn out with his labours for the mitigation of the misery of the people, in the districts where the scarcity was most severe.

In fine, the righteous administration of India is now treated as a matter of high importance. Lord Canning's term of office has expired. He has conducted himself with truth, courage, and honour, in a position of unparalleled difficulties and disadvantages, which overtook him suddenly, and might well have embarrassed and dismayed a ruler more experienced in Indian legislation.

The cardinal error of delay in sending succour to Cawnpoor cannot be attributed to any apathy or indolence on his part, but must be taken as a proof of the dilatoriness and procrastination of the local officials generally. Lord Canning himself was a laborious and methodical worker. He has weathered the storm, and he leaves India in an incomparably better position than he found it. On public grounds he has reason to rejoice, but in his private life he has been sorely stricken by the death of the noble wife, who, supported by high Christian principle, bore up so bravely under the fears and trials of the Mutiny; and then fell a victim to fever, just when peace was restored, and a large circle in England were joyfully preparing to welcome her return.

Lord Elgin, the newly appointed Governor-General, is an administrator of experience, energy, and judgment, with a genial courtesy of manner which is valued everywhere, especially in India. Under his direction, we may reasonably hope, in the emphatic words addressed by Lord Canning to the talookdars of Oude (16th April, 1861), and repeated with cordial concurrence by Sir Charles Wood, that the continued success of England's Government "will be a standing proof that in spite of bygone animosities, and of the broadest differences of race, religion and social usage, a generous and trustful rule is the surest way to make a loyal and dutiful people."

CHAPTER II.

PHYSICAL GEOGRAPHY.

BRITISH INDIA forms the central southern extremity of the continent of Asia, and covers an area of about one million and a-half square miles. It extends from the north-east extremity of the Punjab to Cape Comorin, about one thousand eight hundred miles; and from Kurrachee at the mouth of the Indus river, to Rangoon at the mouth of the Irrawaddy river, about one thousand nine hundred miles: with a land boundary of about four thousand five hundred miles; and a nearly equal amount of coast-line. On the *north*, India is separated from China, Thibet, and Tartary by the Himalaya mountains; on the *east*, from Burmah and Siam by the Yoomadung and the Tenasserim ranges; and on the *west*, from Afghanistan and Beloochistan, by the Afghan chains and plateaux, by the Suliman ridge, the Bolan mountains, and the Keertar, Jutteel, and Lukkee hills. The island of Ceylon is separated from the *southern* extremity of India by the Gulf of Manaar and the Palk Strait. The Malabar or western coast of the Indian peninsula is washed by the Indian Ocean and the Arabian Sea; and the Coromandel or eastern coast by the Bay of Bengal, which forms the western boundary of Arracan, Pegu, and Tenasserim.

Mountains and Plains.

The chief physical features of this great region consist of vast mountain chains, hilly ranges, isolated eminences, and extensive table-lands, intersected by numerous large rivers. The Himalaya (*abode of snow*) is divided by some geographers into Eastern and Western, the division being near Lake Manasarowar, at the southern extremity of the mountain range which, extending from the north-west into Thibet, separates the drainage system of the Indus from that of the Sanpoo (afterwards the Brahmapootra), and probably also from that of the Yang-tze-Kiang. From this culminating portion of the Himalaya the mountains extend in a north-westerly direction for about seven hundred miles, and in an easterly direction for about eight hundred miles, with a nearly uniform altitude of eighteen to twenty thousand feet above the sea, and an average breadth of one hundred and fifty miles. In the eastern section is Kinchinjunga, situated in the north-east angle of Nepaul, which rises 28,176 feet above the level of the sea, and, until the recent discovery of Mount Everest (29,000 feet in altitude), was considered the loftiest mountain in the world; Gosainthan (24,740 feet), rises one hundred and forty miles to the westward of Kinchinjunga. Two hundred and forty miles further to the west is Dhwalagiri, 28,000 feet high. Among the chief summits in the north-west section are Nanda Devi (25,749 feet), Kamet (25,550 feet), Gyu (24,764 feet), Monomangli, or Gurla, in the north-west of Bhotan (23,929 feet). The loftiest peaks generally rise from dividing ridges of irregular height, which extend at right angles from the main chain, and form the great basins that receive the melting snows and drainage of the neighbouring heights, and in which the mighty rivers originate that flow towards the mountain buttress termed the Lower Himalaya, and thence to the plains of Hindoostan. Between the Sutlej and the Ganges there are four ridges connected with the Snowy range, which respectively form the watershed for the rivers Sutlej, Tonse, Jumna, and Ganges. Each ridge consists of a series of rising peaks and corresponding depressions or passes, which form the natural roads through the mountains, and are, with a few exceptions, seldom less than eighteen thousand feet above the sea. On the lower spurs and slopes of the Himalaya, towns and military stations have been established, to which Europeans resort for a cooler climate, such as that of Simla, 7800 feet above the sea, and the Darjeeling ridge, which varies from 6500 to 7500 feet.

The Cashmeer valley is about eighty miles in length by ten to thirty-five miles in width, upwards of 5000 feet above the sea, and nearly surrounded by mountains whose highest ridge is from ten to twenty miles from their base. They are capped with snow for eight months of the year, except at their highest elevation, Diarmal, upwards of 26,000 feet above the sea, on whose steep sides no snow can rest. The Cashmeer river, which drains the valley, finds an exit by a chasm whose almost perpendicular sides are some thousand feet in depth. The river-bed is in one place only seventy feet feet wide, and the waters glide for ten miles with astonishing velocity in an unbroken stream.*

Varieties of climate and of soil are obtainable in the Himalaya at different altitudes. The disintegration of the northern exposed ridges provides a constant accumulation of alluvium, which, mixing with the deposits of decayed vegetation, nourishes noble forests of the Deodar and other pines, and produces naturally at elevations of from eight thousand to twelve thousand feet some of the most delicate European vegetables and flowers. Asparagus, celery, rhubarb, strawberries, gooseberries, and raspberries, the scented violet, primrose, anemone, cowslip, and potentilla are all plentiful in these lofty regions.†

The Suliman mountains, which form the western boundary of the Punjab (or country of the Five Rivers) and of the valley of the Indus, commence in nearly 34° north latitude, and extend due south for three hundred and fifty miles. The loftiest summit, called Takht-i-Suliman, or Solomon's Seat,

* Paper by W. H. Purdon, Esq., Executive-Engineer, on the 'Physical Configuration of Cashmeer Valley.'

† 'Correspondence of Superintendent Briggs relating to Tibet road.' Parl. Papers, 25th July, 1856, p. 82.

sometimes called Khaisa Ghar, in 31° 35′ north latitude, is eleven thousand feet above the sea, but does not enter within the region of perpetual snow. The western side forms a buttress which upholds the lofty table-land of Sewestan. The eastern declivity descends in some places sharply to the valley of the Indus, while in others the hills are comparatively of easy ascent, and the level country not more, on an average, than twelve miles distant from the peaks of the Suliman. The heights are twenty-five miles from the Derajat, a populous tract extending along the western bank of the Indus, and forming a portion of the plain called the Damaun or Border, which is three hundred miles long, by sixty miles broad, and reaches from the Kala, or Salt range, on the north, to the confines of Sinde on the south. The mountain slopes are here remarkable for vigorous and varied vegetation, and the valleys are clothed with many kinds of indigenous trees, shrubs, and flowers. The ranges which divide Sinde from Beloochistan are low, broken, and of irregular height.

Next in political importance to these marked natural boundaries on the north and west, is the Vindhya chain, which crosses India between the twenty-second and twenty-fifth degrees of latitude, from the valley of the Ganges on the east, to Guzerat on the west coast, forming the northern boundary of the valley of the Nerbudda river. The Vindhya may be viewed as the crest of the vast plateau, seven hundred miles long, by one hundred to two hundred and fifty miles broad, with an elevation of nearly two thousand feet, which, on the north of the Nerbudda, constitutes the table-lands of Malwa and Rajasthan, and, with the adjacent regions, is called Hindoostan. On the south, is the triangle termed the Deccan, nine hundred and fifty miles long, by seven hundred broad, with an elevation varying from two to three thousand feet above the sea. The Vindhya also connects the northern extremities of the two series of ranges, called the Western and Eastern Ghauts; the former stretching parallel to the Indian Ocean, the latter to the Bay of Bengal, and both uniting, towards Cape Comorin, to form the southern extremity of the Deccan. The highest portion of the Vindhya does not exceed five thousand feet. The crest of the Jaum ghaut, or pass, proceeding from the Nerbudda towards Indore, has an altitude of two thousand three hundred feet. The Sautpoora range, which divides the Nerbudda and the Taptee valleys, is an offshoot of the Vindhya.

The river system of the Vindhya and Sautpoora is distinct; the dip of the land on the north being to the western coast, and on the south towards the eastern coast, or Bay of Bengal.

The Western Ghauts increase in altitude, from about three to eight thousand feet, as they pass from the Gulf of Cambay to Cape Comorin. They are abrupt in their descent towards the seashore, and gradually decline on their eastern face towards the Deccan. The distance between the mountains and the coast is from twenty to forty miles; the flat country is intersected with streams, very fertile, but insalubrious. The fine lofty region of Coorg constitutes a portion of the Western Ghauts; Mercara, the chief town, is more than four thousand feet above the sea.

The most prominent feature in southern India is the Neilgherry or Blue Mountains. They rise abruptly in mural precipices from the adjacent plains, with an average height, from the crest to the general level below, of about six thousand feet, except on the north side, where the mountains abut on the table-land of Mysoor and Wynaad two to three thousand feet in altitude, between which and the heights the Moyaar river intervenes. The Neilgherry summit forms a varied line of undulations, frequently breaking into lofty ridges and abrupt eminences, but presenting a more generally level aspect than is to be found in any of the tracts of equal elevation in other parts of India, and this, probably, owing to volcanic eruption, or to a subsidence of the surrounding regions. From the plateau, of six thousand feet elevation, there arises a central range, running from north-west to south-east, the highest apex of which, Dodabetta, is 8610 feet above the sea. Another mass of mountains, called the Koondahs, separated from the Neilgherries proper, rises to the north-west, and attains an elevation nearly equal to Dodabetta; numerous spurs, with intermediate rich valleys, adapted for coffee plantations, jut out to the southward. Ootacamund, the chief European settlement, is 7300 feet above the sea; two minor stations (affording different climates), Coonoor and Kotergherry, are each six thousand feet above the sea. At Jackatalla, now Wellington, there is a sanitarium in a well sheltered valley, exempt from the dry cutting north winds experienced at Ootacamund. Although the base of the mountains is granitic or sienitic, the soil of the Neilgherry plateau is very productive. Its fertility is attributed to the decomposition of numerous dykes of rock, especially of trap and hornblende, which, mixing with the quartzose and clayey products of the granite, afford a soil well adapted for cultivation. The greater portion of the country is covered with grass; forests occur in distinct and singularly isolated patches in hollows, on slopes, and sometimes on the very apex of a lofty hill, becoming luxuriant and extensive only when they approach the crests of the mountains, and stretch along the valleys into the plains below.*

The climate is famed for salubrity and for remarkable evenness in its seasons. Although only eleven degrees north of the equator, the mercury falls to the freezing-point in the coldest months, December and January; and seldom reaches 75° in the warmest period of the year, April and May. The fall of rain annually is at Ootacamund, sixty; at Coonoor, fifty-five; at Kotergherry, fifty inches. The soil and climate are very favourable for the growth of wheat.

Connected with the Ghaut ranges are the Pulni, or

* 'Survey of the Neilgherry Mountains.' Parl. Paper, 1st August, 1861.

"Fruit" hills, near Madura. There are two ranges, upper and lower; the highest peaks are more than eight thousand feet high. The upper ridge extends, in long undulations, over a space twenty miles long by fourteen broad, covered with grass; while woods full of timber, some of great size, clothe the ravines and sheltered hollows of the plateau. Elk and bison abound in them. The scenery resembles that of the Scottish Highlands, with extensive ledges of mushroom-shaped rocks, over which the torrents fall; and natural bridges and underground channels, through which they percolate. The vegetation resembles that of England more than that of Simla does, where the nettle will not sting, though it will on the Pulni. Many European fruits, flowers, and vegetables flourish; the turnips, for instance, are excellent, and the potatoes mealy and good. Pure water abounds; horses, cows, and sheep thrive; and the natives are few and peaceable.

The European sanitary station at Pulni, 7,230 feet above the sea, may be reached from Periacolam by a horse-track in four hours; when the sweltering heat of the plains is exchanged for a climate in which blazing fires, carpets, and curtains are acceptable.*

The Eastern Ghauts extend from Balasore, near the head of the Bay of Bengal, to fifty-six miles north-west of Madras, and form the south-eastern buttress of the southern table-land; their length is upwards of eight hundred miles; their height is less than that of the Western Ghauts, seldom attaining 2,500 feet. Bangalore, in the latitude of Madras, is 3,000 feet above the sea.

The Yoomadung and Tenasserim mountain ranges, of from five to ten thousand feet high, on the eastern side of the Bay of Bengal, are little known.

In different parts of India there are several mountain and

* See 'Minute of Tour,' by Sir Charles Trevelyan in 1860. Parl. Papers, 31st July, 1860.

hill ranges, and some isolated heights. The Nepaul plateau rises three thousand to six thousand feet north of Bengal. In Assam, and to the eastward of the Ganges, are the little-known clumps and ranges, termed Cossya, Garrow, Jynteea, and others, with table-lands and heights varying from one thousand to four thousand feet. Sewalik range, near Hurdwar, rises three thousand feet; Ḳala or Salt range, near the Suliman, two thousand five hundred feet. The Aravulli form the western buttress of Central India; on Mount Aboo, the chief peak in this range, five thousand feet high, there is a sanitarium for Western India. The Kattywar hills, near the centre of the Kattywar peninsula, rise one thousand to three thousand feet; the three ranges in Bundelcund do not exceed two thousand feet; the Rajmahal hills, stretching from the Ganges towards the Vindhya have an elevation of from five hundred to seven hundred feet.

Rivers.

The natural irrigation of India is on a grand scale. Viewing the entire region, from the Suliman to the Youmadung mountains, it is the best-watered portion of the globe. No other tract of country of like extent has so many great rivers flowing to the sea, with such numerous fluvial tributaries in the directions needed for agriculture and for traffic.

In the north-west, four hundred thousand square miles of territory are watered by the Indus (Nilab or Blue River), whose whole course is eighteen hundred miles, during which it receives the Five Waters of the Punjab—namely, the Sutlej, eight hundred and fifty miles long; Beas, two hundred and ninety; Ravee, four hundred and fifty; Chenab, seven hundred and sixty-five; and Jhelum, four hundred and ninety —also the Cabool river, three hundred and twenty, and the Zanskar, one hundred and fifty miles long. The Indus is navigable for steamboats from Kurrachee, on the shore of the Arabian Sea, to Attock, on our extreme northern frontier, a distance of about one thousand miles, thus affording communication with the ocean along the whole course of our only vulnerable land boundary.

In the north-east the famous Ganges, one thousand five hundred miles in length, unites with the Jumna at Allahabad, and is navigable for steamboats from Calcutta for nearly a thousand miles. The Jumna, before its confluence with the Ganges, receives the Chumbul (five hundred and seventy miles long), Betwa (three hundred and sixty), Sinde (two hundred and sixty), Nuddea (two hundred and forty-five), and seven other streams, principally from Central Hindostan, draining altogether an area of one hundred thousand square miles. The Ganges has numerous tributaries, many of which are themselves large rivers, such as the Gogra (six hundred miles long), Gunduck (four hundred and fifty), Goomtee (four hundred and eighty), Sone (four hundred and sixty-five), Coosy (three hundred and twenty-five), Ramgunga (three hundred and seventy), and the Mahanunda (two hundred and forty).

Like many great rivers, the Ganges has formed at its termination in the Bay of Bengal, a number of marshy islands called the Sunderbunds, by the deposition of the immense quantities of earth swept down by the stream. These islands are intersected by numerous channels or outlets for the mighty volume of water, which is estimated to pass Benares at the rate of two hundred and fifty thousand cubic feet per second. One of these channels, named the Hooghly, on whose left bank Calcutta is built, is formed by two branches of the Ganges, termed the Bhagruttee and Jellinghee; it runs a tortuous course to Diamond Harbour, and thence to an estuary of the sea, fifteen miles wide, near Saugor Island. The course of the Hooghly is one hundred and sixty miles; during its progress it receives the Dammoodah and Rupnarain rivers.

The entire area drained by the Ganges and its tributaries

is probably not less than half a million square miles, and from time immemorial the Gangetic valley has been the seat of a comparatively high civilisation. Immense cities, densely inhabited, have flourished along this great maritime highway; of many of these nothing now exists but heaps of bricks and ruins; yet despite the ravages of war, pestilence, and famine throughout many centuries, probably half the population of all India dwells on land irrigated by the Ganges and its tributaries; a circumstance which determines that the seat of empire must be somewhere on the navigable part of this great artery, the entire course of which is in the temperate zone.

The Brahmapootra is a noble river. Its early course is still a subject of discussion. Under the name of the Sanpoo or Dihong, it is said to flow from west to east a thousand miles north of the Himalaya; then bursting through a gorge in 28° 30′ N. lat., it enters Assam under the name of the Brahmapootra, and forms a winding channel nine hundred miles long to the Bay of Bengal, near which the stream is called the Megna, and its branches anastamose with those of the Ganges. The river is available for steamboat navigation for several hundred miles.

The Irrawaddy river is more than a thousand miles in length. The British territory of Pegu and the harbour of Rangoon are situated at its termination in the Bay of Bengal; and Ava, the capital of the kingdom of Burmah, on the upper portion of its course. The Bassein branch of the river is navigable for ships of the largest size for sixty miles; steamboats have ascended the Irrawaddy for several hundred miles from the sea, and by this means a communication might be established with western China. Eastward of the Irrawaddy are the Sittang, and the Saluen or Salween, both rising on the highlands of Yunnan, in China, and flowing nearly due south for about five hundred miles, receiving many tributaries from unexplored regions, and entering the British dominions of Martaban and Tenasserim in about the seventeenth degree of latitude.

Returning to "India within the Ganges," and examining the western side of the Bay of Bengal, there will be found eighteen rivers draining the regions southward of the Nerbudda and eastward of the Malabar Ghauts. Among these may be named the Godavery, eight hundred and thirty miles long; Kistna, eight hundred; Cauvery, four hundred and seventy; Mahanuddy, five hundred and twenty; Brahminy, four hundred; Byeturnee, three hundred and forty; North Pennar, three hundred and fifty; South Pennar, two hundred and forty; and other streams flowing from one to two hundred miles.

The western side of India has about twenty rivers, but few of magnitude. The Nerbudda is eight hundred miles long, the Taptee four hundred, Myhee three hundred and fifty, Loonee three hundred and twenty, Bunnas one hundred and eighty, and Bhader one hundred and thirty. The Nerbudda and Taptee flow through Central India—the former between the Vindhya and Sautpoora ranges; the latter south of the Sautpoora—and both fall into the Gulf of Cambay. They are not available for steam navigation, owing to the rocky nature of their beds.

Altogether about fifty rivers in India discharge their waters into the sea. Four of these are each more than one thousand miles long; three are eight hundred and upwards; and five are from four to five hundred miles in length. There are above fifty large tributaries to the ocean rivers. Two of these run upwards of eight hundred miles; two upwards of six hundred; eight from four hundred to five hundred; and ten from two hundred to three hundred miles.

Harbours.

Considering the extent of coast-line from the Arabian Gulf to the Straits of Malacca, there are few good harbours. Bombay is the only one available for the resort and refitment of a large fleet; in its spacious dockyard excellent line-of-battle ships have been constructed. Goa (which belongs to the Portuguese) is a fine port. To the south of Goa an important haven is being formed at Seedashevaghur, which is two hundred and ninety miles south-east of Bombay, and contiguous to Dharwar and the best cotton districts of the Deccan. The Cala Nuddy river here descends from the Ghauts to an inlet of the sea about one mile wide, with a depth of twenty-five feet at high tide, and a roadstead outside sheltered by several islets. The harbour requires skill and capital for its improvement, and these are now being employed by Government. The Manchester Cotton Agency has fixed on Seedashevaghur for the erection of its presses and warehouses, and the port promises to become a valuable emporium. The immense and secure haven of Trincomalee belongs to Ceylon. The Hooghly river, on which Calcutta stands, has its entrance impeded by shifting sandbanks, and the passage of the river itself is barred against very large merchant ships by the 'William and Mary' shoal. Bassein, Rangoon, and Moulmein, are good ports on the eastern side of the Bay of Bengal.

Kurrachee harbour would be one of the most important in the East—in consequence of its proximity to the Persian Gulf and the Red Sea, and as the port of the Indus—if the bar at its mouth could be removed. Operations have been commenced by Government in the hope of effecting this object.

There are many small or barred harbours: on the Malabar side twenty-four, on the Coromandel coast eleven, and on the east side of the Bay of Bengal eight; all well adapted for coasting traffic and for vessels of small draught. Havens or shelter are also to be found among forty islands and groups of islands which fringe the coast, the greater number of which are on the shores of Chittagong, Arracan, and Tenasserim.

Geology, Mineralogy, and Soil.

A complete geological survey of India is now in progress, and museums for the public exhibition of specimens of rocks, fossils, and minerals have been formed at Calcutta, Madras, Bombay, and Kurrachee.

The formation of a road into Thibet has afforded some insight into the geology of the Himalaya. The elevated plain lying between the Sewalik range and the outer spurs of the great chain is composed of loose conglomerate and alluvium; the line passes through tracts of friable sandstone, much indurated in parts; higher up the mountain spurs are capped by masses of granite imbedded in stiff, ferruginous clay, frequently intersected with walls of gneiss and overlying beds of indurated sandstone. At Dhurmpoor, at an elevation of four thousand nine hundred feet, is an extensive mound of half-baked, stratified rock, abounding with fossiliferous remains, especially shells. On Dugshai hill there are thick beds of graphite and marl; on the spur to the north there are masses of yellow sand, perfect rectangular blocks of argillaceous limestone, and other deposits of the oolitic system. The Krole mountain is almost entirely composed of coralline magnesian limestone of fantastic shape and full of fissures and caverns. From the Krole to Tara Devi mountain the formation is of clay-slate, finely laminated. The Tara Devi is of volcanic origin, composed of several of the primary rocks fused into a conglomerate mass; mounds of black scoriæ are here as on the Krole of frequent occurrence. A bright vermilion powder, in considerable demand among the natives, is found here, and at one place quartz veins impregnated with iron pyrites. Between Simla and the uplands of Thibet the mountains are of mica-slate and gneiss, crossed but seldom with any other formation; the mica-slate is piled up in precipices many hundred feet in height, and the gneiss is exposed in equally perpendicular masses, thousands of feet in extent. Veins of quartz pierce every description of rock, and form a network throughout the whole of this formation. The action of the weather on the cliffs causes rocky avalanches to descend with crushing force, carrying ruin and desolation in their impetuous course, and depositing vast quantities of forest trees and surface strata in the glens beneath.*

The mineral wealth of India is of incalculable value; gold, silver, tin, copper, iron, plumbago, lead, and coal have been found in various districts. There is abundance of copper and also of iron ore in Kumaon, easily obtainable, with the materials for working it in the immediate vicinity.† The iron region stretches along the base of the lower Himalaya range, so far as examined, for sixty miles. At Dechowree a wall of ore extends three hundred feet in length, which on being excavated for twenty feet left the depth of the deposit unascertained. At Hurdwar a rich red ironstone, associated with clay, is in many places fifty feet deep, and contains 50·96 per cent. of metallic ore. Dense primeval forests of hard wood peculiarly suitable for making charcoal abound, and water power exists for any amount of machinery.

Near Kundrelah, seven thousand feet above the sea, close to where the two great spurs of Simla and the Chor bifurcate, a large tract of about two hundred square miles extends, containing a magnetic iron ore similar in its external, physical, and chemical character to that of Norway and Sweden; it occurs in very dark iron disseminated in veins throughout the mica schist, has long been worked by the Hill-men, and from its malleability is much prized in the Indian market. The working is extremely simple: a stream of water washes away the friable schist, at an expense of sixpence the hundred-

* 'Report of Lieutenant Briggs,' describing the difficulties encountered in the formation of the Thibet road.

† See 'Tramroads in India in connexion with the Iron Mines of Kumaon and Gurhwal,' by W. P. Andrew, Esq., p. 51.

weight of ore, which contains fifty-two per cent. of fine iron. Lieutenant Briggs erected a rude furnace on the spot, and turned out iron, superior to that of Glasgow and Merthyr Tydvill, at seventy shillings a ton.

In past ages gold was extensively obtained in India, and Professor Max Müller thinks that Malabar is the site of the Ophir whence wealth was brought by the Queen of Sheba to Solomon. The geological formation in different parts of Hindoostan bears a resemblance to that of the auriferous regions in California, and it is supposed that the Deccan and the Malabar coast are rich in the precious metals; fluvial or alluvial gold-dust has recently been found there in the beds of streams. A search has been instituted in Dharwar, and promising quartz reefs discovered, which, it is alleged, will yield a more profitable return of gold than those in Victoria and in New South Wales.

European skill and capital are now being employed in raising metals in Kumaon, on the Nerbudda, and elsewhere. Sulphur, alumina, and natron exist; diamonds, rubies, pearls, cornelian, and various precious gems have for ages been celebrated among the products of India; but more valuable than all these are the coal-mines, which have been found in various localities.

The quantity of coal raised in 1858 from six distinct fields was two hundred and twenty-six thousand tons; in 1860 it had increased to three hundred and seventy thousand. This, indeed, is small compared with the annual yield of the United Kingdom—viz., seventy-two million tons—but in process of time the subterranean fuel of Hindoostan will probably be found adequate to the demands of increasing civilisation.

The alluvial soils of India are of great extent, as may be supposed by examining the numerous rivers on the map. Dr. Forbes Watson estimates that a third of the entire area of the country consists of alluvia, varying in its component parts, but rich in vegetable matter, and, when aided by the organic deposits which irrigation affords, of inexhaustible fertility. The famous black soil, so favourable to the growth of cotton, is chiefly formed by the decomposition of basalt and trap. It extends from the Nerbudda to the extreme south of the Deccan, and contains nodules composed of carbonate, phosphate, and sulphate of lime; of potash, oxides of iron, and aluminium. When dry, it is dark-coloured, and glistens from the presence of nearly pure grains of silica. Occasionally it exhibits minute shells and specks of limestone; in many places scarcely a pebble is to be seen. This soil possesses extraordinary attraction for water, and forms a tenacious mud which does not need irrigation. In depth it equals that of the American prairies; in the North Berar valley wells are sunk through ninety to a hundred and twenty feet of black earth and greyish clay. The soils of Southern India are mainly formed by granitic decompositions, and they contain the elements necessary for vigorous vegetation.*

Climate.

The climate of India is more varied than that of Europe. About half the country is within, and the other half without the tropics; irrespective of which, altitude, aspect, and prevailing winds modify the temperature in relation to the health and character of man, and to the products of the soil. On the Deccan plateau the atmosphere is cool, dry, and healthy. At Ootacamund the mean of the thermometer (Fahrenheit) for the year is 57°; at Delhi, 72°; Bangalore, 74°; Calcutta, 79°; Madras, 83°; Bombay, 84°. The quantity of rain is varied: at Calcutta, fifty to eighty inches; Bombay, sixty to one hundred and eight — average seventy-six; Madras average, sixty-six inches; Ootacamund, sixty; Nagpoor fifty-three. On the Western Ghauts the monsoon breaks with great violence. At the sanitary station of Mahabaleshwar,

* For analysis of soils, see 'Address delivered before the Society of Arts on the Growth of Cotton in India,' March 25th, 1859, by Dr. Forbes Watson.

four thousand five hundred feet above the sea, the mean annual fall is two hundred and fifty inches; but in the Ghauts, as elsewhere, the quantity diminishes with the increased altitude.* Thus, at Kotergherry, eight thousand six hundred feet high, it is only eighty inches. On the Cossya hills in North Assam—exposed to the full force of the monsoon from the Bay of Bengal—the fall is five hundred to six hundred inches (fifty feet); at Darjeeling, on the Himalaya slope, which is above seven thousand feet high, the fall is one hundred and twenty-two inches. At Little Thibet and on the higher portions of the Himalaya rain seldom falls.

The climate of India is not only affected by the great mountain ranges, but also by the south-west and the north-east monsoons, which influence the degree of moisture on the western and on the eastern coasts. The southern parts of the Deccan and of the Neilgherries derive benefit from both monsoons. Generally speaking there are three marked seasons—the cool period, in November, December, January, and part of February; the dry heat which precedes the periodical rains; and the moist heat which follows them. The autumn and winter weather on the Indian plateaux is delicious; so also are the mornings and evenings in spring throughout Hindoostan.

* In Cumberland, England, the diminution in the fall of rain begins at an elevation of two thousand feet.

CHAPTER III.

POPULATION.

AT a period long prior to the Christian era India was peopled by a swarthy race, low of stature, with high cheek-bones, large jaws, flattish nose, expanded lips, little or no beard, and long black shaggy hair; speaking a language different from the Sanscrit, eating animal food, drinking intoxicating liquors, with no system of caste, and practising customs totally unlike those of the Hindoos. Old castles, extensive excavations, Druid-like altars and tombs, with various monumental ruins and works, attest the degree of civilisation which these aborigines attained prior to their subjugation by the Hindoos—a comparatively fair, or rather olive-complexioned race, which Blumenbach designated as of Caucasian, and Pritchard of Iranian origin. The conquerors, as shown by their literature, migrated from a northern clime; they probably entered Hindoostan in large bodies in rapid succession, and gradually reduced the primitive inhabitants to serfdom, or drove them towards the southern districts, and into forest-clad elevations and fastnesses, where our surveyors, on taking possession of new districts, have suddenly come upon them living in small, quiet communities in the mountain recesses.

The famous writings known as the 'Institutes of Menu' afford a good view of the state of Indian society in the ninth century B.C. The Hindoos had not then passed the twenty-second degree of latitude. Caste existed, in its broad divisions of the Brahmin, or sacerdotal; the Cshatriya, or military; the Vaisya, or industrial; and the Soodra, or servile class. Intermarriage between the superior and inferior castes was forbidden, but human passions proved too strong for the fetters of state policy or priestcraft, and marriages were contracted, and other infractions of the laws of caste committed, which gave rise to a numerous and ever-increasing multitude of Pariahs or outcastes. The 'Institutes' do not mention Suttee or infanticide, nor recognise the torture of witnesses or criminals. Great respect is enjoined towards women, to whom, as Sir William Jones has well pointed out, the Code accords important proprietary rights. The gross idolatry of the present period appears to have been to a considerable extent an innovation of later date, like the human sacrifices offered to the goddess Cali; the Bayadères or dancing girls attached to the temples; and other horrible defilements of modern Brahminism. The Vedas, or sacred books of the Brahminical creed, were compiled in the fourteenth century B.C. Six centuries afterwards the invaders are believed to have crossed the Vindhya range in Central India; two centuries more elapsed ere they turned that barrier to the eastward and to the westward, leaving an intermediate wild belt of country, termed Gondwana, unsubdued; and five centuries more passed ere they reached the Mysoor.*

With the proceedings of the Boodhists, as distinguished from those of the Brahminists, we have very little acquaintance. The remains of their temples and the gigantic images of Boodh afford little insight into the period of their erection. By some authorities Boodhism is believed to have been introduced into India before Brahminism, but in both cases the professors appear to have been of the same origin.

The aborigines, under various names, such as Gonds, Bheels, Sonthals, Mairs, Koles, Bengies, Domes, and Bhars, are now scattered over India, and supposed to number about

* See two lectures on the aboriginal tribes of India, delivered before the Royal Asiatic Society in 1852, by Lieut.-General Briggs.

twenty million; they live on the outskirts of towns, in the jungles or on the mountain heights; in some provinces (Malabar, for instance) they are predial slaves; in others, serfs (*adscripti glebæ*); in the Deccan and elsewhere, they roam from place to place; always abhorred by the Hindoos as an impure race; yet brave, truthful, faithful, and honest: they make excellent soldiers, and are now under organisation as armed police, with European officers. The Hindoos, comprising under that designation the master race, found by Alexander in the Punjab, B.C. 330—with whom the invading Mohammedans struggled for supremacy from the commencement of the eleventh to the close of the seventeenth century, and who now constitute under various designations four-fifths of the population gradually subjected to British sway—are, generally speaking, rather of an European than an Asiatic type. In features and in crania the Hindoos bear no resemblance to the Chinese, the Malay, the Tartar, Mongolian, or other races of Central or of Northern Asia; they have some affinity in countenance and in figure to the descendants of Ishmael; but in the harmonious proportions of the head, in regularity of feature, in beauty and force of expression, in perfection of structure, in their delicate hands and feet, and slight, tall, graceful figures, the Hindoos are like the ancient Greeks; to whom they are also akin in love of poetry, eloquence, music, and fine arts; in subtlety of mind, in their half metaphysical half material creed, with its sublime theories and degrading practices; in their contempt of death, their social combinations and municipal institutions; and in devotion to renowned chieftains rather than to monarchical, oligarchical, or democratic forms of government.

The modifying influences of climate and food, and the intermarriage of widely different races, have produced variety of appearance, distinctiveness of character, and peculiarities of customs and manners in India to as great an extent as in Europe; the Native of the cool, dry, elevated regions of

Malwa and the Deccan is as unlike the denizen of the hot and moist plains of Bengal and Tanjore, as the hardy Swiss to the voluptuous inhabitant of the banks of the Tiber, or the industrious Englishman to the slothful Portuguese. Therefore in all questions affecting the people of India, it will be well to bear in mind that we are speaking of nations as distinct in language, appearance, customs, and manners, as are the British, French, Spanish, Italian, German, Muscovite, Greek, and other European peoples; and that we are not dealing with an homogeneous race like the three hundred and sixty million of Chinese, who have one type of face, one written character, one mode of thought, and uniformity of dress, habitation, and social life.

Concerning the origin and progress of the civilisation of which so many proofs exist, we have no knowledge; but Herodotus, Arrian, Strabo, Quintus Curtius, and other writers, place the Hindoos at different remote periods in the first rank of organised communities. They are described as having brought a disciplined army of cavalry, elephants, war-chariots, and thirty thousand infantry, against Alexander, and to have withstood his invincible Macedonian phalanx, for eight hours, on the banks of the Jhelum. Though the Greeks were conquerors, they saw and felt the skill and valour of the Hindoos sufficiently to fear and respect them as foes; and, dreading conflict with the Gangaridæ and Prasii, who dwelt in the region watered by the Ganges and its tributaries, and whose chiefs could bring into the field two hundred thousand infantry, twenty thousand cavalry, and several thousand elephants; the warriors who had subdued Persia, Bactria, and other countries, refused to advance any further, and the leader who had sighed for new worlds to conquer was compelled to retreat from beautiful, fertile, wealthy Hindoostan.

At the period of the Christian era, India seems to have been divided into several independent States, and densely populated in the vicinity of the chief rivers, where large cities and great fortresses then existed; for instance, the city of Palibothra, in the Gangetic valley, is described by Megasthenes as eight miles long by one and a half mile broad; protected by a deep ditch, and a high rampart with five hundred and seventy towers and sixty-four gates. The ruins of Gya and other ancient cities, with many temples and tanks, were evidently adapted for the use of a numerous and flourishing population.

A Chinese Buddhist priest, Chi-fa-Hian, travelled for six years in different parts of India at the commencement of the sixth century; he visited large cities and towns of noble architecture, adorned with sculpture; and described the inhabitants as rich and charitable, delighting in theatrical entertainments and concerts, encouraging literature and the fine arts, providing hospitals for the sick, cripples, and orphans, and carrying on an extensive maritime traffic.

Among other proofs of the early attainments of the Hindoos, it may be mentioned that one of their works, the 'Surya Sidhanta' (supposed to have been written in the fifth or sixth century A.D.), contains a trigonometrical system involving theorems that were not known in Europe until the sixteenth century. Cassini and Bailly state that observations still extant show that astronomy had made considerable progress in Hindoostan three thousand years before the Christian era; Bentley asserts that the Hindoo division of the ecliptic was made B.C. 1442.

The invention of decimal notation is ascribed to the Hindoos, who may have acquired it from the Chinese, to whom, however, they were much superior in their music, which was systematic and pleasing, not monotonous and harsh like that o their neighbours. In architecture and sculpture the Hindoo taste resembled the Greek more than the Egyptian, Indian productions being elegant rather than massive; though the relics of triumphal arches, immense gateways, and broad flights of steps, leading to vast tanks and lofty pagodas, show that size was understood as an element of grandeur. Chemistry and metallurgy were brought to a high state of perfection; mercury and other minerals, as well as vegetable extracts, were used in medicine; inoculation for smallpox was practised, the eye was couched for cataract, and lithotomy and other delicate operations in surgery were performed. Colonies were founded on land and by ocean voyages to distant shores, and marine insurance was practised in the time of Menu; coins were struck, bills of exchange used by traders, royal roads marked by milestones intersected the country, and the police-system was excellent. The Britons were painted barbarians when the Hindoo manufacturers attained the perfection for which they are still remarkable: the shawls of Cashmeer were then as they are now unparalleled for lightness, warmth, and beauty; the muslins of Dacca were fine and transparent as "woven-wind;" the gold and silver brocades of Delhi adorned the Courts of Imperial Rome; and the porcelain of India, its scents and spices, its diamonds and pearls, were prized by all the civilised nations of antiquity.

In their leading characteristics, the Hindoos have changed comparatively little in the course of centuries. The Mohammedan conquest placed them in a position of inferiority, particularly in some of the Moslem kingdoms of the Deccan, and at periods when bigotry was in the ascendant; but the most deteriorating influences to which they have been subjected have been the ambition and pride of the Brahminical priesthood, the increasing Pantheism of their creed, and the sanguinary and impure practices gradually introduced. The warlike race, especially the Rajpoots (king's sons), became addicted to the use of opium, and sacrificed the noble though vague aspirations after one Universal Deity taught by the Vedas, to the intoxicating influences of the hateful drug, which heightened the pleasures of the harem or the excitement of the battlefield, but in exchange took from the mind and body their sustained and tranquil energy, and induced the worst infirmities of age. The Mohammedans also became addicted to the use of opium, bang, and similar stimulants, which they smoked or took in confections. The Great Moguls, with the exception of Aurungzebe, and perhaps one or two others, were opium-eaters; and this sensual and suicidal indulgence tended more than any other single cause to the decay of both Mohammedan and Hindoo power. The same poison is now hastening the dissolution of the Tartar government in China.

Numbers and Distribution.

No complete census has as yet been taken of the people of the numerous countries included in British India. It was to have been done in 1861; but the mutiny in 1857-58 rendered it inadvisable, lest a vast population among whom such a practice was unprecedented might misapprehend the motive of Government, and be seduced by designing persons into panic and disturbance.

The general Table given at the commencement of this work contains a summary of the latest information furnished by the Calcutta Government, and received in London in March, 1862, under the head of a 'Return of Area and Population of each Division of each Presidency in India.' The total population is there stated at above one hundred and fifty-six million British subjects: add to these about forty million under Native princes—more or less controlled by the British Government—and the aggregate approaches two hundred million people. It is difficult to realise the vast number of subjects of the British Crown which the unclassified return of 1862 represents, and it may be useful to analyse and compare it with another area and population return, presented to Parliament 28th July, 1857, which furnishes the proportions of males and females in many districts, and gives the Hindoos as distinguished from the Mohammedan and other classes of the people.

The Bengal Presidency.

The north-eastern side of India contains the provinces of Bengal, Behar, and part of Orissa, which occupy the lower valley of the river Ganges, and of one of its large branches, the Hooghly. The Bengal Presidency also comprises Dacca the district which extends along the Megna, a continuation of the Brahmapootra; and the Cuttack district, on the north-west, with that of Chittagong, on the north-east side of the head of the Bay of Bengal.

The boundaries of the Presidency are: on the north, Nepaul, Sikhim, and Bhotan; on the north-east, Thibet; on the east, Burmah and Siam; on the south, the head of the Bay of Bengal; on the south-west, Sumbulpoor and several small states on the Mahanuddy River and adjoining Cuttack; and on the west, Benares and the districts forming the North-West provinces. The extreme measurement of the territory is: from Champarun in Patna, to Sandoway in Arracan, one thousand miles; from Debroogurh in Assam, to Pooree in Cuttack, six hundred and fifty miles; and from Tipperah in Chittagong, to the boundaries of Nagpoor, six hundred and fifty miles; showing an area more than double the size of Great Britain and Ireland.

A large proportion of this region is an alluvial plain, on the verge of the temperate zone, intersected by numerous rivers; with a hot, moist, and insalubrious climate, except in the months from November to February. Rice is largely cultivated, and forms the chief article of sustenance among the Hindoos of this Presidency. Vegetation is most luxuriant. The zoology of the country is equally varied and rich, and food for man and beast is abundant. The population consists of various races differing in language, appearance, customs, and laws, and with little or no community of interest between the corresponding ranks of the population in each district.

The most numerous class are the Bengallees, who in form and feature are of the pure Hindoo type. They are generally of middle height, dark olive hue, slim, with finely moulded limbs, well-formed skull, slightly aquiline nose, brilliant eyes, and small hands, feet, and ears. Partly owing to long subjugation to the Mohammedans, and partly perhaps owing to the enervating climate and voluptuous indulgences, the Bengallees have acquired the character of being timid, cunning, untruthful, litigious, vengeful, covetous, superstitious, sensual, and fond of show. They are inferior to the Chinese in agricultural and manufacturing skill, but superior to them in taste, in subtlety of mind, and in desire for intellectual enjoyment. Like most Orientals, they are polygamists, and in imitation of the Mohammedans keep their wives in strict seclusion; they are domestic in their habits, charitable to the poor, and hospitable to strangers. Their want of courage and tendency to accumulate wealth made them an easy prey to the Moslem invaders, who ruled them despotically and plundered them without mercy. Under British rule a limited class have been enabled to amass riches, to exhibit them without fear, and to enjoy a degree of individual liberty unknown to their ancestors for many centuries.

The Zemindarree or permanent settlement of the land-tax in Bengal by the Marquis Cornwallis in 1792, gave to the landlords of estates and to those employed as Zemindars in the collection of the Government revenue, the soil in fee simple—the Magna Charta of the country. The annual tax was fixed at an average of ten years' assessment, and the proprietors thus constituted were allowed to bring waste lands into cultivation without incurring any additional tax. Nevertheless the assessment was so high, that very many of the Zemindars were ruined, and their estates sold by auction: these again were bought by wealthy "Baboos" (native traders) and Shroffs (money-changers and bankers), who applied capital in clearing waste lands, and brought large tracts into cultivation. During the last half-century the wealth of Bengal has considerably increased: there has been no famine or even dearth since the fee simple of the soil was relinquished by the Government. A rich native aristocracy is being formed. Since the land-tax has been fixed, the revenue from all other sources has been doubled, and an easily levied property and income tax is now yielding a fair revenue to the State.

During the mutiny and rebellion of 1857-58, Bengal was perfectly quiet. The higher classes had nothing to gain by the expulsion of the British; they were secure in their persons and property, unmolested in their religion, and devoid of any grievance which could give a cause for revolution. It is too true that the great mass of the people live from hand to mouth, in a manner which in a colder climate would be impossible;* but in no part of India is there so large a proportion of the area under tillage, so much accumulated capital, or so many persons possessed of competence. Many of the "Baboos" have acquired enormous fortunes, and their spacious mansions in Calcutta and its suburbs, when thrown open for "nautches" (dancing parties) and the reception of European visitors, exhibit in profusion the ornamental and luxurious appendages which money can procure. It is an evidence of the suspicious character of the Bengallees, that the British

* Mr. Marshman, who lived in Bengal for many years, and edited the 'Friend of India,' declares that "No one has ever attempted to contradict the fact that the condition of the Bengal peasant is almost as wretched and degraded as it is possible to conceive; living in the most miserable hovel, scarcely fit for a dog-kennel, covered with tattered rags, and unable, in too many instances, to procure more than a single meal a-day for himself and family. The Bengal ryot knows nothing of the most ordinary comforts of life. We speak without exaggeration when we affirm that if the real condition of those who raise the harvest, which yields between three and four millions a-year, was fully known, it would make the ears of every one who heard thereof to tingle." The holdings of the cultivators are small, often not exceeding a single acre.—*Friend of India*, April, 1852.

Government, ruling there for a century, and with the seat of the Supreme Government in their midst, has never deemed it prudent to ascertain the exact numbers of the people. The returns for Bengal are even less reliable than for other parts of India; but there can be no doubt, especially in the minds of those who have traversed the districts in the vicinity of the Ganges, that the population is very dense.

In 1854-55, a statement was prepared for Government, with reference to the Village Police, which thus enumerated the villages and houses in the following Districts:—

Districts.	Villages.	Houses.
Patna	21,124	886,606
Bhaugulpoor	17,122	882,662
Rajshaye	25,756	962,045
Dacca	27,606	1,068,618
Chittagong	7,805	508,329
Cuttack	15,531	420,478
Burdwan	29,585	1,229,619
Nuddea	14,780	870,509
Total	159,309	6,828,866

Supposing five individuals to reside in each house, this return would give a population of above thirty-four million. The Lieutenant-Governor of Bengal considers that forty million is a moderate estimate of the numbers in the territories under his jurisdiction, which comprise in addition to the districts above stated, the extensive regions of Assam, the Cossya Hills, a wild district on the lofty upper portion of the Brahmapootra river; the low coast region of Arracan (now being joined to Pegu, as part of British Burmah); an undulating plateau three thousand feet above the sea south of the Ganges; Chota (little) Nagpoor; and part of Sikhim, attached to the sanitary station of Darjeeling.

The population and area return received in 1862, gives the provinces under the Lieutenant-Governor of Bengal thus, excepting Arracan, which will be found under the head of British Burmah:—

Bengal Presidency.	Area in Square Miles.	Population.	Number to each Sq. Mile.
REGULATION PROVINCES.			
Patna—			
Behar	5,689	1,434,132	252
Chumparun	2,612	750,000	287
Sarun	3,781	1,371,729	362
Patna	1,828	566,023	308
Shahabad	4,403	1,044,780	237
Tirhoot	6,114	1,845,000	301
	24,429	7,011,664	287
Bhaugulpoor—			
Bhaugulpoor	4,185	7,00,000	167
Sonthal Pergunnahs	5,480	550,000	100
Monghyr	3,592	1,000,000	278
Purneah	5,712	900,000	157
	18,971	3,150,000	166
Rajshahye—			
Rajshaye	3,035	615,000	212
Rungpoor	4,591	1,285,000	279
Dinagepoor	4,607	1,125,000	244
Moorshedabad	2,634	1,100,000	417
Pubna	1,739	783,000	450
Bogra	1,219	470,000	385
Malda	1,288	312,000	242
	19,115	5,690,000	297
Dacca—			
Dacca	3,011	941,000	312
Backergunge	3,515	903,177	256
Mymensing	6,586	947,240	143
Sylhet	4,900	1,393,050	284
Furreedpoor	1,479	639,709	432
Cachar	650	179,222	245
Jynteea	459	41,300	89
	20,602	5,044,698	244
Chittagong—			
Chittagong	2,717	801,000	295
Bullooah	2,652	566,070	213
Tipperah	2,280	1,000,000	438
Chittagong Hill States	8,200	Unknown.	
	15,849	2,367,070	149

Bengal Presidency.	Area in Square Miles.	Population.	Number to each Sq. Mile.
Nuddea—			
Nuddea	3,577	1,100,000	307
Twenty-four Pergunnahs		840,980	
Calcutta	2,277	600,000	922
Baraset		660,265	
Jessore	3,440	1,075,475	312
Soonderbunds	6,300	*	
	15,595	4,276,720	274
Burdwan—			
Burdwan	2,692	1,038,53	385
Bancoorah	1,348	768,690	569
Hooghly	2,007	1,439,985	976
Howrah		520,000	
Midnapoor	4,017	1,402,908	278
Hidjellee	1,013		
Beerbhoom	1,252	655,096	523
	12,332	5,825,211	472
Cuttack—			
Cuttack	3,061	1,340,000	437
Pooree	2,697	625,000	231
Balasore	1,875	460,000	245
	7,635	2,425,000	318
Total of Regulation Provinces	1,34,532	25,790,363	191
NON-REGULATION PROVINCES.			
Assam—			
Gowalparah		229,937	
Kamroop		390,242	
Durrung	27,555	186,692	49
Nowgong		247,478	
Seebsaugor or Seebpoor		211,478	
Luckimpoor		94,500	
Cossya Hills	3,500	77,625	22
Assam Hill States	21,134	Unknown.	
	52,189	1,437,952	27

* The swampy delta of the Ganges, of which the inhabited portion is very small; it may be considered as included in the several districts of Jessore, the Twenty-four Pergunnahs, and Backergunge.

Bengal Presidency.	Area in Square Miles.	Population.	Number to each Sq. Mile.
Chota Nagpoor—			
Hazareebaugh	62,823	749,000	45
Lohurdagga		802,814	
Maunbhoom		347,466	
Singbhoom		279,268	
Gurhjat Mehals		362,821	
Sumbulpoor	..	294,971	
	62,823	2,836,340	
Cuttack Tributary Mehals ..	15,791	999,827	63
Darjeeling	740	60,000	81
	16,531	1,059,827	64
Total under the Administration of the Lieut.-Governor of Bengal	266,075	41,124,482	

Note.—*Arracan* is transferred to the province of British Burmah.

Notwithstanding its official character, the preceding table is little better than guess-work, and must be considered only as an approximation to the actual numbers. The density of population to area has been added to the official return. Calcutta and its suburbs of the Twenty-four Pergunnahs and Baraset shew nine hundred and twenty-two mouths to each square mile; and Howrah (which is separated from Calcutta by the Hooghly river, across which ten thousand people pass daily to the capital) nine hundred and seventy-six. This density is accounted for by proximity to Calcutta; but the number of people in the districts along the Ganges, where they appear to swarm, is not equal to that in several of the sea-coast provinces of China. For example:

Chinese Sea-coast Provinces.	Square Miles.	Population.	Number to each Square Mile.
Shantung	65,104	28,958,764	414
Kangsoo*	92,661	37,843,501	778
Gan-hwuy		34,168,059	
Chekeang	39,150	26,256,784	670

Several of the inland Provinces are also thickly peopled. Chihle, containing Pekin, has four hundred and seventy-three persons to each square mile; Honan, three hundred and fifty-three; Kiang-si, four hundred and twenty-one; Hoopiih and Hunan, three hundred and seventeen; Shense, two hundred and fifty-three. The area of China Proper is about one million three hundred thousand square miles; the population about three hundred and sixty-seven million; and the average number to each square mile, two hundred and eighty.†

If the territories in India, under British rule, were as densely peopled as China, they would contain more than three hundred million people. When the data given above for the Bengal Regulation Provinces (that is, those under defined laws and regularly-organized administration) is examined, it will be seen that there are only one hundred and ninety-one persons assigned to each square mile. They are all Gangetic and sea-coast districts, and contain probably about two hundred and fifty mouths to each square mile. The average density of population in India will be better understood by a comparison of the number of individuals to each square mile in other countries. The calculation was made a few years since.

England	333	Portugal	130
Wales	134	Prussia	156
Ireland	200	Greece	55
Scotland	100	Bavaria	158
Isle of Man	256	Holland	245
United Kingdom, about	200	Belgium	323
France	186	China	283
Spain	88		

* Contains the city of Nanking.

† See 'China; Political, Commercial, and Social,' 1847, by the author of the present work.

The estimate given of the Non-Regulation districts (that is, those under a Commissioner, without defined laws or system) is utterly unreliable. No guess even is made at the population of the Assam Hill States, which have an area of twenty-one thousand square miles,—nearly as large as Scotland, excluding the islands. Assam itself, probably as large as Ireland, is noted at forty-nine to each square mile; and the density of Chota Nagpoor, with a larger area than England and Wales, is guessed at forty-five; while the mountain ridge of Darjeeling, is supposed to have eighty-one. There are no details as to the number or race of the aborigines. Numerous tribes, some in the wildest savage state, inhabit the districts to the eastward of Bengal. The Mughs are the principal inhabitants of Chittagong, which consists of level land along the coast, and hilly tracts to the eastward of the plain. The Joomea Mughs or cultivators of the land have to the east and south-east of them the Koomeas, the Kookis, the Morungs, the Shans, the Poangs, and others. As is usually the case with uncivilized border tribes, murderous and plundering raids are carried on with a view of making captives for slaves, to obtain women, and to prosecute blood and family feuds. Our Government has considerable difficulty in managing the wild races, whose village and hill fastnesses are stockaded and well defended by art and natural position. A mountain tribe will occasionally descend to the plain, and its foray is marked by rapine and murder. On a recent occasion a tribe of hill Kookies made a sudden descent on the Tipperah plains; fifteen villages were set on fire; a large number were wantonly destroyed; all property of a light and moveable nature was carried off; neither men, women, nor children were spared, except such as were retained for slaves; and the alarm was so great, that many villages on our frontiers were deserted. Before the British Military Police arrived, the marauders had retired to their hills.

Slavery exists in many parts of India, and is in some districts agrestic, in others domestic in its character. From Parliamentary documents published in 1828 and 1838, and from other sources, the following statement of the number of slaves in the chief districts of Bengal has been prepared:*—

	Slaves.		Slaves.
Northern, Central, and Southern Cuttack ..	600,000	Assam	27,000
Moorshedabad	95,366	Dacca Jelalpore	275,190
Behar and Patna	131,280	Tipperah	343,065
Bhaugulpore	40,861	Chittagong	175,200
Purneah	24,560	Sylhet	361,240
Rungpoor	536,140	Mymensing	363,677
Rajeshaye	766,341	Tirhoot	212,210
Shahabad	21,340	Sarun	180,509
		Total in above districts	4,153,978

On the hill districts of Orissa and the plateau south of the Ganges there are various wild tribes; among one in particular, the Gonds, infanticide prevails, female children being not unfrequently offered in sacrifice to propitiate supposed evil deities, or to secure abundant harvests from land sprinkled with human blood. Captain M'Neill, agent to the Governor-General in the Orissa Hills, has been endeavouring to put a stop to these diabolical practices, but could devise nothing better than a governmental reward to the headmen of villages "in which the relative number of the sexes is proportional." † In 1860 about five thousand Gonds assembled at the full moon on the plateau of Tooamool and Karoonde (which is four thousand feet above the sea, fifty miles long by twenty miles broad) to sacrifice a female slave and her three children, but were prevented by an armed force under Captain M'Neill, who fired on the murderous crowd. In 1860 Lieut. Crawford rescued thirty intended victims; and in 1861 twenty-six males and twenty-seven females were saved from destruction by the British Agent. It is full time that attention should be given to the state of

* See 'Annual Report of the Anti-Slavery Society' for 1842, p. 101.

† See 'Report on Suppression of Human Sacrifices and Female Infanticide in Orissa' for 1860-61, p. 2.

the aboriginal population in every part of India; a special agency for this purpose is much needed.

For more than twenty years a large annual emigration has taken place from Bengal and the adjacent provinces, of the labouring classes, who seek to better their condition in the British colonies, from which some return in comparatively comfortable circumstances. The number of emigrants in the year 1859-60 was twenty-three thousand three hundred and twelve statute adults, of whom fifteen thousand nine hundred and eighty went to the Mauritius; four thousand three hundred and ninety-four to Demerara; one thousand six hundred and eighteen to Trinidad; six hundred and seventy to St. Lucia; and six hundred and fifty to Jamaica. Difficulty is experienced in obtaining a proper proportion of women to accompany the males. Emigration agents and medical officers are appointed by Government, with a view to prevent fraud, and mitigate the hardships of the voyage to the colonies.

Calcutta.

Since the battle of Plassy, Calcutta has been the capital of the Bengal Presidency; and under Warren Hastings, the first Governor-General, it became the seat of the Supreme Government of India. In 1717, it was a straggling village interspersed with jheels (small lakes), and bounded by jungle and forest. In 1752, Mr. Holwell, the Governor, estimated the number of houses within the East India Company's bounds at fifty-one thousand; and the constant inhabitants, at four hundred thousand; in 1802, the Police Magistrate reckoned the citizens at six hundred thousand; in 1810, the estimate was one million. Subsequent calculations made the population less; but all these statements were based on vague and unreliable data.

A census of Calcutta,* taken in 1850, showed in round

* The statistics of the capital of British India are "exceedingly defective,

numbers and classes, Europeans, six thousand two hundred; Eurasians (children of European fathers and Native mothers), four thousand six hundred; Americans, eight hundred; Chinese, eight hundred; Asiatics generally, fifteen thousand; Hindoos, two hundred and seventy-four thousand; Mohammedans, one hundred and eleven thousand; giving a total of about four hundred thousand. In the return sent from India, in 1862, Calcutta is put down as comprising six hundred thousand souls; but this is apparently independent of the extensive suburban population. Town and suburbs probably now comprise upwards of one million of inhabitants, where, a century ago, there were a few miserable hamlets. But the whole of this so-called City of Palaces has the same drawback: the princely dwellings at Chowringhee and Garden Reach, and the Hindoo huts beside them, alike stand on a low, hot, insalubrious plain, almost on a level with the bank of the Hooghly river, and at the highest part only thirty feet above the sea at low water.

In 1850 the dwellings in the city were returned at sixty thousand, but of these more than forty-nine thousand were only huts. The finest structures are:—Government House, erected by the Marquis Wellesley, in 1804, which cost one hundred and thirty thousand pounds; the Supreme Court of Judicature, a building superior to the Courts at Westminster; a Town Hall, with some fine statues of Governors-General; the Madrissa and other Native Colleges; the Martinière, an establishment founded by General Claude Martin, Saint Paul's Cathedral, recently erected by the exertions and munificence of Bishop Wilson, aided by a contribution of fifteen thousand pounds from Government;

there being no official register of births, marriages, and deaths; nothing to afford an insight into the extent of the floating population; no public record of arrivals and departures of Europeans, and no official return of the general causes of death: of the population of the town no accurate estimate can be made."—*Government Statement exhibiting the Moral and Material Progress and Condition of India during the year* 1859-60, part ii., page 58.

several handsome Churches—Episcopalian, Scotch Kirk, Dissenters, and Roman Catholic; Writers' Buildings (Civil Service), also Banks, Hospitals, Libraries, Chamber of Commerce, and the Metcalfe Hall, erected in honour of the great and good statesman of that name. On the opposite side of the river Hooghly, which is little wider than the Thames at Waterloo Bridge, there is a large suburb called Howrah; and on the same side, lower down, facing the magnificent esplanade and "Garden Reach," is Bishop's College (for instructing and preparing Native youths as Christian Catechists and Missionaries); there is also an excellent Botanic Garden, stocked with every variety of tropical vegetation.

The Hindoos have one hundred and sixty-seven religious buildings in Calcutta, and the Mohammedans seventy-four; the Jews have a synagogue, and the Chinese a Budhistic temple; the Greeks and Armenians have their respective places of worship, and there is perfect freedom for every religious denomination. The City is now lit with gas; attempts are being made to drain the European quarter, and there are signs of general improvement.

Fort William, near the City on the river bank, is the strongest fortress on level ground in India; and resembles in its site and appearance that of Antwerp. It is of immense extent, and would require ten thousand soldiers to man the works. From its commencement by Lord Clive, after the battle of Plassy, the structure has cost about two million sterling. The esplanade between Calcutta and the fortress forms an agreeable morning and evening drive for the citizens. Every variety of equipage is observable on the crowded course, while the merchants and travellers from different parts of Asia, and indeed from all quarters of the globe, form a motley assemblage, hardly to be seen in any other country.

The Madras Presidency.

The Madras Presidency extends to the south-west of Bengal, from Ganjam in the twentieth to Cape Comorin in the eighth degree of latitude. It forms the southern apex of what is termed the Indian Peninsula, and is bounded on the eastward by the Bay of Bengal, and on the westward by the Indian Ocean. It extends about nine hundred and fifty miles from north-east to south-west; and at its greatest breadth, in right angles to that line, measures about four hundred and fifty miles. The sea-coast of about seventeen hundred miles, has no harbour adapted for the entry of large-sized trading vessels. The area is about a hundred and thirty thousand square miles. A large part of this Presidency is occupied by the Eastern and Western Ghauts, which unite about fifty miles to the north-west of the city of Madras, and form the buttress that upholds the triangular plateau of the Deccan and its southern prolongation. The Eastern Ghauts are thirty to sixty miles distant from the low coast-line, excepting to the southward, at Madura and Trichinopoly, where there is an almost level tract of about one hundred miles in width. The breadth of low land between the sea and the Western Ghauts is less than on the east coast, measuring generally from twenty to thirty miles. The seaward faces of both ranges are more elevated and abrupt than the inward, where they merge into the table-land.

The climate of this part of India varies with the position of the land and its elevation above the ocean. The eastern coast has a more continuous dry heat than is found in any other part of India; the mercury standing not unfrequently above 100° Fahr. at midnight, causing the nails to fall out of doors and tables, wood to shrink and warp, and glass globes and shades to crack. On the western shore the heat is not so sultry, there is much moisture, and a very large quantity of rain falls during six months in the year. On the plateau above the Ghauts there is the mild climate of the warm part of the temperate zone, and at higher elevations still cooler temperatures are attained.

Amidst these diversities of climate the population varies in character and appearance; but generally speaking the people, especially on the coast, are darker, stronger and with more definite characteristics, but less fanatical, than the Bengallees. They are peaceable and industrious; and during the troubles of 1857-58 both the military and the civil population remained loyal.

Madras has not made the progress in wealth and improvement that is visible in some parts of Bengal. The numerous annexations of petty principalities, and the consequent downfall of the hereditary aristocracy, have tended to discourage native trade and arts. The class of wealthy gentry has almost disappeared, owing to the oppressive nature of the land-tax in this Presidency, and their exclusion from offices of trust or emolument.* The ryotwar system of taxing

* Mr. John Sullivan, who was a member of the Madras Council, and a man of acknowledged ability and marked probity, thus described the consequences of "annexation" and "consolidation:"—"Five Native States have fallen within the last ten years. If we put on one side of the account what the Natives have gained by the few offices that have been lately opened to them, with what they have lost by the extermination of these States, we shall find the net loss to be immense; and what the Native loses, the Englishman gains. Upon the extermination of a Native State an Englishman takes the place of the sovereign, under the name of commissioner; three or four of his associates displace as many dozen of the Native official aristocracy, while some hundreds of our troops take the place of the many thousands that every Native chief supports. The little court disappears—trade languishes—the capital decays—the people are impoverished—the Englishman flourishes and acts like a sponge, drawing up riches from the banks of the Ganges, and squeezing them down upon the banks of the Thames. Nor is this all. Native princes and their courts not only encourage Native trade and Native arts, but under them, and because of their very weakness, public opinion flourishes; all that constitutes the life of a people is strengthened; and, though the government may occasionally be oppressive, heavier far is the yoke of our institutions."

MountStuart Elphinstone, Sir John Malcolm, and other high authorities, have expressed similar opinions; and Lord William Bentinck considered that "In many respects the Mohammedans surpassed our rule; they settled in annually the land of every peasant cultivator and taking about fifty per cent. of the produce of the soil has pauperized the mass of the people and caused frequent desolating famines. Mr. Bourdillon, Secretary to the Government of Madras, vividly describes the condition of the cultivator or small farmer, as living from hand to mouth, rarely seeing money, except when borrowed at from twelve to twenty-four per cent. per annum from the bazaar usurer, to pay the Government tax; his dwelling a mud hut, destitute of anything deserving the name of furniture or cooking-utensils; his family food partly thin meal-porridge, and partly rice with a little condiment; his ploughing cattle, wretched animals,

countries they conquered; the interests and sympathies of the conquerors and conquered became identified. Our policy, on the contrary, has been the reverse of this—cold, selfish, and unfeeling: the iron hand of power on the one side, monopoly and exclusion on the other."

Sir Thomas Munro, who was likewise thoroughly acquainted with the condition of the Natives of India, especially in the Madras Presidency, declared:—"The main evil of our system is the degraded state in which we hold the Natives. We suppose them to be superstitious, ignorant, prone to falsehood, and corrupt. In our well-meaning zeal for their welfare, we shudder at the idea of committing to men so depraved any share in the administration of their own country. We exclude them from every situation of trust and emolument; we confine them to the lowest offices, with scarcely a bare subsistence; and even these are left in their hands from necessity, because Europeans are utterly incapable of filling them. We treat them as an inferior race of beings. Men who, under a Native government, might have held the first dignities of the State, who but for us might have been governors of provinces, are regarded as little better than menial servants, are often no better paid, and scarcely permitted to sit in our presence. We reduce them to this abject state, and then look upon them with disdain as men unworthy of high station. Under most of the Mahommedan princes of India the Hindoos were eligible to all the civil offices of government, and they frequently possessed a more important share in them than their conquerors."

The Rev. G. R. Gleig, Chaplain General to the British army, writing four years before the mutiny of 1857, declares that, "By the Native gentry of India,—and it is a great mistake to suppose that India has not its gentry of ancient lineage and proud reminiscences,—the rule of the English is regarded not only without favour, but with settled detestation. All the classes above the mere cultivators see in the English Government a power which, however evenly it may profess to hold the scales between man and man, entertains no sympathy for them or for the traditions of their ancestry."—*India and its Army*, pp. 3, 4.

not worth more than seven shillings to twelve shillings each; and his few agricultural implements equally primitive and inefficient. In a small part of the territory the condition of the farming class is far better than in the Carnatic and the districts north of Madras. Tanjore—a rich alluvial delta producing three crops a-year—is abundantly irrigated, the Cauvery river being by artificial means thrown on the land, instead of wasting itself in the sea, and the district is now one of the richest in India. Sir Charles Trevelyan visited Tanjore in 1860, when Governor of Madras, and says:—"The assessment has been so moderate and fixed, that the feeling and fruit of private property in the soil has been realised. Land sells at a price equal, on an average, to twenty years' purchase; and there are individual landowners with incomes which, when allowance is made for the difference in the value of money, would cause them to be regarded as considerable proprietors even in England. The ancient proprietors are still in possession, and are the greatest gainers by the additional security which has been given to landed property. The mirasdars of Tanjore are more like sturdy English yeomen than any class of people that I have seen in India: they speak out honestly and roundly. The advanced social state is apparent in the face of the country. The high roads are admirably shaded with productive trees, and they sometimes pass for miles through almost a continuous village. The houses and homesteads are well built, the people are well clothed and fed, and there is every sign of abundant subsistence." *

City of Madras, or Fort St. George.

The City of Madras, on the Coromandel coast, with its defences called Fort St. George, is nearly the oldest British possession in India. It is disadvantageously situated for

* 'Minute of Tour in March, 1860,' by Sir Charles Trevelyan. Parl. Papers, Commons, xxv. Feb. 13th, 1861, p. 6.

maritime commerce, having only an open roadstead with dangerous landing during the greater part of the year. This serious defect is being remedied by the construction of a landing-pier, made of iron piles driven into the ground, and carried out so far as to afford four fathoms' water at the extremity. An attempt to form a breakwater was unsuccessful. The sea flows to within a few feet of the ramparts of Fort St. George, which is well designed, armed on the coast-face with heavy guns, and protected on the land-side by a double line of bomb-proof fortifications. A wide esplanade, like that of Calcutta, separates the Fort from "Black Town." The public offices and chief European residences extend several miles along the beach, are well built, and with intervening gardens have a pleasing effect. Good water is abundant and drainage in course of improvement. The Native town and suburbs, being filthy in the extreme, are frequently visited by cholera. The cantonment on the rising ground known as St. Thomas's Mount, about six miles from Madras, is connected with the Fort by a good road well shaded by fine trees and adorned on either side by handsome villas.

The population has, under British government, gradually increased in numbers and in wealth. In 1810, the Natives within the limits of the Supreme Court were estimated at three hundred and twenty thousand. In 1823, Madras and its suburbs contained four hundred and fifteen thousand seven hundred and fifty-one inhabitants, exclusive of the dwellers in nearly three thousand houses within the precincts of the Nabob's palace. In the return for 1862 the population of Madras City is given as in the return for 1857, at seven hundred and twenty thousand, without any attempt at classification. The number of Europeans not employed in the service of Government or on the railways is very small. The variety of races is less than in Calcutta.

The Presidency is divided into twenty districts, the area

and population of which are thus given in the return for 1862.

NAME OF DISTRICT.	Area in Square Miles.	Population.	Mouths to each Square Mile.
Regulation Districts :—			
Madras City	27	720,000	26,666
Madras	3,073	605,221	197
Godavery	7,534	1,276,200	169
Kistna	8,353	1,022,524	122
Kurnool	7,604	683,147	89
Cuddapah	9,727	1,014,257	104
Nellore	8,507	996,877	117
Bellary	11,496	1,077,715	93
North Arcot	6,874	1,588,104	231
South Arcot	4,961	1,135,961	229
Salem	7,608	1,268,200	166
Coimbatoor	8,417	1,192,433	141
*North Canara	4,300	483,336	112
South Canara	3,678	643,602	175
Malabar	6,259	1,587,312	253
Trichinopoly	3,097	809,580	261
Tanjore	3,736	1,657,285	443
Madura	9,076	1,792,737	197
Tinnevelly	5,145	1,339,374	260
	119,472	20,893,865	174
Non-Regulation Districts :—			
Ganjam	3,743	949,747	253
Vizagapatam	5,335	1,284,243	240
	9,078	2,233,990	246
Total under Madras Presidency	128,550	23,127,855	179

Some of these districts are densely peopled. Tanjore delta has four hundred and forty-three mouths to the square mile; the contiguous district of Trichinopoly two hundred and sixty-one; showing an average for both of three hundred and two. Tinnevelly has two hundred and sixty. Ganjam and Vizagapatam, to the northward, have an average of two hundred and forty. Malabar has two hundred and fifty-three to each square mile. The upland districts have a more

* North Canara has been recently annexed to Bombay.

sparse population: thus Coimbatoor, in the Neilgherries, has only one hundred and forty-one. At Ootacamund in the Neilgherries the population consisted in 1848 of Europeans, three hundred and forty-two; Eurasians, one hundred and fifty-four; Hindoos, three thousand and forty-five; Mohammedans, nine hundred and one; other classes, four thousand nine hundred and forty-one; Hill tribes, seven thousand six hundred and forty-four: total, seventeen thousand and fifty-seven, distributed over a space of four hundred and twenty square miles; forty mouths to each square mile. The race termed Todars, who differ so remarkably in appearance and habits from other natives of India, dwell in this locality, and are less than four hundred in number. There is more reliance to be placed on the Madras returns than on those of Bengal, and there is in the former some degree of classification. The return of 1857 gives the following aggregate:—

Madras Population.	Agricultural.		Non-Agricultural.		Total.
	Males.	Females.	Males.	Females.	
Hindoos	6,919,836	6,424,888	3,274,313	3,282,671	19,899,708
Mohammedans and others ..	439,063	409,154	413,927	440,745	1,702,889
	7,358,899	6,834,042	3,688,240	3,723,416	21,602,597

The proportion of agricultural to non-agricultural indicates a large number of people engaged in manufactures and trade. Muslins and various cotton goods are made at Masulipatam and other places. The number of Mohammedans is not separately given, and the "others" jumbled with them consist partly of slaves, of people of no caste, and of wild tribes. The Hindoos are as twelve to one of all the remaining classes.

The proportion of females to males appears larger in this Presidency than in other parts of India from which there are returns; thus there are (excluding Madras city):—

	Males.	Females.		Males.	Females.
Adults ..	7,140,463 ..	7,191,700	Children ..	3,906,614 ..	3,342,296

Total males ..	11,047,614
„ females ..	10,533,996

Emigration from Madras to the Mauritius and the British West Indies is conducted on a large scale. The numbers embarked in 1859-60 from the depôts were: men, eight thousand and one; women, three thousand three hundred and seventy-four; boys, one thousand one hundred and sixty-five; girls, nine hundred and twenty-nine; infants, five hundred and eighty-eight. Four-fifths of these went to the Mauritius. The numbers that returned from the above-named colony and from Demerara during the year were: men, nine hundred and twelve; women, two hundred and eighty-nine; boys, eighty-three; girls, eighty-two; infants, thirty-two. One ship, the *Henry Moore*, brought from the West Indies three hundred and thirty returned emigrants, of whom one hundred and sixty-two were men and ninety-five women; the remainder children. The savings of these labourers, as shown by Government money-orders, were about eight thousand pounds, after ten to fifteen years' residence in the West Indies. Emigration is now diminishing, owing to more remunerative employment being obtainable at home.

The Madras census does not state the number of those who are in bondage; but the following estimate for certain districts has been formed from the documents laid before Parliament in 1828 and 1838:*—

In Malabar	146,000
Canara, Wynaad, Coorg, Cochin, and Travancore	254,000
Tinnevelly	324,000
Trichinopoly	10,600
Arcot, North and South	20,000
Concan, South	2,000
Southern Mahratta Country	15,000
Total in above districts	771,000

* See 'Slavery in India,' by Rev. J. Peggs, page 84. London, 1840 Wightman, Paternoster-row.

The subject of slavery requires careful investigation as a preliminary to eventual abolition. The Hindoo and Mohammedan laws recognise conquest as a legitimate source of slavery; and the sale of children by their parents, and of orphans by those who have possession of them, are prolific sources of the evil, as is also the sale of individuals themselves to those who may be their creditors. A system of bondage extensively prevailed among the Sonthals (near Rajmahal), but it has gradually disappeared under the protection afforded by Government and the remunerative employment which railways, coal-mines, and other commercial enterprises afford. A *Kameotee* bondsman was one who, in consideration of a sum of money, bound himself and his heirs to serve the lender until the money so advanced should be repaid with interest. The *Hurwahee* bondsman bound himself to work for the money-lender whenever his services were required. These liabilities descended to the children. The bonds were legally executed on stamped paper. The Kameotee was an indoor domestic servant; the Hurwahee an outdoor labourer. The British government only became aware of the existence of this practice in 1858, and the bondsmen were at once released from servitude.

Some attempts have been made in the Madras Presidency to diminish the amount of bondage, and to ameliorate the condition of the enslaved. The slaves on Government lands have been manumitted (in Malabar in 1835), and in 1843 an Act of the President in Council ordained that slavery would be no longer recognised in our law courts, and that slaves would be protected in life and in property as if they were freemen. Until a complete census shall be taken, and the condition of the bondsfolk, with the cause of their having become such, be fully known, it will be difficult to give due effect to the benevolent intentions of Government on their behalf.

There are several territories under the government or jurisdiction of Madras, not included in the Presidency census. The first in importance is Mysoor, whose native Hindoo ruler was set aside on the plea of incompetency in 1832, and allowed a stipend of thirty-five thousand pounds a year and a fifth share of the revenues of Mysoor, which amounted in 1860-61 to one hundred and nine thousand pounds; making his income one hundred and forty-four thousand pounds. A subsidy is paid for military charges into the Imperial treasury of two hundred and forty-five thousand pounds a year. A British Commissioner rules the country, and makes an annual report to Calcutta of the proceedings of his administration.

This province, which is larger than the mainland of Scotland, lies between the eleventh and fifteenth degrees of latitude, is upwards of two hundred and fifty miles long from north to south, with an extreme breadth of two hundred and forty miles; and has an area variously estimated at twenty-seven thousand to thirty thousand square miles. The whole country is elevated and skirted on its east, west, and south limits by the East and West Ghauts, which gradually converge from the north and support a triangular-shaped plateau. The altitude above the sea ranges from two to three thousand feet: some parts are higher. The Sevagunga mountains, twenty-five miles to the north-west of Bangalore, have an altitude of four thousand eight hundred feet, and the Bala-budin mountains, near Bednore, upwards of six thousand feet. Isolated rocks, termed Droogs, with bases of one to two miles, rise abruptly from the table-land to a height of one to two thousand feet and upwards. Nundydroog is four thousand eight hundred and fifty-six feet above the sea; Severndroog four thousand. The elevation of Chittledroog and others has not been ascertained. These gigantic pillars are chiefly composed of granite, gneiss, and hornblende, and in former times were crowned with nearly inaccessible fortresses.

Mysoor is much cooler than either coast of the Indian peninsula. From its altitude it is exposed to the violence of both monsoons, and receives a heavy fall of rain. Hailstorms are frequent in the hot season of April and May.

The population differs in appearance and character from the residents on the lower plains. The Hindoo Mysooreans bear a general resemblance to the Mahrattas; but the Natives, both Hindoo and Mohammedan, are a bolder race than the inhabitants of Bengal. All classes are engaged in agricultural pursuits, and are in more comfortable circumstances than the people of the Madras regulation districts. Mysoor was thirty-eight years under the rule of Hyder Ali and his son Tippoo Sultan; who, though they desolated the Carnatic and carried the scourge of war into other kingdoms, were careful of their own territories. After the capture of Seringapatam, in 1799, Colonel Arthur Wellesley, in co-operation with the able Hindoo minister Purneah, and aided by Colonels Barry Close, Malcolm, and Mark Wilks, organized an effective administration, made roads, improved the country, suppressed turbulence, and encouraged agriculture. In 1804 the population was estimated at two million one hundred and seventy-four thousand. Since then Mysoor has prospered, and its inhabitants have increased in number and wealth. (See Table, p. 139.)

The total population in 1860-61 is stated to exceed three million eight hundred and four thousand, and to have increased forty thousand during the previous year. The proportion of Mohammedans to Hindoos is as one to fourteen.

Westward of Mysoor lies the ancient Hindoo principality of Coorg, mentioned by the historian Ferishta as governed by independent princes in 1583. The Anglo-Indian authorities dethroned the Rajah in 1834, and assumed the sovereignty of the country, which is a beautiful mountain region, diversified with hills and valleys—the former crowned with forests of sandal-wood and other valuable timber, the latter well cultivated with rice and other grains. Coorg varies in elevation from

AREA AND POPULATION OF MYSOOR IN 1857-58.

Divisions.	Hindoos.			Mussulmans.			Grand Total.	Area in Square Miles.	Mouths to a Square Mile.
	Males.	Females.	Total.	Males.	Females.	Total.			
Bangalore	562,827	505,992	1,068,819	41,990	39,527	81,437	1,150,256	5,695	205
Chittledroog ..	353,549	300,317	653,866	11,465	9,879	21,344	675,210	7,724	88
Ashtagram	631,488	539,047	1,170,535	25,855	22,357	48,212	1,218,747	7,493	162
Nuggur	353,379	310,511	663,890	17,961	12,863	30,824	694,714	6,091	114
Totals	1,901,243	1,655,867	3,557,110	97,271	84,626	181,817	3,738,927	27,003	138

	Population.	Houses.	Number to each House.
Bangalore Cusbah	42,888	6,075	7
Bangalore Cantonment	132,742	17,821	8
Mysoor Town	55,761	11,130	5
Seringapatam	14,928	5,212	3
Joomkoor Town	9,339	2,362	4
Shimooga Town	14,186	2,615	5
	269,844	45,215	5 average.

from three to six thousand feet above the sea: it is traversed in various directions by ramparts of fifteen to twenty feet high, with ditches in front eight to ten feet wide, and in many places double, triple, or quadruple; their linear extent being estimated at five to six hundred miles—about twenty times the extent of the Pict walls in North Britain. When taken possession of in 1834, some of the territory of Coorg was annexed to Canara, and the present length is about sixty miles from north to south, and thirty-five miles from east to west, with an area which Thornton * gives as one thousand four hundred and twenty square miles, but the Population Return of 1862 as two thousand one hundred and sixteen square miles, with one hundred and eighteen thousand four hundred and sixty-four inhabitants, or fifty-six to each square mile.

The Coorgs are a handsome, athletic, warlike race, usually above the middle size, and nearly as fair as many Spaniards or Portuguese; especially the women, who have pleasing features, with finely proportioned figures. The people are comfortably clad, cleanly in their persons and habitations, and very industrious; they speak the Canarese language, are almost exclusively Hindoos, and entertain a deep aversion to the Mohammedans. Polyandria prevails in some districts among the Nairs. There is no census showing the proportion of males to females.

The condition of the mass of the people of Coorg has not improved under British administration.† The observation

* Thornton's 'Gazetteer,' Article Coorg.

† The Rev. Mr. Mægling, a missionary of standing in Coorg, writing some years after its annexation, states :—"Little or nothing has been done for the education of the people. Nothing has been attempted systematically to raise them in intelligence and character: on the contrary, it is a common complaint that three evils—drunkenness, sexual licentiousness, and lying—have greatly increased during the Company's reign. In former days the Native rulers suppressed drunkenness by summary and violent means; now the government draws a large revenue from the sale of intoxicating liquors. Prostitutes were formerly turned out of the country, and Coorg men severely punished and degraded for intercourse with low-caste women; now, the wicked and shame-

made by Colonel Wellesley in the last century "that the extension of our territory and our influence has been greater than our means," might have been repeated with additional force after every one of our later annexations; especially in the case of the distant minor principalities, for the righteous administration of which it was scarcely possible to provide under the system of rejecting the natural and abundant material offered by Natives of character and position, and delegating almost irresponsible power to the inexperienced youths of the civil service, who were of course compelled to resort for advice to their ill-paid Native subordinates, and tempted to listen to the counsels of interested persons and to the solicitations of money-lenders. These latter, though not more unscrupulous in India than in Europe, have a more dangerous sphere of influence in the Anglo-Indian courts of law, which the Natives of rank and character unite in cordially detesting.

The employment of responsible Native agency, if heartily followed up by the imperial government, will probably tell rapidly on the bold mountaineers of Coorg, to whom reparation is due for the arbitrary manner in which, without any fault or consent of theirs, they were deprived of the independence they had preserved for many centuries.

Coffee thrives well in Mysoor, in the adjacent jungly region of Wynaad, and in Coorg. European planters are now establishing themselves in these healthy districts, where pepper, cardamoms, and other spices are extensively cultivated. Cardamoms are a precarious crop, and the Natives evince skill and care in rearing the valuable production. The seed is thinly strewn in baskets of earth raised on sticks, and placed in the shade in a running stream to prevent the

less do as they please. In times past the Rajah would now and then cut off a man's tongue or his head for having spoken a falsehood; in these days the man who lies most impudently and swears most fearlessly, often gains the cause; when lies do not succeed, bribes do."—*Present and Future of India under British Rule*, by Henry Richard, p. 22.

inroads of ants and reptiles, who eagerly devour it. Snakes are especially fond of cardamoms, and rarely allow them to ripen. The gatherers are obliged to wear a coarse loose blanket dress to protect themselves from reptiles. The areca, betel-nut, and cocoa-nut palms are very productive.

The province of Berar or Nagpoor, recently annexed to the British dominions, has an area, including the Godavery districts, larger than that of England and Wales. The returns of 1862 estimate Berar at nearly seventy-two thousand square miles, with a population of about four million five hundred thousand, or sixty to each square mile. This is evidently little more than a guess; no census nor any classification or territorial subdivision is attempted in the return.

Nearly equidistant from Calcutta, from Bombay and from Madras, with an elevation of from one to two thousand feet above the sea, this region is one of the best portions of India as regards fertility of soil and salubrity of climate. It is well drained by the Weingunga, the Wurda, and other streams; and its black soil when tilled yields in abundance wheat and cotton of excellent quality. The people are brave, but peaceable and industrious; the majority are Hindoos; the Gonds (aborigines) number about a quarter of a million, and the Mohammedans do not constitute three per cent. of the population. Much of the country has never been visited by Europeans, but it deserves to be better known.

Jeypoor and the Hill zemindars in Orissa pay tribute to the British Government, and are under the management of the Madras authorities. Jeypoor, in the nineteenth degree of latitude, one hundred and eleven miles north-west of Vizagapatam; is bounded on the south by the Godavery, and on the west by the Nagpoor territory. It is a wild country, the people are in a semi-savage state, and owing to the dense jungles, the climate is pestilential to Europeans. The area of Jeypoor and the Hill states is given at about thirteen thousand square miles (nearly twice the size of Wales), and the population assigned is about three hundred and fifty thousand, or twenty-six to each square mile: but both the statements of area and inhabitants are conjectural. The "Hydrabad assigned estates" which have been taken by the British government from the Nizam, to pay for the military contingent stationed in his territories, consist of ten estates, containing in West Berar ten thousand nine hundred square miles, with a population of six hundred and twelve thousand souls; and in East Berar five thousand six hundred square miles, and a population of four hundred and eighty-six thousand souls. The total area exceeds sixteen thousand five hundred square miles; and the population one million one hundred thousand souls, showing sixty-six inhabitants to each square mile.

The southern extremity of India is occupied by the district of Travancore, over which British authority was established in 1810, and has been exercised more or less, according to the ability of the reigning prince, ever since. When the Rajah has shown an aptitude for rule, and not been a sensual inmate of the zenana, he has been intrusted to a considerable degree with the management of affairs; when he has proved incapable, or indolent, the British Resident has resumed complete control. This is the case with other small territories in India called "Native States." Travancore has an alleged area of four thousand seven hundred square miles, but as it includes a part of the Western Ghauts, with, in some places, an elevation of seven thousand feet above the sea, the area has been but imperfectly measured. The sea-coast for one hundred and fifty-five miles west of Cape Comorin, and a few miles east of that point, is generally low, with a few cliffs of slight elevation; but fifteen to twenty miles inland the mural fronts of the Ghauts rise in magnificent masses. The population is stated at above one million two hundred and sixty-two thousand, or about two hundred and sixty-five to each square mile; a density which is very improbable, considering the mountainous character of a large part of the district. There are various classes of inhabitants, including Hindoos, Mussulmans, Jews, Native Christians, and others. Of the Hindoos, many are Nairs—a low caste, among whom the custom prevails of one woman becoming the wife of several brothers. The Mohammedans are chiefly Moplahs, a fanatic class descended from the Arabs, who migrated to the western coast of India. The Lubbis are a mixed race between the Arabs and the Hindoos. The Christians are of three denominations: first, Syriac, who recognise the Patriarch of Antioch as their spiritual head; second, Roman Catholics converted by Portuguese missionaries; third, Protestants, who are chiefly descended from converts made by the Dutch.

It is asserted that there are one hundred and fifty thousand Christians in Travancore, of whom about seventy thousand are Syriac, and an equal number attached to the Church of Rome. The Rajahs belong to the Nair caste, and regard the children of their sisters as their heirs.

There are wild and savage races in the hills, who live on game and the spontaneous products of the forest. Their numbers are not known. Slaves are numerous; and a government report describes them as existing "in the lowest state of degradation." A proclamation, issued in 1853, declared that the children of slaves would be in future born free; forbade the seizure of slaves in satisfaction of debts; recognised their right to hold property, and be protected by the law; prohibited, without consent, the sale of parents or separation of children to a greater distance than fifteen miles, and enacted regulations to diminish oppression. It is supposed that this proclamation has produced little or no effect.

Cochin, situated to the northward of Travancore, is, like that territory, subject to British supremacy, and has a Native Rajah under the control of the English Resident and the Madras government. It contains an area of about two thousand square miles, including the contiguous Western

Ghauts, but it is uncertain whether a large back-water on the coast one hundred and twenty miles in length, with a breadth varying from a few hundred yards to ten miles, and a depth in the dry season of one to two feet, is included in the estimated area. The population is stated at somewhat under three hundred and thirty-two thousand, or one hundred and sixty-six persons to each square mile. The Hindoos include many of the Namboories, who constitute the Brahminical priesthood, and here exercise a more remarkable influence over their co-religionists than in any other part of India; yet their conduct is wholly at variance with the austerity inculcated in the Vedas, and they live frequently in a state of promiscuous intercourse with the Soodra (low-caste) women of the Nairs, the largest class of the population. There are many outcasts from Brahminism, who are engaged as fishermen, and in other pursuits; the Mohammedans are few. The aborigines or hill-people are described as so degraded as to be "scarcely human." * The Christians are Syriac and Romanist, and the Jews are of two classes: one black, settled in Cochin from time immemorial; and the other white, of more recent immigration. The number of places of worship for each form of religion was some years since stated to be:—Hindoo, two thousand seven hundred and thirty-four; Moslem, thirty-one; Jewish, eight; Christian, one hundred and eight.

The Tamil, Mahratta, and Teloogoo languages with some dialects prevail in the Madras Presidency, as Bengallee does in the Gangetic Valley.

The Bombay Presidency.

Irrespective of the Native States under British jurisdiction, the Presidency of Bombay has an area of nearly one hundred and forty thousand square miles, and is consequently larger than the United Kingdom. It extends from south-east to north-west upwards of six hundred and fifty miles, and has

* Thornton's 'Gazetteer.'

a breadth varying from two hundred to two hundred and forty miles, with a sea-coast of five hundred and sixty miles, furnished with several excellent harbours. The Western Ghauts stretch from the head of the Gulf of Cambay to Malabar, forming the buttress which supports the Deccan, and the plateau north of the Nerbudda. The western side of the Ghauts is rocky and rugged, except on the borders of the Gulf of Cambay, which are flat and marshy. Eastward of the Ghauts the table land is from one to two thousand feet above the sea, gradually sloping to the eastward and southward, as shown by the courses of the Kistna, Godavery, and other Deccanee rivers. Bombay itself was originally a group of rocky and marshy islets, and was at one time so unhealthy that three years was the average duration of European life there. The gradual recession of the ocean, the exclusion by artificial means of tidal water, and an improved system of drainage, has rendered the surface dry, and as healthy as most other tropical places. The fort was commenced by the Portuguese, and has been enlarged and made very strong by the English; the sea washes three sides of the fortress, which has a town of some size within its walls, together with large barracks, arsenal, and docks, adapted for the building of line-of-battle ships. The native town adjoining the esplanade isthmus, which connects the fortress with the other portion of the island, is like most Native towns, irregularly built, and defective in its supply of water and sewerage. The European and wealthy Parsee and Native merchants' dwellings are scattered in different directions, affording a sea-prospect, with picturesque views of the adjacent island of Salsette and its surroundings; or fine inland scenery, bounded by the distant Ghauts. The climate is sultry; and, owing to the contiguous mountains and the western site of Bombay, the quantity of rain that falls there is very large, sometimes as much as one hundred inches in the year; while in the Deccan droughts are not unfrequent.

The advantageous position of the island for commerce, the

security for life and property afforded by the British Government, added to the recently attained facility for European intercourse by the Red Sea; have concurred in augmenting the population. In 1716 it was estimated to contain sixteen thousand inhabitants; in 1816, the numbers were computed at one hundred and sixty thousand, of whom above a hundred thousand were Hindoos, twenty-eight thousand were Mohammedans, thirteen thousand Parsees, eight hundred Jews, eleven thousand Native Christians, Portuguese, and Armenians, and one thousand eight hundred and forty British (not military). These numbers were irrespective of a floating population of sixty thousand to seventy-five thousand persons. The Parliamentary returns for 1857 give the following classification of the inhabitants:—

Bombay Island and City, and Colaba Island.	Males.	Females.	Total.
Hindoos	196,979	99,952	296,931
Mussulmans to include Siddees (an Arabic and African race) ..	77,359	46,796	124,155
Parsees	60,967	53,731	114,698
Christians	12,348	6,946	19,294
Shrawniks or Jains	1,083	819	1,902
Jews	612	520	1,132
Low Castes	4,742	3,265	8,007

Thus the total population on an area of eighteen square miles is five hundred and sixty-six thousand, or thirty-one thousand four hundred to each square mile. The return for 1862 gives the area at twenty square miles, and the population at seven hundred and thirty thousand, or thirty-six thousand five hundred to each square mile. There are said to be only one hundred and thirteen thousand females to three hundred and fifty-four thousand males. Among the Hindoos the proportion of males to females is as two to one. In all classes the males preponderate.

The motley groups that are to be seen at Bombay converse in a variety of tongues. Throughout the Presidency different languages are spoken. Mahratta and Canarese prevail in the south and south-east; Gujerati in the north; Persian and Oordoo are employed as the languages of etiquette and of business; Marwari, Portuguese, and Arabic are also in use; the Bheels in some districts have a language peculiar to themselves.

AREA AND POPULATION OF THE REGULATION DISTRICTS.

Name of District.	Area in Square Miles.	Population.	Mouths to each Square Mile.
Bombay and Colaba Islands and town of Bombay	20	730,000	36,500
Ahmedabad	4,402	650,223	147
Kaira	1,375	580,631	422
Broach	1,351	290,984	215
Surat	1,482	492,684	332
Tannah or Northern Concan	5,400	874,570	161
Candeish	12,078	778,112	64
Poonah	5,250	666,006	126
Ahmednuggur	10,414	995,585	95
Sholapoor	8,565	675,115	78
Rutnagherry	4,500	672,197	149
Belgaum	13,106	1,033,373	78
Dharwar	6,070	754,385	124
Total	74,013	9,193,865	124

There is more classification in the returns from this Presidency for 1857, than from any other part of India. The aggregate of each district is as follows:—

Classes.	Males.	Females.	Total.
Hindoos	3,009,790	2,642,359	5,652,109
Wild Tribes	485,321	428,655	913,976
Low Castes	408,114	373,429	782,003
Shrawniks or Jains	70,662	58,136	128,798
Lingayets	493,046	272,401	565,447
Mussulmans including Siddees ..	415,980	363,284	779,264
Jews	1,840	1,768	3,608
Parsees	69,354	62,709	132,563
Christians	32,258	25,508	57,766

Males	4,787,325
Females	4,228,209
Total	9,015,534

It will be observed that here, as in the other Presidencies, the Mohammedans bear but a small proportion to the Hindoos and to the general population. The Mahrattas, who cherish an hereditary hatred to the Mohammedans, form the bulk of the people. The Ramosees, a semi-civilised tribe, occupy the hills south of Sattara; the Bheels, an aboriginal race, the valley of the Taptee and the Candeish basin; further west and north are many wild tribes, all sunk in barbarism. The Jains or Boodhists are widely scattered. The Parsees, the most mercantile and best educated class of the people of India, are descended from the fugitive fire-worshippers of Persia; who, being driven from their country by the usurping Mohammedans, sought asylums at Surát and along the west coast of India. They settled in considerable numbers in Bombay, and rendered their adopted home a centre of wealth and industry by their mechanical skill, their mercantile habits, and character for probity. Even the reluctance of the Anglo-Indian Government under the old régime to confer distinction on Natives, was overcome by the public spirit displayed by a Parsee merchant; and the subsequent conduct of the first Indian baronet, Sir Jamsetjee Jejeeboye, was calculated to reflect honour on the class to which he was elected, and on that which he naturally represented. There are many other Parsees—shipbuilders and others—who have risen by their own exertions to the position of merchant princes; and so general is the reputation earned by them as men of business, that it is popularly asserted, that when a Parsee shopkeeper settles in any district, however remote, some trade is sure to spring up there.

Slavery exists in several parts of the Presidency. Mr. Chaplin reports its presence in the Deccan. The number of slaves in Surat alone is stated at three thousand.

Sattara and the jaghires attached thereto are under the Bombay administration. In 1862, their area and population are thus given :—

Sattara and its Jaghires.	Area.	Population.	To each Square Mile.
Sattara	9,327	948,053	101
Jaghires—			
Akulkote	986	74,076	75
Bhore	500	110,193	220
Jutt	700	58,794	84
Oumdee	300	67,967	226
Phultun	400	47,160	117
Wyhee		Not given.	
Total	12,213	1,316,223	107

The other territories under the Government of Bombay, whose Native rulers are still retained, are given in the return of 1862 (see page 151).

Guzerat, including the Kattywar peninsula, is a large, wild, and little known region: flat towards the coast, but the interior broken into hills, rocky tracts, and granitic peaks rising one thousand five hundred to two thousand feet above the sea. The Aravulli mountains run from south to north, towards Delhi, and form the western boundary of the table-land of Hindoostan. Races of diverse lineage, manners, and language, inhabit Guzerat. The Mahrattas are numerous, so also are the Rajpoots. Mussulmans and Parsees are to be found chiefly in the towns; but the latter sometimes engage in agriculture. There are also the Coolies, an aboriginal race, robust and brave, professing Brahminism, but eating flesh and using intoxicating liquors; the Koonbies, an agricultural tribe; the Katties, who migrated from the Indus at a remote period; the Dunjas, the Bhats and Charuns; the Bheels dwell in large numbers along the Myhee river. These and other races require watchful superintendence, just and conciliatory treatment, and the least possible interference with their customs and prejudices.

In several places the country is well cultivated. Cotton is

Guzerat, Cutch, &c.*	Locality.	Area in Square Miles.	Population.	Mouths to each Sq. Mile
Balasinore	Guzerat	175	19,092	109
Bansda	Guzerat	242½	26,713	110
Baroda (Dominions of the Guicowar)	Guzerat	4,399	1,735,432	394
Cambay	Guzerat	350	175,000	500
The Daung Rajah's country	Guzerat	950	70,300	74
Dhurrumpoor	Guzerat	794¼	45,024	56
Chowrar	Guzerat	440	10.582	24
Pahlunpoor	Guzerat	2,384	184,060	77
Radhunpoor	Guzerat	833	46,017	55
Baubier	Guzerat	72	4,089	56
Charchut	Guzerat	Not given.	3,547	
Deodur	Guzerat	240	13,217	55
Seogaum	Guzerat	161	7,365	45
Therwarra	Guzerat	100	5,017	50
Thurraud	Guzerat	644	30,885	47
Warye	Guzerat	204	14,592	71
Wow	Guzerat	360	14,368	40
Morewarra	Guzerat	96	4,712	49
Kankry	Guzerat	507	46,017	90
Kattywar Petty Chief	Guzerat	19,850	1,468,900	74
Myhee Caunta	Guzerat	4,000	311,046	77
Barreea, or Deoghur Barreea	Guzerat	780	64,380	82
Loonawarra	Guzerat	415	37,000	89
Mewassee Chiefs residing on the banks of the Nerbudda and the Myhee	Guzerat	375	27,750	74
Odeypoor (Chota), or Mohun	Guzerat	900	78,366	73
Rajpeepla	Guzerat	1,300	122,100	93
Soauth	Guzerat	500	31,450	62
Sucheen	Guzerat	35⅓	15,959	456
Wusravee (Bheel Chiefs)	Guzerat	450	33,300	128
		41,557½	4,646,280	111·
Cutch	Western India	6,500	409,522	63
Kolapore	Southern Mahratta Country	3,184	546,156	171
Peint and Hursool	Adjacent to Ahmednuggur	780	55,000	70
Sawunt Warree	South Concan	900	163,650	118
Southern Mahratta Jaghires	Southern Mahratta Country	3,700	475,725	128
		15,064	1,650,053	109·
	Total in Bombay	56,621¼	6,296,333	111·

* Very little is known of the condition of the people in these petty states; even their names are so carelessly given in the Government returns, as to render it difficult to verify them. The sparsity of population is remarkable, but the data on which both area and population are based hardly promise even an approximation to correctness.

is the staple product. The railway from Bombay to Baroda, Ahmedabad, and Deesa, will open up this fine country, in which insurrectionary movements have been frequent. Guzerat and the territories nominally under the Guicowar were disarmed in February, 1858, by the late Sir Richmond Shakespear, for which "most wise" act he was complimented by the Supreme Government of India and censured by the Court of Directors in England. From eight thousand villages there were taken one hundred and sixty cannon, twenty-one thousand fire-arms, about one hundred and eighteen thousand swords, and three hundred and seven thousand other weapons. Only two villages attempted resistance, and these were among the worst and most turbulent communities in India.

Sinde, which comprises the lower part of the Indus valley, is under the Government of Bombay.

AREA AND POPULATION OF SINDE.

Non-Regulation Districts.	Area in Square Miles.	Population.	Months to each Square Mile.
Shikarpoor	9,042	650,304	71
Frontier Districts	2,147	47,955	22
Hydrabad	10,974	630,300	57
Kurrachee	19,240	340,000	17
Thur and Packur	13,000	127,035	9
Total	54,403	1,795,594	33

The population of the above districts is not classified in the return for 1862, but in that for 1857 it was given as follows:—

Classes.	Males.	Females.	Total.
Mohammedans	758,164	596,727	1,354,891
Hindoos	203,050	160,245	363,295
Other religions	28,118	22,433	50,551

Males	989,332
Females	779,405
Total	1,768,737

Khyrpoor district, near Sukkur, in the north of Sinde, has an area of six thousand five hundred square miles; and a population of one hundred and fifty thousand, or twenty-three persons to each square mile.

A large portion of Sinde, which is about the size of England and Wales, is sandy, and in many places only cultivable by constant irrigation. The population is sparse, varied in character, and very wild in some localities.

There has been a large immigration of Patans and of Cutch artisans into Kurrachee, induced by the demand for employment on the railway, and the hope of obtaining work under an enterprising Patan, named Moorar Khan, who is expending one hundred thousand rupees on extensive irrigation works near the Hubb river, where he has obtained the lease of a large tract of waste land on favourable terms. Bhawul Khan, chief of the Beloochee hill-men of Tinde, is establishing a village on some waste lands near the Maunchar lake, and has persuaded others of his tribe to settle in the vicinity.

This is the only part of India in which the Mohammedans outnumber the Hindoos; the latter are more lax in their religious profession than their sect in other parts of India, and were largely, but often forcibly, converted to Islamism. These converts are peaceable, and despised by the Beloochee Mohammedans, who are powerful and warlike. The Sindians dwelling on the Indus are a finer people than the Bengallees in the same latitude on the Ganges. The men are brave and the women beautiful, and the mixed race between the Beloochees and the Hindoos is remarkable for symmetry of figure and noble features. The Sindian language is said to be a branch of the Sanscrit or Indo-Germanic root, with merely a little difference in spelling and inflexion from the pure Hindi of Upper India. Colonel Macmurdo says it has fewer modern innovations and a greater number of Sanscrit words than the Gujarati, which is a pure Hindoo dialect. Beloochee, another Indo-Germanic dialect, is largely spoken, especially in the hills; Persian is the language of the higher orders of the people. There are some Afghans among the population, and they speak their native tongue. Camels are bred in large numbers in the salt marshes of the Indus. The horses and asses of Sinde are small but very active and hardy. Buffaloes are reared in extensive herds in the swampy tracts, where they may be seen wallowing in the mud with their heads only above water. The flesh is excellent, and the milk answers better than that of the cow for the production of the *ghee*, or clarified butter, so largely consumed in India.

The Punjab.

The ten districts which constitute this province are under the direct administration of the Lieutenant-Governor. The area and population are thus given in the return of 1862:—

Punjab Districts.	Area in Square Miles.	Population.	Mouths to each Sq. Mile.
Delhi—			
Delhi	786	273,479	348
Goorgaon	2,000	686,086	343
Kurnaul	1,271	369,085	290
	4,057	1,328,650	327
Hissar—			
Hissar	3,156	261,146	82
Rohtuck	2,171	451,005	208
Sirsa	3,219	145,870	45
	8,546	858,021	100
Trans-Sutlej States—			
Jullundur	1,347	698,169	518
Hoshiarpoor	2,188	833,817	381
Kangra	3,206	718,955	224
	6,741	2,250,941	319
Cis-Sutlej States—			
Umballah	1,829	723,992	395
Thanessur	2,038	511,887	251
Loodiana	1,377	525,498	381
Simla	Not given.	27,786	
	5,244	1,789,163	341

Districts.	Area in Square Miles.	Population.	Mouths to each Sq. Mile.
Lahore—			
Lahore	3,608	662,338	183
Goojeranwala	2,651	420,753	158
Ferozepoor	2,730	475,624	174
	8,989	1,558,715	173
Umritsur—			
Umritsur	2,024	884,429	437
Goordaspoor	1,675	787,417	470
Sealkote	1,350	641,782	475
	5,049	2,313,628	458
Rawul Pindee—			
Rawul Pindee	5,996	553,750	92
Goojerat	1,886	500,167	265
Jhelum	3,684	375,800	102
Shahpoor	6,500	261,692	40
	18,066	1,691,409	93
Peshawar—			
Peshawar	2,324	450,099	193
Huzarah	2,424	296,364	122
Kohat	2,840	116,293	40
	7,588	862,756	113
Derajat—			
Dera Ghazee Khan	6,531	238,959	36
Dera Ismael Khan	5,745	434,180	75
Bunnoo	4,500	237,557	52
	16,776	910,696	84
Mooltan—			
Mooltan	5,634	411,386	73
Moozufferghur	2,849	246,912	86
Jhung	5,314	264,314	49
Googaira	5,553	308,020	55
	19,350	1,230,632	63
Total under the Administration of the Lieut.-Governor of Punjab	100,406	14,794,611	147

In the return of 1857, the population (including that of the Delhi districts) was thus classified :—

Classes.	Agricultural.		Non-Agricultural.	
	Males.	Females.	Males.	Females.
Hindoos	2,242,066	1,759,016	1,670,608	1,293,538
Mohammedan and others not Hindoos	2,414,755	2,060,335	1,883,860	1,578,825
Total	4,656.821	3,819,351	3,554,568	2,872,363

The number of the Seiks ought to have been separately stated. It is believed to be less than two million, of which one million inhabit the protected states eastward of the Sutlej; and the remainder, called the Mangha Seiks, dwell to the westward.

The preceding figures, with corrections and additions for 1862, are the result of a census made in 1855-56, since which date the population has considerably increased. It will be observed that in some districts there are more than three hundred mouths to each square mile, but this is chiefly on the river borders; on the arid plains the density is from fifty-six to one hundred. There are numerous small States, under the supervision, and more or less under the control, of the Lieut.-Governor of the Punjab; these are thus described :—

Punjab Native States.	Area.	Population.	Mouths to each Sq. Mile.
Near Delhi—			
Bahadoorghur	Not known.	Not known.	
Bullubghur	Not known.	Not known.	
Doojana	71	6,390	90
Furrucknuggur	60,000	3,000,000	50
Jhujhur			
Loharoo	200	18,000	90
Patowlee	74	6,660	90
Puttiala	5,412	1,586,000	291
Jheend	1,236	311,000	259
Nabha	863	276,000	320
Kulsea	155	62,000	400
Puttiala and Kulsea in shares ..	18	7,200	400
Puttiala and Nabha in shares ..	31	8,680	280
Milair Cotta	165	46,200	280

Punjab Native States.	Area.	Population.	Mouths to each Sq. Mile.
Cis-Sutlej—			
Bhawulpoor	25,200	925,000	
Baghul	180	22,305	
Beejah	5	981	
Belaspoor	360	64,848	
Bussahir	2,700	45,025	
Bujee	80	9,001	
Bulsun	30	4,892	
Dhamee	35	2,853	
Durkotee	3	612	
Goond	10	963	
Hindoor (Hill Estates)	330	49,678	
Joobul (Hill Estates)	324	17,262	
Koomharsein (Hill Estates)	75	7,829	
Koonhear (Hill Estates)	8	1,906	
Keonthut (Hill Estates)	80	18,083	
Kotee	40	3,981	
Kothar	9	3,990	
Mangul	15	917	
Milag	36	7,358	
Mudhan	28	2,431	
Puttiala (Hills)	238	48,836	
Saugree	9	1,994	
Sirmoor	Not given.	75,595	
Theag	36	4,423	
Turoch	48	3,082	
Trans-Sutlej—			
Mundee	1,082	139,259	
Sokeit	420	44,552	
Chumba	3,216	101,631	
Kupoorthullah	598	212,721	
Rhunbeer Singh's Dominions ..	60,000	3,000,000	
	103,442	7,154,538	69

This widely-diversified region is inhabited by a variety of races, but the Seiks and Hindoos generally predominate, and the Mohammedans, except in and near Delhi, form a small minority. The Seiks, who were the dominant class at the time of the British annexation, had their beginning in a peaceable religious sect, founded by a Hindoo, named Nanuk, about the end of the fifteenth century. Driven from

Lahore, their original seat, A.D. 1606, they took refuge in the adjacent mountains, and remained there nearly seventy years. Guru Govind, the tenth spiritual chief in succession from Nanuk, converted the Seiks from an inoffensive and persecuted community into a military commonwealth. He increased their number by abolishing caste distinctions and allowing the use of intoxicating drinks and animal food; the slaughter of kine being alone prohibited. All converts were placed on a footing of perfect equality with the oldest members of the sect, were sworn to fight for the cause, always to carry steel in some shape, to wear blue clothes, and never clip or shave the hair on any part of the body. Brahminism was respected, and an endeavour was made to combine that creed with the teaching of the Koran, on the basis of the unity of God: and the new doctrine was expounded by their Guru or "teacher" in the writings called "Grunths." The Mohammedans becoming alarmed at the growth of the Seik power, caused Guru Govind, his mother and children, to be massacred, and from that time a deadly hostility has existed between the two races. The Seiks overran the Punjab, destroyed the mosques, slew the moollahs, massacred the population of whole towns, spared neither age nor sex, and disinterred the bodies of the dead to expose them as carrion to birds of prey. At length, after alternate successes and defeats, the Seiks established themselves, under separate chiefs, on the banks of the Sutlej, and were gradually united and formed into a nation by Runjeet Sing, a Seik chief of Jât descent, who, by the aid of European officers, French, Italians and others, organised a strong military power on our north-western frontier. After the death of Runjeet, the Sirdars or Native chiefs led the Khalsa or State force against the British; but being defeated in several desperate battles, the Punjab was annexed to the Crown. The Seiks have proved themselves brave enemies and faithful friends: they are now peaceable and prosperous subjects. We know little of the inhabitants of the adjacent Hill districts: some are Afghan, others Hindoo, and all difficult to govern—successful rule depending more on the personal bearing and character of the English official placed over them than on any system of government, however well devised. Men rather than measures are essential for the subjugation and management of warlike tribes, turbulent from hereditary feuds, and impatient of any control over their actions.

The Rajah of Puttiala and other Cis-Sutlej chieftains, exercise their internal jurisdiction with little supervision on the part of the Supreme Government. The Puttiala Rajah is now a member of the Legislative Council at Calcutta, sits by order of precedence next the Governor-General, and is an acknowledged British subject.

Punjabi and Hindoostani are the principal spoken languages.

North-West Provinces.

Eastward of the Punjab and north of Rajpootana lie the British Regulation districts, termed the North-west Provinces, which are situated chiefly along the courses of the rivers Ganges and Jumna, in the country between those streams termed the Doab, and below their junction from Allahabad to Benares. The area of these districts is exactly that of the United Kingdom. The following figures show the distribution of the population, according to the return of 1862; but when the enumeration was made does not appear: it differs regarding several districts from the return of 1857.

Districts.	Area.	Population.	Mouths to each Sq. Mile.
Meerut—			
Seharunpore	1,882	801,325	426
Mozuffernuggur	1,646	570,478	346
Meerut	2.350	1,085,984	462
Bolundshuhur	1,883	771,844	409
Alighur	1,845	817,354	443
	9,606	4,046,985	421

Districts.	Area.	Population.	Mouths to each Sq. Mile.
Rohilcund—			
Bijnour	1,831	672,171	367
Moradabad	2,534	1,111,971	438
Budaon	1,946	693,627	356
Bareilly	2,852	1,305,123	457
Shahjehanpoor	2,483	895,651	360
	11,646	4,678,543	401
Agra—			
Muttra	1,613	759,058	470
Agra	1,865	1,001,961	537
Furruckabad	1,685	887,974	527
Mynpoory	1,579	599,229	394
Etawah	1,625	580,000	357
Etah..	1,468	561,532	382
	9,775	4,389,754	449
Allahabad—			
Cawnpoor	2,348	1,102,980	469
Futtehpoor	1,583	679,787	429
Banda	3,024	718,359	287
Allahabad	2,788	1,079,788	387
	9,743	3,581,427	
Benares—			
Benares	996	857,757	855
Goruckpoor	7,340	3,087,874	420
Azimghur	2,516	1,481,359	588
Jounpoor..	1,552	1,143,749	736
Mirzapoor	5,152	1,104,315	214
Ghazipoor	2,181	978,718	448
	19,737	8,647,772	438
Total Regulation N.W. Provinces	60,507	25,344,481	418
NON-REGULATION PROVINCES.			
Kumaon including Gurhwal	..	606,687	54
Jaunsar and Bewar	..	24,684	138
Dehra Doon	..	37,500	55
Ajmeer	..	291,666	141
Mhairwarrah (British)	..	50,800	165

Districts.	Area.	Population.	Mouths to each Sq. Mile.
Jubbulpoor—			
Saugor	3,556	409,173	115
Dumoh	2,831	232,385	81
Jubbulpoor	6,237	442,771	70
Seonee	3,980	211,003	53
Mundlah	5,105	83,532	16
Hoshungabad	5,000	238,000	47
Baitool	3,421	209,456	61
Nursingpoor	2,003	214,205	106
	32,133	2,040,525	63
Jhansie—			
Jhansi	2.275	413,736	181
Jaloun	2,025	565.550	279
Humeerpoor	2,318	477,968	206
Lullutpoor	2,850	256,500	90
	9,468	1,713.754	181
Nemaur (British)	362	25,400	70
Total under the Administration of the Lieutenant-Governor of the N.W. Provinces	116,493	30,110,097	257

It will be observed that many of the foregoing Regulation districts are very thickly peopled, the number of mouths to each square mile ranging from three hundred to five hundred and upwards; the average density being four hundred and eighteen. There is an acre and a half of land for each person, but this average includes irreclaimable wastes. The loss of life during the recent famine is entirely unknown; Colonel Baird Smith states that it was not possible to form even an estimate. Neither has any calculation been attempted of the number of the natives of the North-West Provinces who perished during the mutiny and rebellion of 1857-58.

The relative proportion of classes in the Regulation districts is thus given in the return for 1857:—

N.W. Provinces.	Agricultural.		Non-Agricultural.	
	Males.	Females.	Males.	Females.
Hindoos	8,955,270	7,655,669	3,967,826	3,533,098
Mohammedans and others	835,691	758,265	1,230,407	1,140,640
Total	9,790,931	8,413,934	5,198,213	4,673,378

This enumeration shows about twenty-four million Hindoos to less than four million Mohammedans and all other classes; the proportion being six to one.

The Hindoos of the slightly-elevated, hot and dry regions of the North-West Provinces differ in appearance and character from the denizens of the low, sultry and moist Bengal plains. They are more athletic in figure, and braver and more independent in bearing; they feed on wheat and pulse rather than on rice, which is an expensive grain; they use some descriptions of animal food; and are not such slaves to ritual nor so superstitious as the Bengallees. The Hindoostani language, which was formed chiefly during the reign of Akbar from a combination of Hindi, a primitive language of the Hindoos, with Arabic and Persian, which were introduced by the Mohammedan conquerors, is used generally throughout Hindoostan as the medium of colloquial intercourse.

The "Non-Regulation" territories, under the administration of the Lieutenant-Governor of the North-West Provinces, are as large as Ireland and Scotland united.* Some are situated on the great plateau of Central India, others (as Kumaon) on the lower ranges and buttresses of the Himalaya. The

*	Area in Square Miles.
Ireland	31,874
Scotland, without its Islands	26,014
Scotland with its Islands	30,238

population returns may or may not approach to correctness. In the Hill districts the density is not great. Jhansi, whose Queen perished in the rebellion of 1858, is comparatively well peopled; the territory has been recently transferred to Sindia, the Maharajah of Gwalior.

Nemaur, or Nimar, in the Nerbudda valley, bounded on the north by the Vindhya mountains, and on the south by the Sautpoora mountains, has no area or population assigned to it in the preceding table. The length from east to west is estimated by Sir John Malcolm at one hundred and thirty miles, and the general breadth at thirty to forty miles. The area exceeds two thousand two hundred and twenty-five square miles. A portion of Nemaur, about three hundred and sixty square miles in extent, with a population of twenty-five thousand Hindoos, is under direct British rule; other tracts are in the territories of Sindia, of Holkar, and of the Dhar Rajah.

Oude.

The recently annexed province of Oude lies north of the Ganges between the twenty-sixth and twenty-eighth degrees of latitude; is two hundred and fifty miles long by one hundred broad; and has an area of nearly twenty-eight thousand square miles. The country is from four hundred to eight hundred feet above the sea-level, well watered by the Goomtee and other streams, which flow to the south-east and fall into the Ganges. The climate is salubrious, the soil fertile and well tilled by a brave and martial race, strong in body, keen in mind, and attached to feudal institutions.

The population has been variously estimated. Thornton gives it at about three million; the return of 1857 at five million; and that of 1862 as follows:—

Divisions.	Population.
Baraitch	2,330,500
Lucknow	2,014,822
Khyrabad	1,826,398
Bainswarra	1,899,355
Total	8,071,075

showing two hundred and eighty-two mouths to each square mile.

No classification is given; but the Hindoos largely predominate over the Mohammedans, probably in the proportion of ten to one, although Oude was for a long period under Moslem sway.

Colonel Sleeman's writings well describe the turbulent character of the people, whose disarming has now been completed. The arms taken by Government consisted, in round numbers, of—*cannon*, seven hundred; *fire-arms*, one hundred and ninety-two thousand; *swords*, five hundred and seventy-eight thousand; *spears*, fifty-one thousand; *miscellaneous weapons*, six hundred and forty-two thousand. The demolition of forts has been accomplished, except fifty retained for Government use; and a few that have been deserted for years have been left standing because from the immense size of the works their destruction would have caused considerable expense: the total number destroyed is one thousand five hundred and eighty-five. Of these the walls and bastions have been entirely thrown down, the ditches filled up, and the jungle that surrounded them cleared for a space of four hundred yards all round. The Commissioner reports in 1860, that "in a few years travellers in Oude will have difficulty in discovering even the trace of a fort."

The Hindustani language is in general use: Persian and Arabic are also spoken.

British Burmah.

Eastward of Hindoostan and the Ganges, across the Bay of Bengal, there is a large tract of territory situated on and near the Irrawaddy, about being formed into a Province under the designation of British Burmah. It extends along the eastern coast of the Bay, from Arracan in the twentieth to the Mergui Archipelago in the eighth degree of latitude, a distance of about seven hundred miles; and consists of a generally flat, alluvial, rice-growing region backed by hills rising into ranges of forest-clad mountains.

The area and population of British Burmah is thus described in the returns of 1862:—

Provinces and Districts.	Area in Sq. Miles.	Population.	Number to each Square Mile.
Arracan Province—			
Akyab	14,124	224,382	26
Ramree		117,631	
Sandoway		32,113	
Total	14,124	374,126	
Pegu Provinces—			
Rangoon	9,800	252,507	25
Bassein	8,900	225,876	25
Prome	5,494	232,867	42
Henzada	2,200	118,614	8
Tharawady	2,160	128,248	59
Tonghoo	3,900	66,773	17
Total	32,454	1,024,885	31
Martaban and Tenasserim Provinces—			
Martaban	10,000	108,768	9
Amherst	12,000	134,872	11
Tavoy	7,168	56,497	7
Mergui	5,670	33,696	6
Total	34,838	333,833	9
Grand Total	81,416	1,732,844	21

The density is small; even Arracan, many years under British rule, has only twenty-six mouths to each square mile.*

Pegu, until it became British territory seven years ago, was tyrannized over by the King of Ava, and treated as a hive for plunder by the Burmese. There are a variety of races, as shown in the following return for 1860:—

* Burmah Proper contains only about 1,200,000 inhabitants.

Burmese	700,888
Karens	171,821
Taleins or Peguers	104,499
Shans	17,123
Khyengs	13,548
Yabaings	8,141
Indians	13,818
Chinese	2,058
Europeans and their descendants	1,429
Jews	80
Other races	7,935
Total	1,041,340

Males	355,017
Boys under Fifteen	205,597
	560,614
Females	316,419
Girls under Fifteen	184,307
	500,726

This census is exclusive of the population within the cantonments at military stations, but includes the chief town Rangoon and its suburbs, which has the following inhabitants:—

Men	19,850
Boys under Fifteen	10,097
	29,947
Women	16,263
Girls under Fifteen	9,674
	25,937

Total 55,884, irrespective of a large floating population.

The Burmese, who form more than half the inhabitants of Pegu, appear to be an offshoot of the great Chinese family, modified by climate and intermarriage with mountain races. The original Peguers, called Taleins by the Burmese, denominate themselves "Mon," and appear to have attained civilisation at an earlier period than their conquerors. They were centuries ago a maritime and commercial people.

The Karens are a singular wild race distributed over a

mountain tract of country, about two thousand square miles in extent. They are divided into various tribes; the highland race, east of the Sitang river, are thus estimated—True Karens, sixty-two thousand; Red Karens or Ka-ya, eastern and western, two hundred thousand. The former reside within British territory; of these, twenty-five thousand, including women and children, are under the influence of Christian missionaries, who require their converts to promise to forsake their heathenish practices, obey the teachings of the Bible, support a Teacher, send their children to school, and take the temperance pledge, as preliminary conditions ere they enter on their new career.

The Tenasserim and Martaban Districts contain less than ten mouths to each square mile. In 1860, a classified return was given as follows:—

European and other Christian immigrants ..	2,015
Burmese and Taliens	205,377
Shans and Thoungthoos	24,042
Karens	83,224
Chinese	4,351
Malays	1,058
Jews	57
Natives of India	12,418
Total	332,542

Burmese is generally spoken; the Mugh language resembles the Burmese, and has the same written character; the Mon language is spoken by the Taleins. Boodhism is the prevailing form of religion; ignorance and superstition abound.

Protected Native States.

Having now examined the territories under direct British administration, it remains to notice the states governed by Native rulers, aided by the advice of a British resident stationed at the court of the reigning prince. The right of adoption, in case of the failure of direct heirs, will probably be sanctioned by the British government as a general rule.

The information possessed regarding these states is so scanty and vague, that it is hardly possible to prepare a tabular view of their number, area, and population. There is no official document extant describing the Native Princes or chiefs, showing their religion, whether Hindoo or Mohammedan, or their political standing in relation towards superior Native administrations or to the Supreme Government. Where it has been necessary, for a special reason, the area has been calculated by some more or less irregular process; in many instances by weighing a piece of paper which covers the surface of the unknown area as exhibited on a flat map, and comparing it with the weight of paper required to cover a known area on the same map. The population is frequently guessed at by allowing a small or large number of persons to each square mile according to the idea formed by the calculator of the extent of the cultivation and apparent density of population.

Oude exemplifies the imperfect manner in which these estimates have been made. Mr. Edward Thornton, the late head of the Statistical Department at the East India House, furnished for Parliament, shortly before the annexation of Oude, a return giving the area at twenty-three thousand seven hundred and thirty-eight square miles; population two million nine hundred and seventy thousand, or one hundred and twenty-five to each square mile; in the official returns transmitted from Calcutta to the India Office, London, in 1862, the area is given as twenty-seven thousand eight hundred and ninety miles, and the population at eight million seventy-one thousand and seventy-five; or two hundred and eighty-nine to each square mile—more than twice the number estimated by Mr. Thornton. The following tabular view of Native states must therefore be considered merely as an attempted approximation to truth; the number of inhabitants is probably much larger than that here given:—

STATES ruled by NATIVE PRINCES and CHIEFS under the Political Supremacy and Protection of the British Government.*

Designation.	Area in Square Miles.	Estimated Population.	No. to each Square Mile.	Locality.
Gwalior (Sindia)	35,650	3,500,000	98	Central India.
Indore (Holcar)	8,318	815,164	98	,,
Allee Mohun, and other small States	17,000	2,200,000	130	,,
Bhopal	6,764	663,656	98	,,
Rajpoot States, fifteen in number	114,391	7,412,426	65	Rajpootana.
Dhar	1,070	104,860	98	Malwa.
Rewah and five other States	9,327 2,417	1,200,000 360,000	128 107	Saugor and Nerbudda Territory.
Bundlecund States, thirty-two in number	8,354	856,600	102	Bundlecund.
Dholpoor	1,626	550,000	338	Near Chumbul River.
Bhurtpoor	1,978	600,000	303	Near Agra.
Rampoor	720	320,450	445	Rohilcund.
Cashmeer	60,000	3,000,000	50	North of Punjab.
Nepaul and Sikhim ..	56,170	2,001,766	36	North of Bengal.
Cooch Behar, &c., Cossya and Garrow Hills	13,295	277,445	21	N.E. of Bengal.
Tipperah	7,632	360,000	50	Near Burmah.
Hydrabad (Nizam) ..	95,337	10,666,080	102	The Deccan.
Cuttack Mahals, &c. ..	40,054	1,913,884	47	Orissa.
Total	570,103	36,802,204	62	

Foreign Territories.

The Foreign European States on the Indian Continent are:

Name.	Locality.	Area in Square Miles.	Population.
French—			
Chandernagore ..	On the Hooghly River ..	Not known.	32,670
Karical	Coromandel Coast	Not known.	
Pondicherry ..	Coromandel Coast	188	171,217
Yanon	Orissa Coast	Unknown.	
Mahé	Malabar Coast	Unknown.	
Portuguese—			
Goa	Western Coast	1,066	313,262
Damaun	Concan Coast	Not known.	
Diu	South Coast of Kattywar		

* It is possible that some of these States have been included in the returns of British territories, and that others which ought to be named here are omitted.

The area and population of the foreign settlements or rather factories, marked as "not known," are very small.

The French territories, like the colonies of France generally, are as far as possible miniatures of Paris. Sir Charles Trevelyan says, "Pondicherry is more European than any Anglo-Indian place; it is like a small Continental town transported to the shores of the Indian Ocean; it is teeming with intelligence and enterprise." *

Little can be said in favour of the Portuguese settlements; they exhibit in India, as on the African coast, the filth, sloth, corruption, sensuality, and priest-ridden weakness which have become the characteristics of a once great and enterprizing nation.

Efforts have been recently made by Government to ascertain the number of Europeans in India not in the service of the Crown, but the returns are imperfect, and have not yet been arranged by the Registrar-General.

The Commissioned Officers in 1859 in the Anglo-Indian army consisted of—in the Royal troops, four thousand and thirty; Indian troops, four thousand five hundred and sixty-three—total, eight thousand five hundred and ninety-three.

It remains to be said that the Government is as imperfectly acquainted with the relative proportion of the various classes of the people as with their aggregate number; the time, perhaps, has not yet arrived when a census could be attempted; it may, however, be gradually accomplished district by district, when an efficient Native constabulary shall have been organized in every province. It may be assumed that out of the alleged two hundred million, twenty million are of the aboriginal class, slaves, pariahs, or devoid of caste; the Mohammedans may number from twelve to fifteen million; the Seiks (on or near the Sutlej) about two million; the Boodhists and Jains, about five million; sundry others, Hill tribes, &c., perhaps eight million; and the remaining one

* 'Minute of Tour' in January and March, 1860.

hundred and fifty million, Hindoos of the Brahminical creed. An important fact is shown in the preceding pages. So far as there are statistics giving a return of males distinct from females, among the Native population, it appears that there is in every district a preponderance of males, and in some places to a large degree. There is unfortunately no census of Bengal, but in other presidencies or provinces, the sexes, according to the returns of 1857, are:

	Males.	Females.
Madras	11,047,139	10,534,558
Bombay	4,787,325	4,228,209
North West Provinces ..	16,495,651	14,382,144
Punjab	7,029,912	5,687,909
Total	39,360,027	34,832,810

This shows an excess of four million and a half of males, in a population of seventy-four million. It may to some extent be exaggerated in consequence of the seclusion of women, and the difficulty of ascertaining their number in a household, owing to the jealousy of their husbands, whether Hindoos or Mohammedans. It is to be feared also that female infanticide still prevails in certain parts of the country, to a greater extent than is known to Europeans. But neither of these surmises fully accounts for the disparity. The mysterious law which governs the increase or diminution of population by causing a preponderance of male or female births, can be traced only in its operation. The disproportion in India must indicate either an excess of people in relation to the area of land available for their subsistence, or an enfeebled state of life owing to general and long-continued impoverishment. In a new country, with a fertile soil, abundance of food, and no severe toil for women, there appears to be an effort of Nature to increase and multiply the human race, to replenish the earth and subdue it. For the accomplishment of this great end, the number of female preponderates over that of male births; the law, so far as I could trace its results in Australia, in North America, in South Africa and elsewhere, holds good in relation to domesticated animals as well as to man; every colonist or stock-farmer may observe its operation in the rapid increase of his horses, cattle, sheep, and swine; and an examination of baptismal registers in Australia, New Zealand, Canada, and other sparsely-peopled but healthy regions shows that Europeans multiply in the proportion of girls to boys almost at the rate of two to one. When the cause for this preponderance no longer exists, as the country becomes more densely inhabited, the inequality of births gradually ceases, and the relative proportions become more equal. If, however, there be a high state of social prosperity, plenty of food, activity of life devoid of injurious labour, abstinence from pernicious practices, and political liberty, the population will continue to augment by the preponderance of female births; and relief from overcrowding will be obtained by the natural remedy of emigration.

But if the number of mouths to each square mile of area be large in proportion to the food raised, and to the means of procuring the other essentials requisite for a comfortable existence; and if unceasing toil be enforced on both sexes, whether as bondfolk by the whip of the overseer, or under free institutions by the necessity of earning the pittance required to maintain life from day to day; then, by some law of which we are at present ignorant, the male exceed the female births, the population becomes enfeebled and diminishes in number. With the effect, the cause of the evil increases in an accelerated ratio; until finally, regions which at one period were well cultivated and tenanted by a large industrial population, become waste, overgrown with jungle, unhealthy, and at length almost deserted, or scantily peopled by a spiritless, sickly and degenerate race. Under this deteriorating process we can understand why empires decline and fall; why countries once swarming with millions of prosperous inhabitants now sustain with difficulty a few thousand wretched beings who struggle with wild beasts and noxious creatures for possession of the pestilential climate and the marshy, or it may be, arid soil in which they vegetate. This apparent exhaustion but real perversion of the "powers of Nature," as men term the laws of Omnipotence, usually originates in some form of misgovernment; in desolating wars (such as Napoleon I. carried on when he drained France for a decade of its virility) *; in the rapacity which sweeps away wealth, and gives no stimulus to skill and labour for its reproduction; in the tyranny which attempts to crush an entire nation to a dead level of apathetic poverty, affords no sphere for public spirit, no stimulus to exertion or mental ambition, and makes the desire for personal distinction almost necessarily a crime against the ruling power.

Such has been the state of the people of India for a long period. During the Mogul sway the brave and intelligent Hindoo aristocracy found honourable and lucrative employment in the administration of civil affairs, and in the armies of the Delhi Emperors; but when province after province fell under the absolute control of a mercantile corporation wielding a sharp sword, Hindoos and Mohammedans found themselves alike trodden under foot by their new masters, who, guided chiefly by the instinct of self-preservation and the desire to maintain or increase the annual dividends on their capital stock, had little time or thought to spare for the initiation of just principles of government, and contented themselves with enunciating high sounding sentiments which read well on paper, but were never carried into practice. For nearly a century a large part of India has been subjected to a

* The population of France was enfeebled by the wars at the end of the last and the beginning of the present century, and the number of males exceeded that of the female births. A turning point has now been reached; the census in 1861 shows:—males, 18,642,604; females, 18,739,721: total, 37,382,325.

"paternal government," administered by inexperienced youths, sent from England to make their fortunes, under the superintendence of their relations sitting at a Board of Direction in London: hence an irresponsible despotism, enforced by an enormous standing army, obliterated every distinctive feature of society, while the extortionate system of annual land taxation ground the whole class of cultivators into an uniform mass of struggling poverty, and kept them in a state of continued deterioration. The noblest families in the land, with ancestral honours traceable for centuries, and with hereditary associations venerated by the people, became the victims of territorial spoliation and of personal humiliation. At first indeed, while few and yet strangers in the land, the servants of the Merchant-Adventurers spoke of themselves and their employers as plain traders desiring only to exchange merchandize with the people of India. Even English readers who know something of the decline of the Mogul Empire, and the manner in which the trading Company turned their measuring wand into an iron sceptre, see much to be deprecated and even sharply censured in the process, but to Indian eyes it must appear in a far stronger light. They can only look at their Anglo-Indian rulers as servants who by force and wiles sought favour and pension from their "Honorable masters" in England by the annexation of Indian kingdoms and the dethronement of monarchs,—who were left to linger out a brief and calamitous existence as prisoners, or as pensioners on the bounty of those who professedly came to the country as friends and traders, and were changed by the love of power and lucre into the most deadly enemies. It would be useless to revert to the past, but for the hope that the British people may be induced to understand the atonement which is due to India. Should this be done, should the representatives of the nation appreciate the extent of their obligations as the Christian rulers of one hundred and fifty million Indian subjects, acknowledge the responsibility thus voluntarily assumed, and perceive that the rule of these intelligent and industrious myriads must be either a fearful curse or a national blessing; then will arise cheering hopes for Hindoostan, and instead of the heathen darkness of the past, the internecine wars, awful famines, and various phases of suffering and degradation which history in successive ages records,—there will spring up light and plenty and peace. A new and glorious epoch of political freedom will commence for Hindoo, Seik, Boodhist, Moslem, Parsee, and Pariah, when admitted to share, as they have a right to do, in the best privileges of the English-born subjects of the British Crown; but, incomparably greater will be their gain and ours should they be influenced from on High to receive the truths of the Gospel, and, abandoning their jarring creeds, polygamy, idolatry, and caste, become one with us in the grand Unity of the Christian Faith.

CHAPTER IV.

GOVERNMENT, CIVIL AND MILITARY.

THE general administration for India is vested in a Secretary of State, and a Council composed of fifteen members, who are nominated by the Crown, and hold office during the pleasure of the Sovereign. The Secretary of State is empowered to act independently of the Council. He is assisted by an Under-Secretary, who is required to be a member of either the House of Lords or the House of Commons. Both these secretaries lose office with the Cabinet to which the Secretary of State belongs, but the Indian Council does not change with the ministry; neither does the Under-Secretary of State for India, who superintends a large and permanent establishment arranged under various departments.*

The local administration is regulated by the "Indian Councils" Act of Parliament of 1861, by which the provisions of former acts respecting the local government of India are consolidated and amended. The council of the Governor-General is composed of five ordinary members, three of whom are appointed by the Secretary of State in Council (with the concurrence of a majority of members present at a meeting

* The salary of the Secretary of State is 5000*l.*; of the Parliamentary Under-Secretary, 2000*l.*; the permanent Under-Secretary, and Assistant ditto, 1500*l.*; the Members of the India Council, 1200*l.* each; heads of departments, 1200*l.* to 1000*l.* each; and the subordinates, from 800*l.* to 500*l.* per annum. The annual expenditure of the establishment is about 150,000*l.* A new India Office is to be constructed in Westminster, the cost of which is estimated at 215,000*l.*

Every item of charge connected with the Indian administration in England is defrayed from the revenues of India; not a shilling expended on any account at home or abroad is charged on the British Exchequer.

of the Council) from among persons who have been, at the time of appointment, servants of the Crown, or of the Company and the Crown, for at least ten years; but no military man can hold command while acting as a member of the Council: the remaining two ordinary members are appointed by Her Majesty's warrant, and one of them must be a barrister, or a member of the Faculty of Advocates, of not less than five years' standing. The Secretary of State may appoint the Commander-in-Chief of Her Majesty's forces in India an extraordinary member of Council, and while so serving he takes rank and precedence after the Governor-General at the Council-board. There is a financial member of the Supreme Government, who may be termed the Chancellor of the Indian Exchequer; he need not be a civil or a military servant, but may be sent direct from England—as was the case with the late Mr. Wilson and his successor, Mr. Laing; both of whom were members of the British Legislature, and high in office in England. The Council thus formed discusses with the Governor-General all matters of administration; but the Viceroy may act independently, even in questions of war or peace, after placing his reasons on record. The Executive Council is formed into a Legislative Council for the enactment of laws and regulations, by the Governor-General's nomination of not less than six or more than twelve members; one half of whom must be non-official, that is to say, must not hold any civil or military appointment under the Crown in India; and the seat in council of any non-official member becomes vacant, on his acceptance of office. The members of the Legislative Council are nominated for two years. The Governor-General, if absent from the seat of government, may appoint any member of the Council to preside during his absence; he is likewise empowered to assemble the Council anywhere in British India. If this be done at Madras or Bombay, the Governor of the Presidency is authorised to act as an extraordinary member of Council; in a province, where there is a Lieutenant-Governor, the latter sits as an additional councillor at meetings held for the purpose of making laws only. The power of the Council is very limited. No member is permitted to introduce any motion affecting the public debt or revenues; the religion, or religious rites or usages of any class of Her Majesty's subjects in India; the discipline or maintenance of Her Majesty's military or naval forces in India; or the relations of the Government with foreign Princes or States—without the previous sanction of the Governor-General. On other subjects, the ordinary motion for leave to introduce a measure is submitted to the Council. Laws for the regulation of the Council require the assent of the Governor-General, and are subject to disallowance by the Crown. The Governor-General, in cases of emergency, may make and promulgate from time to time ordinances for the peace and good government of British India, or any part thereof; such ordinances to be valid for a period of not more than six months, unless disallowed by the Crown in the meanwhile, or superseded by an act of the Governor-General in Council.

The Governors of Madras and Bombay are empowered to appoint each a Legislative Council consisting of not less than four or more than eight members, and to add thereto the Advocate-General of the Presidency. Such assemblies are under regulations similar to that of the Supreme Council. The measures passed by the respective Governors in Council at Madras and Bombay require the assent of the Governor-General to become valid, and are subject to disallowance by the Crown. In addition to the restrictions imposed on the Legislative Council of the Governor-General, as before stated, the Legislative Councils at Madras and Bombay cannot, without the consent of the Governor-General, take into consideration any proposition affecting custom duties, currency (coin or bank notes), post office, telegraph, penal code, patents, or copyright. The Governor-General may extend the provisions of the "India Councils Act" to the North-West Provinces and the Punjab, or may constitute new Provinces, and apply the provisions of the "aforesaid Act" thereto, subject to the previous assent of the Crown. If a vacancy happen in the office of Governor-General, and no provisional successor be in India to supply such vacancy, the Governor of Madras or of Bombay, according to seniority of appointment, is to act until the arrival of a successor.*

The Governor-General, or as he is now generally styled, the Viceroy of India, is appointed by the Crown; the term of office is about six years, and the salary twenty-five thousand pounds per annum, with a palace and establishment at Calcutta, and a charming country residence with a spacious park and gardens, at Barrackpoor, fifteen miles from the capital.

The new Legislative Council was brought into operation in January, 1862, by Lord Canning; it comprised among its members five European gentlemen, of the class formerly termed "Interlopers"—*i. e.*, not belonging to the Indian civil or military services; and three natives of India:—first, the Rajah of Puttiala, who stood zealously and usefully by the British Government in the North-West provinces during the crisis of 1857-8; second, the able Brahmin, Dinkur Rao, the prime minister of Sindia at Gwalior, whose loyal attachment was of the highest importance in Central India, during the mutiny; and a petty Rajah, Deo Narrain Sing, who rendered signal service at Benares, at the period of the levy of the Income-tax. By the appointment of un-official European and Native gentlemen to assist in enacting laws for India,

* The salary of each member of the Legislative Council of India, is 5000*l.* a year; the Clerk of the Council, 3000*l.*; Assistant Clerk of the Council, 1500*l.*; the Registrar and Official Reporter, 360*l.* a year. The total cost, independent of the salaries of members of the Council, is 10,000*l.* a year.

the barriers of caste as regards station and colour, which have so long and so banefully existed, have at length been partially broken down; and a step has been taken which has facilitated sound legislation for the time, and may prepare the way for the extension of constitutional freedom to all classes of Her Majesty's Indian subjects.

The Presidencies of Bombay and Madras had become cyphers in the government of India, their most trifling acts had fallen under the control of the supreme authority at Calcutta; but in January, 1862, Legislative Councils were assembled at these Presidencies, un-official English and Native members being nominated as at Calcutta, among the newly constituted functionaries.

The Province of Bengal, with its forty million people, and immense area, is ruled by a Lieutenant-Governor, who since January, 1862, is also aided by a Legislative Council composed of four official and four non-official Europeans, with three Native gentlemen: the Europeans comprising two merchants, a lawyer, and an indigo planter; the Natives—a Zemindar (landlord), a Hindoo (Prussunu Comar Tagore) who was formerly assistant clerk in the Supreme Legislative Council, and a Mohammedan deputy magistrate. Similar Councils are to be appointed for the North-West Provinces and the Punjab.

The duties of a Governor or a Lieutenant-Governor include the making from time to time official tours through the large provinces under his rule. He holds Durbars, or ceremonial courts, for the presentation of the Chiefs and Native gentry in their several districts; confers *khelauts* (dresses of distinction) and presents on meritorious individuals; hears complaints, redresses grievances, sanctions and inspects public works; reviews the various police battalions and stations; visits schools, gaols, lunatic asylums, dispensaries, offices, and other Governmental institutions; inquires into frontier disputes, and the condition of the wild hill tribes; and is expected to exercise a rigid supervision over all the Government functionaries.

The affairs of Oude are administered by a Lieutenant-Governor, who will probably be eventually assisted by a Legislative Council.

The British Government assumed the administration of this Province early in 1856; during the ensuing year, the officials were occupied in making summary settlements of the land revenue, and organizing various courts of judicature; the mutiny of the Native troops broke out in June, 1857; the country was not re-subjected to British rule until 1858-59; and the year 1859-60, when tranquillity was restored, is the first period for which returns have been furnished by different departments, working under a regular system in the transaction of public business.

An uneasy and alarming state of feeling prevailed throughout Oude in 1859-60, in consequence of the proprietors of land doubting the permanence of the arrangement promised by Government. The Governor-General visited Lucknow; held a Durbar, which was attended by one hundred and fifty of the chief talookdars, who were assured by His Lordship that the ancient talookdaree system of Oude had been revived and perpetuated; in confirmation of which *sunnuds*, or title-deeds, were given for their estates to every landholder present. "It is impossible," says the Commissioner, "to overrate the beneficial results of the assurance thus given by His Excellency in person."

By investing the leading talookdars with magisterial functions among the people on their respective estates, the interests of the landlords have become identified with the British Government, and they now heartily co-operate with European functionaries in promoting social improvement.

The present mode of conducting affairs works well, for obvious reasons. In Oude, for the first time in Anglo-Indian history, "the administration is conducted on the great principle of recognizing a powerful landed aristocracy as an important element of national prosperity." The conduct of the new magistrates "has been almost without exception exemplary, and this is no doubt attributable, in a great degree, to their having been treated with friendliness and confidence, instead of with jealousy and distrust. . . . . The relations between the Native aristocracy and the servants of Government are on a freer and kindlier footing than in most parts of India."*

It will be well if the system which has proved so useful in Oude be generally adopted. In the Punjab a number of chiefs (about thirty) have been invested by the Governor-General with a limited jurisdiction in Magisterial and Revenue departments, subject to an appeal to the district European officers. "This measure has given great satisfaction to the higher classes."†

These proceedings have influenced the authorities, who preside over the thirty-two million inhabitants of the North-West Provinces. The Lieutenant-Governor in his report for 1860-61, says, "During the period which has passed [more than half-a-century] since the 'Ceded and Conquered Provinces' came into our possession, no power has been conceded to the Native aristocracy, or, in other words, to the chiefs and representatives of the people. The tendency of our institutions and our systems, it can hardly be denied, has been to obliterate all distinctions, and to reduce all to one common level. The time has now come when, following the guidance of Her Majesty's representative in this country, and the example of younger administrations, this Government might initiate a more generous policy, and give an opening to the heads of Native society for the useful occupation of their intellectual

* 'Report of Oude Commissioner, 1859-60.'

† 'Punjab Report, 1859-60,' p. 39. Printed at Calcutta, 1861.

energies, and for the beneficial exercise of the large influence, both local and personal, which they possess, in the service of the State."

This policy, the Lieutenant-Governor remarks, has been "attended with marked success" in Oude and in the Punjab, where the chiefs "have discharged the new functions justly, diligently, and intelligently, with no arrogation or abuse of authority; and with a high appreciation of the honour of being associated with the European officers of the Government, even though in a very limited degree, in the administration of criminal justice, and in the disposal of revenue business." Had this justly praised system been tried in the North-West Provinces, it might have averted the disastrous rebellion and famine by which they have recently been desolated. The more generous course of action adopted in Oude is still only advocated as fit for the North-West Provinces, and not proposed for other parts of India. It is to be hoped that the Home Government will enforce the extension of a beneficent policy calculated to call forth the intellect, energy, and affections of millions of men in India, and thus secure their fidelity to the Crown and the increasing prosperity of the vast region which is now an integral part of the British Empire.

Pegu, Arracan, Tenasserim, and Martaban are being united in one province, called British Burmah. There are now, therefore, three Presidencies—Bengal, Madras, and Bombay; and four Lieutenant-Governorships, viz.—the North-West Provinces (which require some more accurate designation), the Punjab, Oude, and British Burmah; and a Central Province, composed of Berar and the Saugor and Nerbudda territories, under a Commissioner.

A municipal spirit is being encouraged in different parts of India; its operation is familiar to the Hindoos, who are accustomed to local government and organized action.

Money is being raised in various towns for sanitary purposes, schools, and hospitals; and it would seem advisable to encourage the movement by a general Municipal Act of the Supreme Legislature authorising the establishment of elective corporations in every large city in India.

Calcutta has a Municipality composed of Commissioners who levy rates for the cleansing, lighting, road-making, and improvement of the city. A house-tax yields about fifty-three thousand pounds per annum; a lighting rate, thirteen thousand pounds; and a carriage and horse tax about nine thousand pounds. The city is lit by six hundred gas-lights. There is no efficient water supply to habitations; and the sanitary regulations are defective.

There is a Municipality at Madras, with an income of forty-five thousand a-year, employed in making and repairing roads, lighting, scavengering, watering, and other purposes.

Similar associations have been voluntarily established at Bombay, Kurrachee, Salem, and Vizagapatam; and have effected considerable sanitary improvements.

The forms of administration vary among the Native States; in general there is an hereditary prince invested with despotic power exercised under the eye of a British resident; in some places the rajah or chief is aided by a Council of nobles: in Bhootan, the country is administered by two rulers (the *Deb* and the *Dhurm* Rajahs), who exercise respectively supreme jurisdiction in temporal and spiritual affairs. These offices are not hereditary: the *Deb* Rajah is chosen by election from time to time from among the great officers of state; the *Dhurm* Rajah holds his office for life, is regarded as an incarnation of the Deity, and is supposed to be miraculously invested in infancy with spiritual authority. Sometimes the action of government is paralysed by disputes between the temporal and spiritual rulers.*

The constitution of the Cossyas in the Jynteea Hills is democratic: the Doloies or chiefs are elective and removable

* 'Moral and Material Progress of India, 1859-60,' part ii. p. 64. Parl. Papers. Commons.

by the people. The turmoil occasioned by the absence of any fixed duration of office induced our Government to cause the Doloies to be appointed for three years certain; these functionaries adjudicate civil suits to the value of fifty rupees, try in open Durbar all criminal cases which are not of an heinous nature, and conduct the public business of their respective districts. Some villages are under the charge of head men or chiefs called Sirdars.

The general administration of British India is conducted in its higher departments by Europeans, who form what is designated the Covenanted Civil Service. Appointments therein may now be contended for by all natural-born subjects of Her Majesty, above eighteen and under twenty-three years of age, of sound health and good moral character. The elections are decided by the result of public examinations, the first of which is in English composition, the literature (including the laws and constitution of Britain) and history of England, Greece, Rome, France, Germany, and Italy; in mathematics, pure and mixed; in natural science (chemistry, electricity, magnetism, natural history, geology, and mineralogy); in moral science (logic, and mental, moral, and political philosophy); and in the Sanscrit and Arabic languages and literature. Six months afterwards the candidates are subjected to a further examination in English composition, in the history and geography of India, and in the elements of the Bengalee or of the Hindoostani languages.

The "Covenanted" Civil Service comprises nearly eight hundred members. Their salaries range from three hundred to eight thousand pounds per annum, and they subscribe to a fund, which after twenty-five years' service or twenty-two years' residence, yields under certain conditions a pension of one thousand pounds per annum.

There is also an Uncovenanted Civil Service, the members of which are not subjected to the training above described. Their number and salaries are shown in the following table:—

UNCOVENANTED CIVIL SERVICE in India, 1861.

Locality.	Classes.	Number.	Salaries per Annum.
			£. £.
Bengal	Europeans and Eurasians	1305	12 to 2400
	Natives	418	72 ,, 1200
North-West Provinces	Europeans	219	36 ,, 1500
	Eurasians	293	21 ,, 720
	Natives	643	36 ,, 840
Punjab	Europeans	179	36 ,, 1800
	Eurasians	107	36 ,, 720
	No Natives apparently.		
Madras	Europeans	309	12 ,, 1800
	Eurasians	236	16 ,, 1200
	Natives	557	120 ,, 960
Bombay	Europeans and Eurasians	329	24 ,, 3000
	Natives	556	18 ,, 900
Other parts of India	Europeans and Eurasians	1007	12 ,, 1800
	Natives	54	90 ,, 1500
In all India	Europeans and Eurasians	3984	12 ,, 3000
	Natives	2228	18 ,, 1500

Formerly the patronage of the Covenanted Civil and Military Services was monopolised by a few families connected with the East India Company. Considering that the members sprang from the middle and higher classes, and that ample emoluments, high prizes, and an immense field for the development of talent was afforded them, it is remarkable how few rose above mediocrity. The "Civil Service," partly from paucity of numbers and mistaken notions of economy, but also from the absence of efficient men, was constantly strengthened by officers who were drafted from their regiments for the fulfilment of civil duties. The readers of Anglo-Indian history will find that the names of Governor Child, Streynsham Masters of Madras, and honest Job Charnock; of Warren Hastings, with Wilkins, Colebrooke, Wilford, and a few scholars of that day; of the men of the Wellesley school, Metcalfe, Edmonstone, Webbe, Elphinstone, Jonathan Duncan, Barlow, Adam, Bayley and St. George Tucker; of Teignmouth, Frederick Shore, Cleveland, Orme, Stuart, Law,

Walter Hamilton, Wilson; and in the present epoch, of John Lawrence, Montgomery, Halliday, Hamilton, Frere, and Grant, almost exhaust the roll of able civilians; while Clive, Barry Close, Malcolm, Munro, Gillespie, Ochterlony, Todd, Wilks, Grant Duff, Briggs, the lamented Henry Lawrence, Outram, Nicholson, Baird Smith, Cotton, Abbot, Edwardes, Kay, Balfour, and some others constitute the leading celebrities of the Indian army for a century.

The abolition of monopoly, the open area for election, and the healthy principle of emulation, are believed to have infused new and vigorous blood into an effete system. In 1859-60, one hundred and twenty candidates were elected after severe competitive examinations for the Indian Civil Service; they have sprung from every class of English society: sons of druggists, ironmongers, tailors, upholsterers, drapers, undertakers, farmers, stewards, millers, butchers, printers, have obtained appointments by the exercise of talents which they would not formerly have been permitted to bring inside the walls of Haileybury. And now, says the 'Friend of India,' "there is no official from the Governor-General down to the district officer, who has not expressed his satisfaction with his competitive subordinates, with only a few exceptions. The superiority of the new men as industrious, conscientious, and able officers is as undoubted, as the fear that they would prove mere bookworms has proved unfounded."

The Indian Military Service is undergoing a change similar to that effected in the Civil Departments: an entirely new class of officers is being introduced with every prospect of satisfactory results.

Individual character has a powerful influence in India for good or for evil; since the ordinary class of Natives naturally judge the British Government by the conduct of the Englishman who is their immediate ruler. If he be a man of sound judgment, just yet merciful, consistent in his actions, making allowance for the ignorance, the cunning, the prejudices, and the superstitions fostered by long years of oppression; not grasping at a momentary increase of revenue, but allowing the honey to be accumulated in the hive for seasons of famine or pressure; and enlightening, encouraging, and guiding the people and their chiefs in promoting useful works, his administration becomes a benefit to those intrusted to his care, the extent of which may be conjectured by considering not only the good obtained, but also the misery averted from a helpless and much-oppressed peasantry. Englishmen who have thus ruled provinces and districts, equal in size to small European kingdoms, have been venerated by the Natives almost as deities in the shape of men. Long after they have quitted India, their names and deeds are held in remembrance by the affectionate Hindoos; and such functionaries deserve equal gratitude from the Government, to which they are indeed "towers of strength," more valuable than legions of armed men in maintaining the stability of British dominion in the East.

Henry Lawrence is the recognised exemplar of the rare class of self-sacrificing rulers, who in the dark era which we have now happily passed, realised the idea of a "Paternal Government;" and his bright example will, it is to be hoped, be extensively followed by the new race of officials which competition has provided for the public service. To obtain the grateful homage of millions for exercising a humane sway over them is a reward far greater than Parliament and the Crown can bestow, but there is reason to believe that rank and honours will be freely granted to those who fulfil the high expectations formed of them by their country.

The official reports, now annually laid before Parliament, on the moral progress, social condition, and government of every section of the Anglo-Indian empire, will place on record the names of those intrusted with various degrees of power, and they will be treated according to their deserts.

Military Force.

This is an important branch of the Indian administration. The number of armed men maintained has increased with the accession of territory to be protected. The troops forming the Indian army have been composed—1st, of regiments of the line and cavalry, belonging to the Crown, serving for a limited period in India, and paid for from the revenues of that country; 2nd, of European corps of artillery, infantry, and cavalry, enlisted in Britain by the East India Company for exclusive service in India; 3rd, of Native artillery, cavalry, and infantry, composed of Hindoos, Mohammedans, and other Indians, officered by Europeans. At the commencement of the present century the Indian army contained about one hundred and fifty-five thousand men, of whom twenty-three thousand were Europeans (in the proportion of about one European to seven Natives); in 1810, two hundred thousand (one European to six Natives); in 1820, two hundred and fifty-six thousand (one European to nine Natives); in 1830, about two hundred thousand (one European to six Natives); in 1840, two hundred and fifty thousand (nearly one European to seven Natives); and in 1850, two hundred and seventy-seven thousand, viz., Europeans forty-nine thousand, Natives two hundred and twenty-eight thousand: proportion, less than one to six. In 1857, when the mutiny commenced, the Indian army consisted of above forty-five thousand Europeans, and two hundred and thirty-two thousand Natives; in all exceeding two hundred and seventy-seven thousand men, exclusive of the contingents of protected states.

The Native army of Bengal was almost entirely extinguished during the mutiny of 1857-58, and levies were hastily raised in various districts to supply the immediate necessity. When the mutiny and rebellion was finally suppressed the whole military force was reorganised, the irregular levies, the regular Native cavalry, and the Native artillery were disbanded; troops and companies that had remained faithful were broken up, the men were discharged with gratuities, pensions or land; or transferred at their own request to other corps of cavalry or infantry, or to the police. The only troops of the former Native artillery remaining in Bengal are the Punjab batteries and mountain-trains, and a local company in Assam. Of the Bengal regular Native infantry sixty-one regiments were disbanded or destroyed, as were also ten regiments of irregular infantry, ten regiments of regular light cavalry, nine of irregular cavalry, three battalions of foot and seven troops of horse artillery. At the end of 1860 there remained of the old Native army of Bengal only fifteen regiments of regular Native infantry, six of which were never disarmed; the local infantry—the majority of which had proved faithful; the Ghoorka and irregular line regiments; eight regiments of irregular cavalry, which had retained their arms; and the sappers and miners. The remnants of the partially mutinous irregular cavalry were reorganised.

On the transfer of the government of India from the East India Company to the Crown no reference was made to the Anglo-Indian army, which had been raised in the name and for the service of the East India Company. The local European corps in 1858 began to manifest uneasiness on the subject; the men considered that they had a right to their discharge, and to be enlisted anew. The agitation ceased on an explanation from the Commander-in-Chief, and an intimation that the question would be referred for the consideration of her Majesty's Government in England. In April, 1859, the men were informed that the law officers of the Crown in England had decided that their claim was inadmissible, and in the following month the Bengal Artillery and the 3rd European Light Cavalry at Meerut renewed, in a threatening manner, their claim to be discharged. The discontent became so strong throughout the European local army that Government deemed it prudent to yield, and allow every man who desired his discharge to receive it and have a free passage to England. This privilege was accepted by six thousand two hundred men of the Indian army, who were immediately embarked for England: about three thousand seven hundred men preferred continuing in the service.

Thus both the Native and European armies of Bengal were broken up in the three years 1857, 1858, 1859.

In 1860 the Commander-in-Chief of the Indian army drew up a statement detailing the amount and nature of the troops required for India. It enumerated—*Europeans*, forty troops or batteries of artillery, seventeen reserve companies of artillery, ten regiments of cavalry, and forty-three of infantry; *Natives*, two regiments of sappers, twenty-nine regiments of irregular cavalry, and sixty regiments of regular and irregular infantry. The civil corps and contingents under the control of the Government of India; the Punjab irregular force and the military police are not included in this estimate. The irregular cavalry and infantry regiments have each six officers; the police are officered by one hundred and twenty-four Europeans. The total number of effective Europeans, including officers and staff, in November 1861, in India, was seventy thousand five hundred. The remainder of the British army at home and in the colonies at same date was one hundred and forty-eight thousand six hundred.

The number of European officers attached to the army in India is upwards of three thousand. In 1860 there were three thousand and sixty-three, of whom only about one thousand seven hundred and fifty-four served with their regiments. Of the remainder, two hundred and ten held staff appointments, and seventeen civil employ; seventy-one were colonels of regiments, three hundred and twenty-nine in depôts at home, one hundred and forty-four absent on medical certificate, two hundred and twelve on their private affairs, two hundred and thirteen "absentees from other causes," and eight in transit of exchanges to England.* Madras and Bombay have still distinct armies, but their Commanders-in-Chief are subject to the General commanding the Bengal force. The staff is very large, and there is a well-organised staff-depôt. There are eight hundred highly educated commissioned medical officers.

STRENGTH AND COST OF EUROPEAN TROOPS IN INDIA FOR 1862.

	Strength.	Cost.
Bengal	44,916	£4,940,760
Madras	15,161	1,667,710
Bombay	13,509	1,485,000
Total	73,586	£8,093,470 †

The regular troops of the Native army may be stated at one hundred and twenty thousand men. The report of the military department for 1861 shows a reduction in the Native army of more than sixty-four thousand men, and a saving of one million sterling. The Native commissioned and non-commissioned officers discharged receive grants of land in their respective villages. Further reductions, especially in the Native cavalry, are contemplated; and by diminishing the Native troops, fewer Europeans will be required in proportion. Necessarily our chief garrisons are on the North-Western frontier. In the Punjab, the European soldiers at different stations number about twenty thousand, of whom fifteen thousand consist of infantry; of the remainder, more than one-half are cavalry and the rest artillery. The Native troops at the different stations and out-stations on the 1st of

* 'Parliamentary Paper,' Commons, 159, April 12th, 1861.

† The standing armies of Europe are as follows:—France has six hundred and twenty-six thousand men; Russia, eight hundred and fifty thousand; Prussia, seven hundred and twenty thousand; Austria, seven hundred and thirty-eight thousand; Italy, two hundred thousand; Spain, Portugal, Sweden, Denmark, Greece, the smaller German States, and European Turkey, probably not less than two hundred thousand men. Total three million three hundred thousand. The estimated cost is about £50 per head—or £165,000,000 sterling.

May, 1859, consisted of two thousand five hundred cavalry and nearly thirteen thousand infantry. There is also a frontier irregular force, which protects the line of trans-Indus country from Kohat to the boundary of Sinde, about five hundred miles long; has a detachment in Peshawur, and holds Eusofzi and Huzara. This force consisted in May, 1861, of about six hundred artillery, three thousand cavalry and nine thousand infantry; with an addition of two thousand two hundred mounted and foot levies.

Excellent barracks for European troops have been erected at Delhi, Ferozepoor, Mooltan, Rawul Pindee, Mean Meer, Subathoo, Murree, and other places; and five permanent rest-houses have been formed for the convenience of the European troops when marching between Umballa and Delhi.

Most of the treasuries and police-stations are now fortified.

There are churches for the soldiery at Peshawur, Umballa, Sealkote, and other places where European garrisons are stationed.

Oude was the chief locality where the old Bengal army was recruited, and became the scene of the severest struggle of the mutiny and insurrection of 1857-58. The military garrison in 1860 consisted of four battalions of Royal Artillery, 713; one troop of Horse Artillery, 100; two companies of Foot Artillery, 174 = 906; one regiment of European Cavalry, 693; five regiments of Irregular cavalry, 2582 = 3275; six regiments of European Infantry, 4969; four regiments Native Infantry, 3039 = 8008; total, 12,279 men. It is expected that this force will be diminished, as Oude is now considered to be one of the most contented provinces of the empire.

The Madras army is being largely reduced, and the military expenditure curtailed, owing in great measure to the exertions of Colonel Balfour, who has laboured zealously during several years for the re-organization of the Anglo-Indian Army.

The military strength of the Bombay Presidency is reduced

to one troop of Horse Artillery, four batteries of Foot Artillery, five regiments of cavalry, and nine of infantry; all Europeans. The Native Artillery has been abolished; each Native regiment has been reduced to seven hundred rank and file; various local corps have been disbanded; many small military posts abandoned; several brigade and station commands and staff offices diminished; and the number of horses in cavalry corps lessened by ten per cent. below the number of troopers. The whole of the Native regular cavalry is to be disbanded, the barrack-department re-organized, and the commissariat establishments much curtailed.

The annual cost of an European regiment of the line of one thousand strong serving in India is eighty-five thousand pounds; and of a regiment of Her Majesty's cavalry of one thousand men (comprising fifty-eight officers) one hundred and two thousand four hundred pounds. The casualties in regiments serving in India are about ten per cent. per annum.

The value of an European soldier when landed in India is estimated at one hundred pounds; his annual cost is one hundred and ten pounds; that of a sepoy about ten pounds. The number of Her Majesty's troops who died in India from 1825 to 1853 was above thirty-six thousand, and of the East India Company's European troops above sixteen thousand, together exceeding fifty-two thousand (exclusive of three years for which there are no returns), or an average for twenty-six years of two thousand per annum. This does not include invalids. The ratio of deaths in Her Majesty's troops for the same period in India was sixty-three per thousand. From these facts some estimate may be formed of the cost of the European army stationed in the East.

In various directions, on the slopes of the Himalaya, on the Neilgherries, at Mount Aboo, and on other elevations, military sanitaria have been formed; and at different cantonments plots of ground are laid out for the use of the soldiers, who are encouraged to grow vegetables, and to compete for prizes in fruits and flowers. Bowling-greens and, where practicable, bathing-houses are attached to the grounds, which are neatly laid out, with summer-houses, rustic seats and artificial water. The regimental bands play at intervals, and the gardens form an attractive recreation for the families of the soldiers. Permanent museums are being established at large stations, in the formation of which there is an inducement for the exercise of industry, skill and taste.

The chief sanitarium in Southern India, Wellington formerly Jackatalla, originated in 1847 with the Marquis of Tweeddale, when Governor of Madras. Fifty thousand pounds have been expended in the construction of excellent ranges of buildings for single and married men, with large verandahs, plunging-baths, shaded avenues, and every accessory which can conduce to the comfort and health of the troops.

Regimental savings' banks are inspected annually by two or more auditors appointed by Government.

Independently of the reading-rooms and libraries attached to most regiments, there are station and garrison libraries supplied with newspapers, periodicals, maps and standard works. Normal schools for the special education of masters and mistresses for army and regimental schools have been established in several places.

Non-commissioned officers who have served ten years in India, and whose health requires change of climate, if fit to do duty with invalids and discharged men, are allowed to visit England, their furlough to expire in England one year from the date of their quitting India. The period of absence does not reckon as service, and pay is issued during the time as for men of the same rank in the army serving in the United Kingdom.

Police.

In addition to the regular army, European and Native, there is a very large police force, civil and military. Before the mutiny of 1857 its civil strength was about seventy thousand men, maintained by an expenditure of half a million; its military strength was thirty-nine thousand, and cost nearly six hundred thousand sterling. During and subsequent to the Mutiny the number of the military police was raised to about seventy thousand. The system is undergoing revision, and the following arrangements are to some extent experimental, and may or may not be permanently adopted.

In the Bengal presidency the police consists of two distinct bodies: one entirely of a civil character, employed in the detection of crime, and the serving of criminal processes; the other used for the suppression of riots, and violent breaches of the peace. The military police comprise ten battalions of infantry, each seven hundred strong, three squadrons of cavalry, and some local levies, altogether about ten thousand men, with forty European officers. The men are of various races; some of them belong to the formerly despised aborigines: the wild but simple Coles furnish one regiment; the Sonthals, a supposed savage race, from the Rajmahal hills another; the people of the unfrequented Munnipoor hills a third; the "filthy Mughs" (of Burmese extraction) from Chittagong a fourth; Orissa supplies a fifth; the Seiks two regiments; and two more are chiefly composed of the hardy hill Ghoorkas. A single battalion of the old Behar station guards remain to represent the Hindoostani sepoys, who, before the Mutiny of 1857, formed almost the entire of the Bengal army, regular and irregular, and the police. Now, none of the Bengal police battalions have anything in common with each other except what they learn under discipline; they differ in language, appearance, customs and creed. Each battalion has a commandant and four lieutenants, Europeans, and the usual complement of Native officers. The whole body is directed by an Inspector-General. Its duties are to guard gaols and treasuries, escort treasure, and secure submission to the executive authority of Government; by this display of force the tendency to riot and disturbance is repressed, and life and property are rendered secure. On the frontiers, where wild tribes exist, the military police (who were themselves only yesterday deemed untameable savages) prevent incursions and maintain peace; so that there are but few troops of the regular army employed in Bengal. Thirty-seven large districts, with each a magistrate, are being subdivided, and are to be presided over by one hundred and seventy deputy-magistrates. Justice will be thus brought at least near to the poor man's door.*

There are no connected statements yet prepared which show the number and organization of the civil police under the sole control of Government. The village chokeydars, or rural police in the Bengal provinces in 1854, numbered one hundred and sixty-five thousand, and were spread over one hundred and sixty thousand villages; they were chiefly appointed by the zemindars or by the heads of villages, and were paid—partly in cash, partly in grain—to the value of about four to six shillings each, monthly; some rent-free land was generally allowed, and presents made them. Each chokeydar watched a given number of houses, ranging from twenty-four in Burdwan to eighty-six in Tipperah, or, on an average, forty dwellings to each watchman.†

An organized police, in Madras as in Bengal, is taking the place of the regular troops. An act constituting the new police was passed 6th September, 1859; and by the end of the official year, nine districts, with an area of fifty-five thousand square miles and a population of ten million five hundred thousand persons, had been more or less placed under the control of a civil and military police, whose numbers were fixed at ten thousand seven hundred men—in the proportion of about one policeman to every thousand of the inhabitants, at a total cost of one hundred and twenty

* 'Report on Bengal, 1859, 1860.'

† 'Police in Bengal Presidency,' Parl. Paper, p. 52, Aug. 14th, 1857.

thousand pounds, equal to twelve pounds per annum for each policeman.

The duties of guarding gaols and treasuries, and forming escorts, which heretofore devolved on the regular troops and veteran battalions, are now performed by the police. The system thus far works well and economically, and its advantages are appreciated by the people; violence is prevented, bad characters are hunted down, crime detected and diminished. The English county constabulary has been adopted as a model, with modifications adapted to the circumstances and wants of the country, and to the duties to be performed. The highways are patrolled daily by the general constabulary under the supervision of district inspectors. The petty officers are generally raised from the ranks; the inspectors are drawn from the superior classes of Native society, and they can appreciate the conduct and spirit of the ranks without being too intimately connected, either in interest or in sympathy, with the bulk of the force. Some of the inspectors are Europeans and Eurasians. The constabulary learn the use of firearms, and a few simple evolutions; but on ordinary occasions they only carry a truncheon —the badge of office. Corruption is unsparingly punished. A village police watches over circles of villages, conveniently clubbed together, under the superintendence of well-selected inspectors, who fulfil duties to some extent analogous to those which devolve on justices of the peace in England.

In Oude the police force consists of one mounted regiment numbering one thousand four hundred sabres, and thirteen regiments of six hundred men each, or nearly eight thousand foot police—the whole under European officers invested with the authority of assistant magistrates. The men are recruited from all castes and classes; the greater number are Seiks, Punjabees, Brahmins, Rajpoots, Jâts, and other races. Each district has one troop (one hundred sabres) and one regiment of foot police. Lucknow district has two troops and one regiment of foot, and there is in the city a force organized after the manner of the London police, with eight inspectors, fixed stations, subordinate beats, and two hundred and seventy constables on duty day and night. The city is divided into parishes or mohullahs, and each parish selects a representative who is the medium of communication with the police. The system works well, and is being extended to other Indian cities.

The rural police of Oude is of great antiquity, and identified with the Hindoo village system. Each village had its chokeydar or watchman. The office was hereditary, and much valued; the emoluments were derived from rent-free land, dues on each harvest, and several gratuities. The remuneration sufficed for the maintenance of a large family, the members of which assisted in the performance of the various duties attached to the office: thus, while one patrolled the village at night, another watched the outlying crops of the cultivators—a duty of much importance in an open, unenclosed country. When the British took possession of Oude this system was altered; the old chokeydar was replaced by a functionary appointed by Government, who received a good salary, and undertook the charge of several villages grouped together. The change caused general dissatisfaction; the landowners complained that they no longer had any control over the village police, and that it was unfair to make them responsible for functionaries over whom they had no authority.

It has been determined by Government to revert to the indigenous rural police, which is formed almost exclusively of Passees, a numerous and influential race in Oude, who are noted for fidelity when in service, and for thieving propensities when unemployed. The chief commissioner reports that in Native states where the people are left to manage their own village police, petty theft is comparatively rare; but that in British territory, although heinous crimes have diminished, owing to the increased force and vigilance with which the law is wielded, minor offences have increased. "This is the great blemish of British rule in the eyes of the poorer classes, who are the principal sufferers." * The landed proprietors now nominate their own chokeydars, and provide for their payment in the ancient manner.

The police in the North-West Provinces consists of three hundred and sixty-one inspectors, seven hundred and thirty-five chief constables, two thousand two hundred and sixty-nine head constables, nine hundred and fifty-seven mounted constables, and eighteen thousand six hundred and seventy-four constables; thus the constabulary comprises about twenty-three thousand men, maintained at a cost of about two hundred and seventy thousand pounds per annum, of which sum one-fifth is paid by the chief cities, and the remainder by Government. The force is distributed over twelve hundred stations and outposts, with an average of three policemen to each square mile.

In the Punjab there has been a fusion of the civil and military police. Inspectors, sergeants, and constables, have been formed into battalions, numbering eight thousand two hundred and twenty-eight men; there is a mounted patrol of three thousand four hundred men; and a well-organized urban force, with appointed *beats*, and day and night duties.

The preceding details indicate the system now being organised throughout India. European and Native gentlemen have been appointed unpaid magistrates in various districts, and their number will be extended according to circumstances. By these means, and in consequence of the increasing and more remunerative employment of the people, crime of every description is decreasing.

Marine Department.

The Indian military marine stationed at Bombay is ably

* 'Official Report to Government,' 1861.

commanded by Commodore Wellesley, of the Royal Navy, and comprises several vessels of war, under steam or sail. This department has rendered good service in the suppression of piracy in the Eastern seas, in extensive hydrographical surveys, and also in hostile expeditions. The Bombay dockyard is in a high state of efficiency for building and refitting ships of war.

The Marine department of Bengal consists chiefly of a large pilot establishment for the use of vessels entering or leaving the Hooghly river, the mouth of which, at Saugor, is one hundred miles from Calcutta.

The navigation at the head of the Bay of Bengal is dangerous, owing to numerous sand-banks and the frequency of bad weather. The pilot service consists of one hundred and forty-seven Europeans, or the descendants of Europeans born in the East. Fifteen are branch-pilots, thirty-four are masters, fifty-two mates and second mates, thirty-eight volunteers (who form the junior class), and twenty-four licensed pilots, of whom sixteen belong to the regular covenanted service. The pilot schooners employed are first-rate sea-boats of one hundred tons and upwards, well manned and found: they are capable of withstanding any weather. A master-attendant of the port of Calcutta superintends the establishment, which costs about eighty-two thousand pounds per annum, while the yearly receipts are about fifty thousand pounds. The pay and allowances of the branch-pilots and their subordinates are liberal, as they well may be considering the dangers and privations of the service.

There are lighthouses at Saugor Island, at False Point, and other places, where European light-masters reside. There are also buoy-vessels, with lights. Houses of refuge for the relief of shipwrecked mariners are erected at different parts of Saugor Island, and supplied with fresh water and biscuit; flagstaffs direct attention to their position.

The shipping for the benefit of which the Bengal pilot-service is maintained, amounted in 1860 to a million and a half tons, as will be seen by the following statement of arrivals and departures:—

Ports.	Tons.
Calcutta	1,258,871
Aykab in Arracan	161,992
Chittagong	79,035
Total Tonnage	1,499,898

Several steam-vessels belong to Government, and are used as transports and otherwise for the public service.

The government dockyard at Kidderpoor is adapted for the construction and repair of steam-vessels, ships of war and transports. An engineer school containing about fifty youths is connected with the dockyard.

There is a useful steam flotilla on the Ganges, which consists of eleven steamers and nine flats and troop-boats, besides several steam gun and ferry-boats employed in protecting commerce from pirates, who frequent the lower branches of the river, and from Dacoits or robbers, who infest its upper portions.

A small flotilla of steamers and flats is stationed on the Irrawaddy for the conveyance of troops, stores, passengers, and mails between Rangoon and other stations on the river. The annual expenditure is about thirty-two thousand pounds, and the income about twenty thousand pounds. A government Naval yard at Rangoon costs eleven thousand seven hundred pounds a year; the earnings for private work done bring in two thousand six hundred pounds. There is a patent slip for repairing ships at Rangoon; and an iron steamer sent out from England in pieces, for the King of Burmah, has been put together by the workmen in the Naval yard.

Laws, Crime and Police.

No code of civil or criminal law has yet been published. In 1835 the late Lord Macaulay was appointed, with a salary of ten thousand a year, as a fourth or legal member of the Calcutta Council, and as chief of a Law Commission established for the purpose of framing a code for India. Twenty-seven years have since elapsed, and it is on record that the salaries of the successive legal members of Council between 1835 and 1857 have amounted to two hundred and thirty thousand pounds, and the expenses of the Commission in India from 1835-36 to 1849-50 to above two hundred and thirty-four thousand pounds, and in England to about thirteen hundred pounds, forming an aggregate cost of nearly half a million sterling,* and yet no practical result has been attained, nothing effective has been done. The Moslem criminal and the Hindoo civil codes, notwithstanding their complexity, inconsistency, and defectiveness, are still in general use, except at the Capitals of each Presidency, where English laws are in force, under the superintendence of judges selected from the British bar.

An act of parliament in 1861 decreed the abolition of the Supreme (Calcutta) and Sudder (Mofussil, or country) Courts, and the establishment of high courts of judicature at each Presidency, and in the North-West provinces, superintended by a Chief Justice and as many judges, not exceeding fifteen, as her Majesty may appoint. These high courts are to exercise civil, criminal, admiralty, testamentary, intestate, and matrimonial jurisdiction, original and appellate, by single judges or by division courts. Trial by jury has been long established at Calcutta, Madras, and Bombay.

In Bengal there has recently been a marked improvement in the administration of civil justice. Under a new and simple procedure technicalities have been swept away, which delayed, if they not prevent the course of justice ; a disputed claim can be adjudged on verbal statements without

* Parliamentary Paper, Commons, xc. July 10th, 1859.

any written pleading, and the majority of small cause cases can be decided within six weeks. The Bengallees are pre-eminently litigious; but cheap and speedy justice has caused a diminution of suits. In 1860 there were in Bengal eighty-eight thousand six hundred and eighty-four original suits, of which fourteen thousand four hundred and thirty-five were connected with land, seventy-one thousand two hundred and fifteen with debts and wages, four hundred and seventy-one with caste, and two thousand five hundred and sixty-three with indigo, silk, and sugar contracts.

At Calcutta the number of small cause cases entered in 1860-61 was nearly thirty-two thousand; of which six thousand five hundred were English, and the remainder Native suits; the cases under one rupee (two shillings) approached sixteen thousand. Small cause courts upon the English system have been established in the provincial cities of Patna, Dacca, Moorshedabad, and other places. These courts are generally presided over by Native judges, termed Principal Sudder Ameens, with salaries varying from forty pounds to sixty pounds a month.

The following statistical table respecting the administration of civil justice shows the extent of litigation in each Presidency. (See p. 205).

The criminal law of India has been modified by the abandonment of torture and other severities practised under Moslem rule; and with the strong police now established it is to be hoped that life and property will be effectually protected.

The recorded amount of crime is not large in proportion to the number of inhabitants and the wide diffusion of property. In certain districts of Bengal, having a population of about thirty-eight million, the criminal offenders brought under trial in 1860 numbered about one hundred and twenty-four thousand, averaging one to above three hundred people. The cases of murder, suspicion of murder, and

STATEMENT EXHIBITING THE ADMINISTRATION OF CIVIL JUSTICE IN BRITISH INDIA FOR THE YEAR 1860.

Presidencies or Provinces.	Aggregate of Original Jurisdiction.							
	Total Number of Cases Tried in the Year.	Total Number of Cases Decided in the Year.	Number decided		Number of Cases Pending at close of the Year.	Value of Suits.		Average Duration of Suits.
			In favour of Plaintiff.	In favour of Defendant.		Under Litigation or Decided.	Pending at close of the Year.	
						£.	£.	Mths. days. Yrs. mths. days
Bengal, Regulation Districts	151,717*	99,478	40,764	20,441	52,239	..	6,118,676	5 11 to 1 0 10
Bengal, Non-Regulation Districts	21,118*	16,155	7,193	719	4,963	..	Not given.	0 19 to 0 6 1
North-West Provinces, Regulation Districts only	74,754	62,260	43,327	7,581	9,079	3,405,016	760,110	1 24 to 0 5 8
Oude	6,944	6,594	3,856	1,126	238	147,103	..	24 days.
Punjab, including Delhi	104,221	101,096	56,092	19,204	2,236	570,915	..	33 days.
Madras	225,966	157,111	133,536	23,575	68,855	..	1,481,566	7 11 to 1 4 16
Bombay	139,757	117,571	77,508	9,292	22,406	..	365,684	2 24 to 3 0 12
Sinde	12,065	11,722	Not given.		343	Not given.		Not given.
Hyderabad, Assigned Districts	2,517	2,161	1,153	253	356	153,543	..	44 days.
Mysoor	13,625	12,977	10,706	2,271	648	183,437	..	Not given.
Pegu	26,138†	25,761	Not given.		377	242,111	..	0 8 to 0 2 15
Tenasserim and Martaban	22,452	22,122	Not given.		330	Not given.		Not given.
Total	801,274	635,008	..	..	162,070	..	..	.. ..

* These are for 1859, being the latest complete return received; all the other information is for 1860.

† Including Appeal Cases.

and wounding with intent to kill, were six hundred; offences against property attended with violence, one thousand six hundred and six. Murder, generally speaking, in India is not the result of premeditated malice, but the effect of momentary and ungovernable passion. The crime seems to diminish in the districts where civilization advances. A prevailing belief in witchcraft has been known to occasion the massacre, not only of the individual suspected of sorcery, but of the whole family, as it is considered an hereditary taint.

Dacoity, or robbery by gangs of armed thieves, is on the decrease in the Bengal Presidency; it is under the supervision of a commissioner charged with the suppression of this offence. In 1852 the number of cases was five hundred and twenty; in 1859, one hundred and seventy-one. The river Dacoits are watched and chased by small steam gunboats.

The character of the population influences the description and amount of crimes: in some places poisoning is the mode of violence resorted to, in others assassination. At Madras in 1860, among a population of twenty million, there were fifty-one criminals sentenced to be hanged, and thirty-three to be transported for life. In Martaban crimes of a heinous nature average one to four hundred and sixteen inhabitants. In Pegu, among a population not much exceeding a million, the convictions for murder were eighteen; attempted murder, five; robbery with murder, twenty-two; robbery on water, with murder, fourteen. There were eighty capital convictions out of one hundred and fourteen trials, but only seven persons suffered the penalty of death. The number of recorded murders was forty-one in 1858, twenty-five in 1859, and twenty-two in 1860.

In the Punjab in 1860 nearly thirteen thousand persons were charged with heinous crimes: of these fifty-six suffered capital punishment; eighty-three were imprisoned for life; and twenty-four for periods exceeding twelve years.

Murder has been prevalent in Oude; one hundred and eighty-three cases were reported in 1860, exclusive of a smaller number connected with attacks on property. The District Deputy Commissioners have power to award seven years' imprisonment, or stripes and fines in lieu thereof. Their authority extends to ordering two hundred stripes, but the number inflicted has not exceeded one hundred. The efficacy of the punishment is alleged to be demonstrated by the fact that, out of above four thousand seven hundred flogged in one year, only eighty-three were flogged twice, and sixteen three times. The Commissioners assert that "this punishment may be made effective as a deterrent, without being carried to the point of brutality."

Infanticide has diminished within the last few years in India generally, and particularly in the Punjab, as shown by the careful register (made under penalties) of female births.

A special agency is in operation in the Punjab for the detection of Thugs, Dacoits, and poisoners; the extinction of Thuggee is delayed by the number of old hardened practitioners still at large; but every year their number is diminished. Thirty Thugs were arrested during 1860; one man, executed at Lahore, had three murders proved against him. No case of Dacoity was reported for 1859.

Poisoning is on the increase by means of an herb named *dutoora,* which grows in many parts of the Punjab. The detection of the crime is difficult; no organised gangs practise it; and its commission is not peculiar to any class. The poison is given in a sweetmeat to a traveller; or mixed up in the family dinner by the poisoner, disguised as a fakeer or as a Brahmin; or administered to a dancing-girl to obtain her ornaments; or to a carrier for the sake of his bullocks. The accomplices remain in the background until the drug has taken effect, and they are seldom identified. A Punjabee Mussulman confessed to seventeen murders effected by *dutoora;* and a religious impostor, a Seyed or descendant of Mohammed, who had long travelled about the country, was hung at Lahore in November 1860, five dutoora cases having been proved against him.

Since the rebellion of 1857-8 the authorities have been on the watch to check sedition and punish incitements to destroy Europeans. A fakeer, named Hubeeb Shah, was convicted of distributing seditious papers in the Sealkote district for about a year, and making overt proposals for rebellion and the murder of Europeans. Hubeeb declared himself the deputy of the "Imaum Mehndi," who was to appear in Arabia at the end of the world, which he predicted would shortly occur; he called on the Mohammedans and Hindoos to assemble under their respective standards. The fakeer was executed, and the sensation he had created subsided, but during the year 1859-60 the Native newspapers gave ostentatious accounts of the expected immediate appearance of the "Imaum Mehndi." The subject was much discussed by the Mohammedans of Lahore, and several persons were convicted of publicly uttering sedition, and sentenced to various slight punishments, which had the effect of quelling the temporary excitement. In the course of the investigation it became known that certain Mohammedans employed in the educational department had discussed the legality (in reference to their faith) of serving the British Government. It may reasonably be expected that under the new policy this feeling will pass away.

Gaols.

The gaols of India have long been a disgrace to our Government: the buildings being insecure, devoid of means for classifying prisoners, and filthy in the extreme. There is no uniformity in discipline, and the ratio of mortality is believed to be greatly dependent on the humanity and sense of justice of individual officers.

STATISTICS OF CRIMINAL JUSTICE IN BRITISH INDIA FOR 1860.

PRESIDENCIES OR PROVINCES.	Number of Persons brought to Trial.	Number of Persons Convicted.	Number of Persons Acquitted.	Proportion Convicted of Persons brought to Trial.	Proportion Acquitted of Persons brought to Trial.	Proportion of Acquittals to Convictions.
Bengal	123,962	78,516	40,611	64 per cent.	32 per cent.	51 per cent.
North-West Provinces	72,904	44,587	25,896	61 ,,	35 ,,	58 ,,
Punjab, including Delhi	69,929	52,388	15,737	73 ,,	23 ,,	30 ,,
Oude	23,018	12,789	9,464	55 ,,	41 ,,	74 ,,
Madras	254,597	146,498	105,985	55 ,,	42 ,,	72 ,,
Hyderabad, Assigned Districts	2,181	1,324	268	60 ,,	12 ,,	20 ,,
Mysore	30,757	19,862	Not given.	64 ,,	Cannot be shown.	
Bombay, including Sinde	50,068	37,968	12,100	75 ,,	24 per cent.	31 per cent.
Pegu	20,596	12,898	7,357	62 ,,	35 ,,	57 ,,
Tenasserim and Martaban	5,629	3,703	1,752	65 ,,	31 ,,	47 ,,
Total	653,641	410,533	219,170	62 per cent.	33 per cent.	53 per cent.

Fifty-two gaols in Bengal received in 1859-60 fifty-two thousand prisoners, of whom nineteen thousand remained at the close of the year. In some gaols the total cost of each prisoner is not more than two pounds ten shillings a year. The convicts are employed in road-making, on works inside or near the gaol, on ordinary manufactures, as servants or otherwise within the precincts, and are taught useful handicrafts. The educated were in the proportion of 1·73; the partially instructed 4·90; while the entirely ignorant formed 93·36 per cent. of the accused.

In the Punjab the gaols seem well managed; committals to them fell from thirty-three thousand in 1858 to twenty-two thousand in 1859; the mortality was only 2·35 per cent., the cost of each prisoner about thirty-three shillings per annum, and the escapes have been reduced to a minimum, viz. 0·08 per cent. Out of ten who got away seven were recaptured. Monitors selected from the prisoners are entrusted with the duty of maintaining order within the walls; they are exempted from labour and irons, and otherwise favoured, and are found to be more trustworthy than paid free constables. The punishment of solitary confinement is limited to fifteen days at a time, and to four inflictions during the year; and it is asserted that no mental injury has resulted from a penalty which is necessarily uncertain in its operation and results. The buildings are kept in repair entirely by convict labour. Some prisoners are employed in manufactures, and earn as much as fifty shillings a year.

An experiment has been made of working convicts on the roads. Fair wages are paid to them for task work; their presence is ascertained by frequent roll calls, and any attempt to escape is punished. The men become accustomed to labour; they see their friends, begin to save money, grow habituated to the sweets of rewarded industry, are freed from old temptations, and have a better chance of reformation than if they remained choking up the gaols. The immediate result is satisfactory.

STATISTICS OF GAOLS IN BRITISH INDIA IN 1860.

PRESIDENCIES OR PROVINCES.	Years.	Number of Gaols.	Average Strength of Prisoners in Gaols.	Number of Deaths.	Ratio of Deaths to Strength.	Total Expenditure on account of Gaols for the Year.	Average Cost of each Prisoner per Annum.
						£.	£. s. d.
Bengal, Regulation and Non-Regulation Districts	1859–60	54*	19,003	2,499	13·15	79,510	4 3 8
North-West Provinces, including Saugor and Nerbudda Territories	1859	40	13,865	1,375	9·91	64,193	4 12 7
Punjab, including Delhi	1860	34	10,504	245†	2·33	41,804	3 19 7
Oude	1860	12	1,720	305	17·73	9,373	5 8 11
Madras	1860–61	33	5,955	400	6·71	29,632	4 19 7
Bombay	1860	15	3,435	180	5·23	28,995	8 8 9
Hyderabad, Assigned Districts	1859–60	5	1,226	72	5·87	6,305	5 2 10
Mysoor	1859–60	4	1,784	106	5·94	8,458	4 14 9
Pegu	1859–60	6	2,024	307	1·51	28,336†	14 0 0
Tenasserim and Martaban	1859–60	5	2,154	20	·92	11,718	5 8 9
Total	..	208	61,670	5,509	8·93	308,324	4 19 11‡

* Not including 80 "lock-ups."

† These figures are estimated, the amounts not being given in the Administrative Reports.

‡ Average cost of each prisoner in the United Kingdom, exclusive of Convict and Military Prisons, for the year 1859, was 26*l.* 2*s.* 11*d.* See 'Miscellaneous Statistics of the United Kingdom,' Part III., 1861. Published by Board of Trade.

N.B.—The above information has been abstracted from the Administrative Reports, with the exception of the two first, which have been taken from the Reports of the Inspectors of Prisons of the several districts.

The gipsy tribe of Sansees in Sealkote are notorious for thieving, and yet can always obtain bail for good behaviour by feeing the head men of a village according to a well understood tariff. In 1859 a Sansee tribe was collected and placed on some uncultivated land in which wells had been dug; the territory, with cattle and ploughs, was made over to them, money was advanced on loan, and they were set to work under surveillance. Their prejudices were strong against ploughing or any fixed occupation; but they have now commenced operations and there appears to be a good prospect of their forming a permanent settlement.

An establishment for convicts was formed in 1858 at Port Blair in the Andaman Islands for mutinous sepoys. Port Blair now contains about two thousand five hundred prisoners; the first difficulties have been surmounted, and it will probably become a thriving settlement. The aborigines, who are wild and savage, were at first hostile; but their enmity to the new comers has almost ceased. The excellent havens of the Andamans will be useful to navigators in the Bay of Bengal. Coal has been found in these islands.

Revenue, Expenditure, Debt, and Currency.

The revenue of India has increased during the present century, but not in proportion to the acquisition of territory.

GROSS REVENUE FROM 1800 TO 1860.*

Year.	Bengal.	Madras.	Bombay.	Total.
	£.	£.	£.	£.
1800	6,658,334	3,540,268	286,457	10,485,059
1810	10,682,249	5,238,576	758,372	16,679,197
1820	13,547,423	5,403,506	2,401,312	21,352,241
1850	18,167,455	5,087,333	4,430,772	27,625,360
1860	25,877,178	6,550,980	7,277,664	39,705,822

* The total revenue for 1862 is estimated at 44,000,000*l.*

COMPARATIVE STATEMENT SHOWING THE SOURCES OF REVENUE OF BRITISH INDIA FOR THE YEARS 1849–50, 1854-55, 1859–60.

SOURCES OF REVENUE.	1849-50.	1854-55.	1859-60.	1860-61.
	£.	£.	£.	£.
Land	15,248,696	16,419,031	18,757,400	No returns received.
Excise	27,180	37,828	51,036	
Sayer and Abkarry *	1,060,536	1,218,873	1,653,186	
Moturpha †	115,519	110,076	109,242	
Mint	70,647	78,711	392,892	
Post-office	192,110	201,462	661,505	
Stamps	482,887	542,394	737,527	
Customs	1,447,796	1,532,657	3,872,053 ‡	
Salt	2,580 380	2,887,653	2,926,436	
Opium	4,497,254	4,710,352	5,887,778	
Tobacco	88,106	Tax abolished.		
Miscellaneous ..	1,711,226	1,394,013	4,656,767	
Income Tax				
Total	27,522,337	29,133,050	39,705,822	

* Taxes on sale of liquors, drugs, &c.
† Tax on houses and trades—levied chiefly in Madras.
‡ In March, 1860, the customs duty on imports was raised from 5 to 10 per cent.; the duty on exports remained as before, at 3 per cent. The import duty on spirits was raised from 1 r. 8 a. to 3 r. per gallon, and on cotton thread, twist, and yarn, from 3½ to 5, and finally to 10 per cent.
In April, 1862, the duty on manufactured cottons was reduced from 10 to 5 per cent.; and on yarn from 5 to 3½ per cent.

Opium forms a large source of revenue; in Bombay the tax is raised by issuing passes for the conveyance of the drug from the interior to the port of shipment; in Bengal the Government advance money to more than half a million cultivators of the poppy, and when the opium is prepared, from four rupees to three rupees ten annas per seer is paid for the drug. The quantity produced varies considerably; sometimes it rises to about fifty thousand chests; in 1860-1 there were only twenty-one thousand three hundred and sixty-three chests. The opium is sold by auction to the public, and the price varies according to the quantity in the market and to the demand in China: for instance in the year 1854-55, fifty thousand chests yielded three million six hundred thousand pounds sterling; and in 1860-61, about twenty-one thousand chests yielded four million two hundred thousand pounds. The net receipts for the two periods were two million two hundred thousand, and three million six hundred thousand pounds sterling.

The quantity of land occupied with the poppy in Behar and Benares is about half a million beegas.* The Chinese are now largely cultivating opium on the rich flat lands which border the Yang-tze-Kiang river, and in other localities.

The consumption of salt is a test of the increasing numbers of the people, and in some degree of their condition. In 1841-2, the amount used in Bengal was five million four hundred thousand maunds; in 1860-1 the demand increased to eight million six hundred thousand maunds,† notwithstanding an augmentation of the salt tax in 1859. There has been little or no fluctuation in the selling price during the last twenty years.

On 31st July, 1860, a property-tax of three per cent. per annum was levied on all property in and profits arising from lands and houses in India; and on all other property accruing to any person residing there, whether the property were situated in India or elsewhere; and also on incomes derived from any profession, trade, or employment of profit in India. The income-tax is now under revision.

One per cent. duty is assessed on persons residing in, or carrying on business in any house or land in any Presidency town; and on property and profits derived from roads, canals, and other reproductive public works.

A tax of ten shillings and of twenty shillings per beega is to be levied on all lands in Bengal cultivated with tobacco and with pawn,‡ respectively; the proceeds to be applied solely to public works.

* In Bengal the *beega* contains an area of about a third of an acre, or 1600 yards. Like other measures, it varies in different parts of India.

† In Bengal the common *maund* weighs 80 pounds, but the opium maund only 75 pounds. The common *seer* weighs 2 lbs. avoirdupois.

‡ *Pawn* or *pán* is the aromatic leaf of the betel, which is rolled round a mixture of the areca-nut, lime, spice, and sometimes a little catechu. The natives chew the preparation as a carminative and antacid tonic, and offer it to their guests wrapped in gold or silver leaf.

A great change has been made in land taxes and tenure: * wastes are now sold in fee simple. The tax on cultivated land is to be settled on a permanent basis throughout India, and a right given to the proprietor to redeem, at a certain number of years' purchase, the assessment levied by the State; thus converting short and arbitrarily taxed leaseholds into freeholds. The proceeds of the sale of waste lands are to be capitalized. If this determination be persevered in, an accumulation will be formed, which might constitute a sinking fund for the liquidation of the Indian debt. No more just or generous measure could be adopted by the British Government.

The aggregate charges on the revenue are: military, including troops, stores, and buildings, twenty-three million pounds, or above half the entire revenue; police, civil and military, two million; civil and political establishments, three million; the administration of justice, two million; public works, exclusive of military disbursements and private outlay, but including guaranteed interest on railway capital, about four million; interest on public debt in India and in England, four million sterling. The proprietors of East India Stock receive from the Indian revenues six hundred and thirty thousand pounds per annum, which payment is to be continued until their capital of twelve million pounds sterling is paid off.

The financial estimate of the Government of India for 1860-61 states the amount of—

	£.
Pensions, allowances, and assignments payable out of the revenue, in accordance with treaties or other engagements, at	1,422,865
Allowances to districts, to village officers and enamdars, with charitable grants, amount to	1,152.272
	2,575,137

The total does not appear to include jagheers or rent-free tenures.

The amount of allowances and assignments in 1859-60 was	234,673

* For an exposition of the land tenure and taxation, see '*Indian Empire*,' vol. i. pp. 567–582.

	£.
During the last session of Parliament a return showing the pensions paid to deposed princes and chiefs in India was moved for, but has not yet been furnished. Only imperfect details can therefore be given on this head, but the above-mentioned sum includes pensions to the late Government of Oude of	179,870
120,000*l.*, of which is understood to be appropriated to the ex-King, who is to receive an annual stipend of that amount.	
The family of the ex-Rajah Coorg	4,000
Under the Government of Bengal the allowances, &c., amount to	164,577
Of which sum the Nawab Nazim receives as a personal allowance, 73,255*l.*, and other members of his family, 41,309*l.*	
Under the Government of the N.W. Provinces the total amount is	120,947
Of which the Baiza Bye has an allowance of 20,000*l.*	
Under the Punjab Government the amount charged in account is .. .. 104,873 }	129,073
Paid in England about .. .. 24,200 }	
Of which the Maharajah Dhuleep Sing receives a life pension of 25,000*l.* per annum.	
Stipends to Ranees of Runjeet Sing's family, their dependents and adherents 8,400*l.*, and other members of the family, 840*l.*	
Under the Government of Madras the total amount is	321,464
Of which the Rajah of Tanjore and family receive 47,855*l.*	
The family of Tippoo Sahib of Mysoor, 28,022*l.*	
The families of the Nawabs of the Carnatic, including shares of one-fifth of revenues, 152,493*l.*	
Compensation and allowances to Native princes	77,217
The Maharajah of Mysoor receives 35,000*l.* a-year stipend, and a fifth part of the net revenues of Mysoor, which made his income in 1860-61, 114,000*l.*	
Under the Bombay Government	101,269
Including allowance to the Ameers of Sinde, 39,254*l.*	
Pensions to the Surat family, 12,000*l.*	
These payments are apparently exclusive of Jagheers and rent-free tenures.	
The following additional charges occur in the Financial Statement:—	
Under Madras Government, payments at Collectorates in lieu of resumed lands, privileges, and offices, including charitable grants	92,915
Under the Bombay Government these charges amounted to	1,021,666
Including Enamdars (holders of land in free gift) 410,034*l.*	
Allowances to district and village officers, including charitable institutions, 595,604*l.*	
Compensation to Enamdars and others, 16,028*l.*	
Under the Government of Sinde the charges were	49,460
Including Enamdars, 48,507*l.*	
Allowances to Zemindars and others, 953*l.*	

The Indian Debt.

The debt of India has increased in the following ratio:—

In 1800 it was—

	£.	£.
In India	14,125,384	
„ England	1,487,112	
		15,612,496

In 1857—

In India	60,704,084	
„ England	2,905,000	
		63,609,084

In 1859-60—

In India	71,969,460	
„ England	21,338,000	
		96,307,460

In 1861-2 it will probably amount to one hundred and twenty-five million pounds.

The total interest paid in 1859-60 on the Public Debt was—

	£.
In India	3,374,245
„ England	1,036,780
Total	4,411,025

The total amount borrowed in India and in England from 1800 to 1857 was above one hundred and ninety-five million sterling. The loans paid off amounted to one hundred and fifty-two million. The total interest paid on these loans exceeded one hundred and seventeen million sterling.*

From 1800 to 1833 the rate of interest paid by Government for the loan of money in India ranged from eight to twelve per cent.; the average was nine per cent. From 1835 to 1852 the interest averaged six and a quarter per cent. A diminution to five, four, and three per cent. took place in 1854, 1855, and 1856; the rate is now steady at five per cent. In England money was lent to the East India Company on terms ranging for the whole period from two and a half to five per cent.

The percentage pressure of the interest of the debt, in

* Parliamentary Paper, Commons, cci., August 12th, 1858.

relation to the gross revenue, has varied from above sixteen to under eight pounds, which latter is nearly the present proportion. No statement has been made showing the numbers who have paid the interest, or are liable for the principal of the debt contracted in or since 1800. If the existing Anglo-Indian population of one hundred and fifty million are to be made responsible for the debt of one hundred and twenty-five million pounds, their individual liability will still be under twenty shillings per head; whereas that of the people of the United Kingdom for their National Debt of eight hundred million is about twenty-seven pounds per head.

The latest return laid before Parliament shows that, up to April 1860, the debt and liabilities of India amounted to one hundred and twenty-two million two hundred and fifty-eight thousand seven hundred and ninety-eight pounds, of which sum thirty-six million pounds is payable in England, exclusive of the capital stock of the East India Company.

The estimated cost of the late rebellion, up to the end of the financial year 1859-60, including deficiencies in collections, loss by plunder, destruction of public buildings, and the probable amount payable of compensation to sufferers, approaches twenty-nine million sterling.*

When the trading privileges, or rather monopolies, of the East India Company were abolished in 1832-33, a quantity of tea and other property was sold, and the proceeds invested in the three per cent. annuities to accumulate at compound interest for the payment of the capital stock of six million pounds belonging to the East India Company, to be repaid at the rate of two hundred pounds for every hundred pounds stock. In March 1861, this redemption-fund amounted to above five million sterling; and it is calculated that in 1889 it will have augmented sufficiently for the discharge of the twelve million sterling.

The cash balances in the Government treasuries in December 1861 were upwards of seventeen million pounds; and

* Parliamentary Paper, xc., July 13th, 1859.

by the latest accounts there was great buoyancy in the public funds; the five and a half per cent. stock being at ten per cent. premium.

It is estimated that the amount annually remitted from India to England, in payment of interest of public debt, dividends to East India Company proprietors, civil and military charges, pensions, guaranteed railway and other dividends, and the savings of Europeans for their own retirement or for the support of their families at home, is about ten million pounds sterling.* This is an enormous drain, and its effects

* Enclosure in Financial Letter to India, dated 2nd February, 1861, No. 22, para. 17 :—

Estimate of the Disbursements of the Home Treasury of the Government of India for the year 1861-62.—(P. P. Commons, No. 32, 18th February, 1861.)

Charges on the Revenues of India:	£.
Dividends to proprietors of East India Stock	629,970
Interest on Home Bond Debt, Debenture Loans, and India 5 per cent. Stock	1,255,760
Interest on temporary loans	17,070
Amount to be paid under the postal arrangements	64,000
Red Sea and Indian Telegraph Company: Her Majesty's Paymaster-General, for the portion of interest chargeable to India	17,500
Transport of troops	88,866
Furlough and retired pay to military and marine officers, including colonels' allowances	820,400
Retired pay and pensions of St. Helena establishment ..	2,000
Imperial Government, regimental and other claims ..	1,400,000
Payments under 4 Geo. IV., c. 71: Retired pay, pensions, &c., of Her Majesty's troops serving or having served in India	60,000
Civil establishments of India:	
Absentee allowances	60,000
Annuities of Madras Civil Fund of 1818	6,000
Mission to the Court of Persia	12,000
Her Majesty's establishments in China	12,000
Her Majesty's Paymaster-General on account of convicts transported from India to Australia	6,000
Charges General: Home establishments, civil, military, and maritime pensions, recruiting charges, allowances for outfit, &c.	656,500
Amount that may be required for the New India Office	215,000
	5,323,066

Other

on any country, however intrinsically rich, would need to be counteracted by the influence of a fostering government for the development of internal wealth, the promotion of maritime commerce, and a continuous effort for the elevation of all classes of the people.

Currency.

There are gold, silver and copper coins in circulation, and a limited amount of paper, based on the precious metals, of which the quantity imported into India of late years has been considerable. In 1849–50 it amounted in value to three million pounds; and in 1857–58, to nearly fifteen million pounds; the total for nine years being upwards of sixty-seven million pounds, or more than seven million sterling per annum. The coinage at the mints of Calcutta, Madras, and Bombay during ten years ending 1857–58 is thus shown—

	Number of Pieces.	Value.
In Gold	519,317	£. 778,975
„ Silver	608,315,658	54,281,031
„ Copper	449,594,518	671,539

Making a total of nearly fifty-six million pounds sterling. The

---

Other disbursements in England on account of India:

	£.
Military and other public stores exported and to be exported	944,470
Coals for use of steam vessels in India	37,176
Freight of stores to India	24,000
On account contract for constructing a pier at Madras ..	36,616
	1,042,262
Bills of Exchange from India	36,000
Dividends on India loan property transferred to books in England	80,000
Advances on account of civil, military, and other funds	445,000
India Annuity Funds: Civil Service Annuities payable in England	245,000
Family remittances, remittances by Administrator-General, and miscellaneous disbursements on account of India	325,000
	1,131,000
Interest on railway capital guaranteed	1,851,210
	£9,347,538

Calcutta mint alone issued about thirty million sterling in rupees and fractional parts of that coin.

The mint and assay-offices at each Presidency are at full work, and issue annually a very large amount of coins, which now bear the impress and stamp of the Queen and the Royal Arms, instead of as formerly those of the East India Company.

The value of the coin in circulation is not known. It must be very great. Probably a quantity is hoarded, or melted into ornaments—a favourite mode of preserving wealth.

Banks.

The Indian Government holds a considerable amount of the capital of the banks of Bengal, Madras, and Bombay and nominates *ex-officio* directors to co-operate with the directors appointed by the proprietors of shares in these institutions, the notes of which are received by Government in payment of taxes and dues. In March 1862, paper currency to the extent of four million sterling was issued in state notes, through the agency of the Bank of Bengal, which acts as the Bank of England does for the British administration. The banks of Madras and Bombay are to exercise similar functions. Branch banks are to be established at the large cities in the interior; and through them the Government notes will be widely circulated. Irrespective of these chartered associations, there are several other joint-stock banks; three of which have establishments in London and in China, and carry on large exchange transactions.

The paid-up capital of the banks operating in India is—

	£.		£.
Bank of Bengal ..	1,070,000	Commercial Bank ..	476,000
Bank of Bombay ..	522,500	Mercantile Bank ..	328,000
Bank of Madras ..	300,000	Delhi Bank	180,000
Oriental Bank.. ..	1,215,000	Simla Bank	63,000
Agra and United Service Bank	1,000,000	Dacca Bank	30,000
		Total	£5,184,500

The capital subscribed exceeds that which has been paid up by more than two million sterling.

The quantity of paper representing bullion issued by the Indian banks has not been ascertained.

There are many Native private banks with large capital and good credit throughout India. The bankers, under various designations, such as Shroffs, Soucars, and Banians, transact much business by *hoondees*, or bills of exchange, which circulate by means of corresponding agencies established in the various Asiatic cities.

The Indian rate of interest for money is high, among the Natives not unfrequently one or two per cent. a month.

CHAPTER V.

RELIGION, EDUCATION, AND THE PRESS.

THERE is no Church Establishment in India connected with the State, enjoying peculiar privileges, and endowed as in England. The prevailing form of Christianity is the Episcopalian, but Presbyterian, Wesleyan, Baptist, and other Protestant denominations are unrestrained in their operations; and Roman Catholic Priests, as well as Church of England Clergymen, are supported by the State as ministers of religion in the Anglo-Indian army. Government now abstains from all interference in Hindoo worship, has withdrawn its supervision from idolatrous temples, and restricts its functions to the prevention of Suttee, of human sacrifices, and other proceedings repugnant to humanity. Neither Brahminist nor Boodhist, Seik nor Moslem, has the smallest ground of complaint in reference to religious liberty; the ruling Power makes no covert attempt at proselytism, but leaves every man free to perform his religious duties in the manner he deems best, and secures to all, immunity from interruption to the utmost limit consistent with the welfare of others and the preservation of public tranquillity. Bigotry and intolerance have never been displayed by the English in India. We have erred in the contrary direction, by apathetic sufferance of cruel and immoral practices, which the natives themselves honour us for having at last had the courage and energy to prohibit; by neglect of the external forms of the creed we ourselves profess, and even by public acts and private lives too often utterly opposed to the letter and the spirit of the Gospel. At the commencement of the East India Company the Directors made no provision for the ordinary observances of religion; and it was said that their servants left their Christianity at the Cape of Good Hope when on their voyage to India, and resumed it on their return home. Partly from the fear of exciting suspicion and giving offence, but chiefly from the absence of earnest belief in themselves, the Directors checked every attempt for the extension of Christianity. The first English Church in India was erected in Fort St. George by Streynsham Masters, the Governor of Madras, in 1680, "without any aid or countenance of the Company in order thereto." * The biography of Dr. Claudius Buchanan and other records attest the continuous efforts made to prevent Christian ministers from landing in India. By degrees the number of Chaplains to the Army and Government was increased; in 1814, a Bishop of Calcutta was appointed, and subsequently Madras and Bombay were provided with Bishops; but no other sees have been created; and the charges attendant on the three bishoprics have been diminished from fifteen thousand four hundred and twenty-seven pounds, to twelve thousand seven hundred and fifteen pounds. The number of Chaplains has been augmented from seventy-seven to one hundred and twenty-nine, and their allowances from seventy-one thousand to ninety-five thousand pounds; those to Roman Catholic Priests have been extended from eleven hundred to above eight thousand pounds; while between 1832 and 1855 sixty-seven thousand pounds were expended in building and repairing churches. Between 1852 and 1855, Government appropriated thirty-five thousand pounds to the erection of seventeen Churches in the Punjab.

In the Bengal Presidency the Church of England is represented by a bishop, archdeacon, thirty-two chaplains, and

* Hough's 'Christianity in India,' vol. iii. p. 377.

† Parliamentary Paper, No. 33, February 5th, 1858.

fifty-seven assistant chaplains, appointed to the different stations in Bengal, the North-West provinces, and the Punjab. In addition to these, there are ninety-four missionaries and other clergymen belonging to the Church of England. The Church of Scotland has ten representatives in Government service, and nine ministers of the Presbytery or Free Church of Scotland; London Missionary Society, fifteen ministers; British Baptist, seventeen; American Baptist, twenty-one; American Presbyterian Mission, twenty; American Episcopal Mission, ten; Episcopal Church of Moravians or United Brethren of Germany, three; Welsh Presbyterian Missions, five; German, Lutheran, and Evangelical Missions of Prussia, six; and some others.

In the newly-acquired province of Oude churches are being erected at Lucknow, Fyzabad, Seetapoor, Roy Bareilly, and Gonda; and a Roman Catholic chapel at Lucknow. An Episcopalian church has been erected in the capital from a fund obtained by heavy fines levied on the citizens.

This mode of providing "church accommodation" for the Lucknow civilians is particularly objectionable. To have raised some necessary Government building from this fund would have been justifiable; to have founded a hospital for Europeans and Natives would have been a practical lesson on the forgiveness of injuries, which is one of the most prominent tenets of Christianity: but to erect a place of worship for "the governing caste" with funds raised from the subjugated Mohammedans, whose king we have so recently deposed, and whose supremacy we have overpowered, is of doubtful political expediency; but, in a religious point of view, is peculiarly ill-judged, because calculated to make the structure which ought to be opened as a house of prayer for all nations, hateful in the eyes of the people of Lucknow as the monument of our triumph raised at their expense.

The Madras Presidency has a bishop and an archdeacon;

thirteen Government chaplains; twenty-five assistant chaplains; one hundred and fifty licensed clergymen of the Church of England in the service of Government or under the direction of the Church Missionary and other Societies. There were forty-three consecrated churches within the diocese of Madras in 1860, and thirteen licensed buildings awaiting consecration.

The Church of Scotland has four chaplains and two missionaries; Free Church of Scotland, eleven European and three Native missionaries; London Missionary Society, thirty-five missionaries; American Board of Missions, twenty-three; Wesleyan Missionary Society, thirty-two; Leipsic Evangelical Lutheran Society, thirteen; Basle Evangelical Mission, fifty-four (ten of whom are laymen), assisted by fifty-seven catechists and schoolmasters and five schoolmistresses (mission begun to India in 1834). The Church of Rome is represented at Madras, Cranganoor, and Cochin, by an archbishop, a bishop, and forty-four priests: the "Armenian Street establishment,"* by the bishop of Custoria and vicar-apostolic of Madras, with eight priests, and seven at out-stations; at Pondicherry, by a vicar-apostolic and forty-nine priests; at Coimbatoor, by a vicar-apostolic and eight priests; at Hyderabad, by a vicar-apostolic and six priests; at Mysoor and Bangalore, by a vicar-apostolic and sixteen priests; at Vizigapatam, by a vicar-apostolic and seventeen priests; at Verapoly, by a vicar-apostolic and forty-eight priests; at Madura, by a vicar-apostolic and thirty-three priests.

In the Bombay Presidency the Church of England establishment consists of a bishop, and thirty chaplains and assistant chaplains. There are several Christian missionaries of various denominations.

It appears by the following table (see pp. 228-9) that there are four hundred and twenty European missionaries, and one hundred and fifty-four ordained Native ministers, connected

* See 'Madras Directory,' 1860-61.

with Protestant Societies, labouring in India; under these are sixteen hundred Native catechists. The number of so-called Christians is one hundred and six thousand or on an average two hundred and fifty to each European missionary. The Communicants only number twenty thousand, or about forty to each European missionary.

It must be confessed that these are unsatisfactory evidences after many years of laborious zeal, a considerable sacrifice of life, and a heavy pecuniary expenditure. The money spent on Indian missions in efforts for the Christian education of the Natives and in printing and circulating the Bible in the vernacular, amounted during the last twenty-five years to above three million sterling, and the product (humanly speaking) is twenty thousand Christians who receive the Sacrament, which is viewed by the missionaries as the test of Church-fellowship. The result is still more distressing when it is noticed that the great bulk of nominal Christians belong to the South of India, where Swartz and others made many converts in the last century, from whom most of the present race are descended.

Southern India contains more than eighty thousand nominal Christians, but only thirteen thousand Communicants: a large number in Western India also come under the well-known old-established Churches of Malabar and others: so that in the whole of Northern India, out of one hundred million people, there are not twenty thousand even nominal converts, and only about five thousand Communicants; over whom there are one hundred and fifty European, and seventy Native ordained ministers. Thus, there are in all two hundred and twenty ministers, with an average of about one to twenty-two Communicants each.

There are no details extant of the number of Syrian and of Roman Christians; they exist chiefly in Southern and in Western India. Their creed is very latitudinarian in respect to polygamy, caste, and other Anti-Christian practices;

STATISTICS OF CHRISTIAN MISSIONS IN CONNEXION WITH

Missionaries, Stations, Schools, Communicants, Church Services, &c.*	Society for the Propagation of the Gospel.			Church Missionary Society.			London Missionary Society.		Wesleyan Missionary Society.
	North India.	South India.	Western India.	North India.	South India.	Western India.	North India.	South India.	South India.
European Missionaries	14	19	2	62	40	16	19	28	25
Ordained Natives ..	8	12	..	5	25	4	3	15	9
Native Catechists ..	73	347	..	37	70	7	96	563	12
							including	Teachers.	
Missionary Stations ..	12	23	..	28	29	6	5	17	15
Native Churches	6	..	..	39	464	6	7	23	45
Communicants	1154	3,597	..	1041	6,394	126	145	1,736	494
Native Christians ..	3385	16,288	..	7705	40,132	526	1147	13,163	4015
Vernacular Day-schools	..	73	..	92	229	20	25	214	53
containing Boys ..	..	..	..	6038	7,512	599	1059	7,761	2517
Boarding-schools	..	21	..	10	14	..	..	9	..
containing Christian Boys	..	..	..	434	584	..	..	219	..
Superior English Schools	..	Total scholars: Boys, 4846; Girls, 1539.	..	2	5	1	3	5	..
instructing Boys and Young Men	..		..	695	562	394	954	988	..
Day-schools for Girls ..	..		..	26	201	14	8	56	16
containing Scholars	..		..	763	3,297	208	263	1,728	320
Girls' Boarding-schools	..		..	9	23	1	..	12	1
containing Christian Girls	..		..	426	624	50	..	540	60
English Services ..	..	..	..	..	..	..	5	2	15

N.B.—The tables above given have been, for the most part, furnished by the respective Societies; and the returns are, in general, for the year 1861. In the cases in which information could not readily be obtained to a later date, recourse was had to 'Revised Statistics of Missions in India and Ceylon,' by the Rev. S. Mullens, 1852.

* The terms employed in this column are thus explained by Mr. Mullens :—" Under the term *Missionaries* are included those who have been specially ordained to the work of preaching the Gospel; together with a few, both from Europe and America, who, though not strictly ordained, left their country in the spirit of missionaries and for the same end. All the missionaries are named, whether they were absent from ill-health or labouring at their proper stations. The ordained Native Missionaries are distinguished by the term (*nat.*), except in cases where their name alone suffices to point them out. By *Native Catechists* are meant those Native Christians who have been appointed preachers. The term does not include *Readers* and Schoolmasters, who form a different class of Native agents. The term *Native Churches* refers not to the buildings wherein Native congregations meet, but to the separate *bodies* of Native *Communicants* or (as some term them) *Church members*, resident in one place. *Admitted* points out the number who were admitted into Church-fellowship and to the ordinance of the Lord's Supper *for the first time* during 1851; and *excluded* describes those put away from the body of communicants for misconduct in the same period.

" The term *Native Christians* includes the whole body of Natives who, by breaking their caste, have separated themselves from their fellow-idolators, and are now placed under regular Christian instruction and influence. So far as they have any religion, it is the religion of the Bible. Some of this numerous class are the unbaptised children of Christian parents; others are unbaptised adults, who have broken caste; others have been baptised, but have not entered the body of communicants. All, however, are under regular Christian instruc-

THE PRINCIPAL PROTESTANT SOCIETIES LABOURING IN INDIA.

Baptist Missionary Society.		General Baptist Missionary Society.	Moravian Missionary Society.	Free Church of Scotland Mission.			Basle Missionary Society.	American Board of Missions.		Established Church of Scotland.	American Presbyterian.†	American Baptist. †
North India.	South India.	North India.[a]	North India.	North India.	South India.	Western India.[b]	Western India.	South India.	Western India.	All India.	All India.	All India.
37	2	9	3	7	7	9	51	16	10	6	27	10
37	..	12	..	4	3	2	2	7	4	2	..	..
71	2	8	..	8	23	9	40	90	59	55	16	7
27	2	4	1	9	8	6	14	16	9	5	9	4
49	1	5	..	3	8	5	24	30	22	..	8	4
1984	105	354	..	48	96	182	1361	1183	576	..	151	39
6157	235	950	..	56	90	370	2880	6670	1700	..	407	139
50	..	6	1	8	9	14	48	84	10	1	17	14
2092	..	126[c]	6	542	360	927	1926	1202	250	720	706	460
..	..	2	..	..	..	..	5	1	1	..	3	2
..	..	70	..	..	..	..	148	40	10	..	48	60
2	..	1	..	4	9	3	6	..	..	1	10	..
520	..	55	..	2543	1581	1158	551	..	..	306	963	..
3	..	1	..	14	10	13	5	..	..	..	2	..
50	..	21	..	486	756	640	131	301[d]	..	..	63	2
1	..	2	..	1	1	2	4	1	..	..	3	4
30	..	92	..	43	60	109	214	54	..	..	62	44
10	2	2	..	2	3	6	6	..	..	..	6	1

[a] The above particulars are entered under North India, but Orissa is partly in Bengal and partly in Madras.
[b] Including Nagpoor, which is ecclesiastically connected with Western India.
[c] Probably two-thirds boys and one-third girls.
[d] In the 84 schools given above.

tion. The best portion of these native Christians are the Church members or communicants who are admitted to the ordinance of the Lord's Supper. Of the varying degrees of knowledge and character by which such admission is regulated among different denominations of Christians, the compiler has of course taken no account.

"Missionary *Schools* have been divided into three classes: the *Vernacular day*, the *Boarding*, and the *English day* schools. This division is naturally suggested by the different values of these schools and the different classes which attend them. *Vernacular day* schools are attended chiefly by the poorer classes, and give but a simple education. In *English day* schools a much higher system of education is carried out; they are frequented by the children of most respectable and wealthy families, and their scholars often remain in them for eight or ten years. The *Boarding* schools contain almost exclusively Christian children, who, by residing on a missionary's premises, have the advantage of a superior Christian training. So different is the influence exercised by these different species of schools, that to class all their scholars in a lump as 'receiving a Christian education' can only produce confusion and error.

"The last item points to the efforts of missionaries to benefit their European countrymen, and shows the number of services maintained in the English language for their instruction. Other items might have been added to these tables, as the number of Readers, Christian Schoolmasters, and Teachers; but it was thought that those already given were enough to convey a pretty correct view of the agency employed in Indian missions and its results. It would greatly facilitate the compilation of missionary information were all Societies to adopt some such common items in their tables, however much they might add others of a different kind."—*Statistics of Missions*, p. 4.

indeed, generally speaking, the moral standard of many professing Christians of all denominations is so low, and their drunkenness and dissolute habits so manifest, that the epithet "Christian" has become a bye-word of reproach and contempt among orthodox Hindoos and Mohammedans.

It might be expected that though little could be done in the way of adult conversion, much might have been accomplished in the Christian education of children; but here too there is cause for disappointment. In the whole of India there are only fifty-five thousand boys and thirteen thousand girls, in nominal attendance at the mission schools. Altogether there are less than seventy thousand scholars, with about two thousand teachers (including catechists and ordained ministers), showing an average of thirty scholars to each paid teacher. Individuals who have had opportunities of examining the facts of missionary conversions and teachings in different heathen countries, will be cautious in accepting the numbers set forth in official returns. A large percentage must usually be allowed in consequence of the over-zeal which leads to exaggeration, and also of the natural desire to make the supporters of missions in Britain think favourably of the enterprise. Unhappily, stern facts compel the belief that little has been yet effected in India for the establishment of active Christianity.

With the early Mohammedans subjugation and conversion went hand in hand. The Portuguese Romanists did not disavow the connexion; but the English Bible Protestants or, as they are called in India, "Christians of the Book," when earnest in their religious views, reverenced the Gospel in their own undemonstrative manner, and even erred in their anxiety to keep it unprofaned by contact with the sword or the ledger.

Many difficulties which existed under the rule of the Company have been swept away in the recent revolution. The welfare of India is now anxiously desired, and few will deny that the greatest boon which can be conferred by the British nation on India, is such an exposition of the tenets and practices of Christianity as shall induce the Natives to commend its results and desire its teaching.

The Christian system is the only one by which individuals or nations can be morally and intellectually elevated and sustained. We see that the doctrines of Confucius, of the author or authors of the Vedas, of Menu, of Boodh, of Zoroaster, and of Mohammed, have alike failed to realise the social or spiritual anticipations of their propounders.

Under the influence of Christianity (though warped and weakened in its operation by human frailty) Europe—peopled in former ages by hordes of savages and fierce barbarians—has become the wisest, the most industrious and the most powerful quarter of the globe. Freedom of thought, intellectual activity, social comfort, honourable position for women, protection for the weak, sympathy for the suffering, aid for the poor, have all been developed, more or less strongly, according to the degree of observance shown to the precepts and practice of One whose lifelong sacrifice was designed for no single race or nation, but to restore fallen humanity to the image and likeness in which it was created.

England may establish peace throughout India, may in process of time improve its material condition, may confer political freedom, and secure individual liberty; but she will still fall far—very far—short of her duty, unless the light and truth of Christianity, and the saving and healing virtues for time and for eternity which they originate, be so manifested in the character and conduct of her administration that the vital principle shall permeate through the vast mass of mankind, who have involuntarily become subject to British rule, and who now lie helpless at our feet, plastic as the potter's clay, to be moulded at the will of the temporal power, which, for some mysterious reason, has been suffered to assume this tremendous responsibility.

STATISTICS OF EDUCATION IN BRITISH INDIA FOR 1860.

PRESIDENCIES OR PROVINCES.	Number of Schools and Colleges.	Number of Scholars in attendance during the Year.	Total Cost.	Cost of each Pupil's Education.
			£.	£.
Bengal	816	49,654	79,446	1·41
North-West Provinces	9,621	151,112	79,833	·53
Punjab, including Delhi	8,191	108,776	50,080	·46
Madras	477	22,202	49,451	2·23
Bombay	3,577	124,469	55,256 (Bombay and Sinde)	·40
Sinde	712	11,017		
Mysoor	Not given.	1,661	4,195	2·52
Hyderabad, Assigned Districts	18*	551*	Not given.	..
Oude	103†	1,513†	Not given.	..
Pegu	203	3,514	1,382‡	·39
Tenasserim and Martaban ..	11§	440	5,214	14·1
Total	23,727	474,909	324,857	·66

* The average for the year 1858-59; no change has taken place since.

† These figures represent an average only, as there are no complete details.

‡ This approximation includes Ecclesiastical and Educational charges on the part of Government, which cannot be shown separately.

§ There are many other schools of an indigenous character widely dispersed throughout the province, but their numbers cannot be correctly estimated.

N.B.—The above statement is compiled partly from the Reports on Public Instruction and partly from the Administration Reports of each Presidency, Province, or District.

In BENGAL the educational department is under a Director of Public Instruction, aided by five inspectors of schools, who superintend the five divisions or circles into which the lower provinces are divided; and by forty-seven deputy-inspectors. Three hundred colleges and schools maintained by Government are attended by eighteen thousand scholars; and three hundred schools with twenty-two thousand scholars are aided by Government funds. About one hundred thousand pounds are expended yearly for educational purposes.

Oriental education is imparted at the Calcutta Madrissa establishment and at the Sanscrit College. In the Madrissa English and Persian are now taught to Mohammedan youths, who have a more varied literature than the Hindoos. The Sanscrit College has about three hundred students.

In five Government Colleges for general education there is a progressive increase on the rolls: at the close of the session 1859, there were two hundred and thirty-four students. These colleges are recruited from the vernacular schools, where there are one hundred and sixty scholarships annually attainable: they can be held in district schools for four years, and carry with them the privilege of education in the colleges free of cost, in addition to stipends of four rupees a month. Thus a youth commencing in a vernacular school may work his way up to the University, retaining throughout his career stipends and scholarships sufficient for his maintenance. The Government Colleges and Zillah or district schools are in number forty-four, and in April, 1860, had on their rolls six thousand six hundred and twenty-eight scholars.

Female instruction, although opposed by the Bengallees, is spreading, but much good cannot be expected when girls are betrothed at four or five and are mothers at thirteen or fourteen years of age. The education of men will in time lead to that of women. At present there are ten female schools, containing three hundred and sixty-seven children; and it is supposed that teaching in the Zenana is now being adopted.

There is an ably conducted University at Calcutta, which confers academical degrees, and that of Bachelor of Arts is much prized. There are also Licentiates in law, medicine, and civil engineering.

The Bengal Medical College has a high reputation for imparting sound practical instruction. Each student costs the State one hundred pounds per annum.

A College of Civil Engineering is as yet quite in its infancy. In 1859-60 there were sixty-five students on the rolls, and the demand for native civil engineers is yearly augmenting.

The Associations for the promotion of Literature and Science include the *Asiatic Society of Bengal*, founded by Sir W. Jones in 1784: its twenty volumes quarto of 'Transactions,' and twenty-eight volumes of 'Journals,' are a mine of wealth to the Oriental student. The Society receives from Government fifty pounds a month for the maintenance of its valuable zoological collection, and a like sum for the encouragement of Oriental publications. The *Dalhousie Institute* was established for the diffusion of general literature and science. The *Agricultural and Horticultural Society* has an extensive and beautiful garden, filled with choice plants and trees; and has done much good in diffusing sound instruction on its special subjects. There are Mechanics' Institutions, a Geological Museum, a Photographic Society, British India and Mohammedan Political Associations; and seminaries for promoting industrial and useful Arts.

Calcutta would not be complete without its "Clubs," of which there are several: the *Bengal Club* (1827), *United Service* (1845), *Union* (1859), *Turf*, *Regatta*, and *Cricket Clubs*, &c. Masonic lodges abound, and have their periodical meetings in a large Freemasons' Hall. There are twenty lodges in Calcutta and thirty in the provinces; also an "Encampment of Red Cross Knights," a "Royal Arch Chapter," with "An Order of High Priesthood," the "Ancient degree of the Royal Ark Mariners," the "Encampment of Superexcellent Masons," and branches of the Grand Lodges of England and of Scotland.

At MADRAS three grades of education have been established —a superior or University, a secondary or middle class, and a primary or popular. A commencement has been made in the first, and considerable development attained in the second, but in the third scarcely anything has been effected (regard being had to the magnitude of the work), owing to the indifference of the people to the acquisition of any knowledge not immediately conducive to pecuniary profit. Elementary education has made progress in some localities; at Tinnevelly the great field of missionary labour, at Coimbatoor, and a few other places.

At the University, a degree as Bachelor of Arts or as Bachelor of Laws is granted, after a severe examination. Matriculation is not easily obtained: of fifty-two candidates examined in 1860, only twenty-three passed—four of whom secured places in the first class and nineteen in the second. The Presidency College has qualified teachers, with two hundred and eighty-six scholars. The Normal school at Madras, in its several departments, with five hundred students, is working well, as are also those in the country districts. The Provincial, the Zillah, and the Talook (village) schools are increasing: the latter are seventy-two in number, with three thousand one hundred and seventy-one pupils. They are all supervised by inspectors. At the Madrissa College, established and supported by the late Nawab of the Carnatic—now under the control of Government—only Mohammedans are eligible for admission, and English study is added to that of Hindustani, Tamil, Telugu, Arabic, and Persian: the pupils number two hundred and forty-two. The masters, mistresses and teachers of Government schools undergo strict examination, and receive pecuniary rewards for degrees of proficiency. In the assignment of marks, most weight is attached to language, arithmetic, method, and teaching power, as being of the greatest importance to masters. Government funds are given in aid of private and missionary schools, under defined rules. A Medical College imparts instruction in surgery, in clinical medicine, and in practical pharmacy to one hundred and fifty pupils, and grants diplomas, after a searching *vivâ voce* examination. A primary medical school prepares candidates for the medical college classes. A Civil Engineering College is in course of formation. There is also a Gun-carriage manufactory school for artificers, with one hundred and thirteen pupils; one of Industrial Arts, in which is taught free-hand, plan, chalk, and botanical drawing, flower-painting, engraving on copper and on wood, with perspective; the manufacture of bricks, tiles, glazed and porous vessels, waterpipes, construction of cooking-ranges, &c. The artistic department has one hundred and twenty-six scholars; the industrial, eighty-eight. Military schools, regimental and station, are increasing. Young Zemindars (landed proprietors of rank), who are wards of the Board of Revenue, a position resembling that of English wards in Chancery, are being educated to fit them to take a proper position among their countrymen, and co-operate with the authorities in the diffusion of general enlightenment.

In Madras as in Bengal, there are Civil and Military Male and Female Orphan Asylums; Native Girls' schools; the Henry Lawrence establishment at Ootacamund for the children of European soldiers; a Magdalen Asylum, a Sailors' Home, and several other benevolent institutions.

The Educational department, which costs the Government about fifty thousand pounds per annum, has a Printing establishment attached thereto.

There are Botanical Gardens at Madras, Bangalore, and Ootacamund for the rearing and distribution of useful plants and seeds. An experiment is being made in the Neilgherries to naturalise the Chinchona plant from South America, for the production of quinine, of which the annual importation is to the value of fifty thousand pounds sterling.

Government Museums have been formed at Madras, Cuddalore, Bangalore, Rajahmundry, Ootacamund, Bellary, and Kurnool, which promise useful results. An Astronomical and a Magnetic Observatory are in working order.

District printing presses form useful and economical adjuncts to the collectorate offices in Madras. Local Gazettes are issued, and the income arising therefrom is in excess of the expenditure, reckoning the value of the work done at the usual rate of charge for typography. A lithographic establishment is attached to the Grand Trigonometrical and to the Revenue Surveys, village maps are printed in colours, and topography is becoming generally understood.

Cattle-shows have been recently established, at a very trifling cost to the Government and with highly satisfactory results, by causing emulation among the farmers.

BOMBAY is not behind its sister Presidencies: its colleges are turning out excellent scholars. The first matriculation examination at the *Bombay University* took place in October, 1859. One hundred and twenty-six candidates were examined, of whom one hundred and nineteen were from Government institutions: twenty-one passed. Four institutions have applied for affiliation to the University, viz., the Elphinstone College, Bombay; the Grant Medical College, ditto; the Poona College; and the Poona Government Law School. There are Colleges at Ahmedabad and at Belgaum, and an Engineering and Mechanical school at Poona. Numerous English and Vernacular schools; viz., twenty-three of the former, with three thousand scholars; and five hundred of the latter, with twenty-eight thousand scholars, are established in various parts of the Presidency and in its provinces, besides several seminaries founded and maintained by private individuals and by missionaries. Works in the English and Native languages are extensively printed.

Government has formed a Botanical and Medicinal Garden at Dapoorie, near Poona. The latter yields colocynth, hyoscyamus, croton and castor oils, senna, taraxacum, and other useful drugs for the use of the public hospitals. Mahogany, logwood, Brazil wood, Sappan wood and other foreign trees, are now being naturalised.

Although Sinde has been so recently acquired, there are several schools in operation at Kurrachee, Hyderabad, and Shikarpoor.

The NORTH-WEST PROVINCES contain ten thousand governmental schools, with two hundred and twenty-five thousand boys. There are colleges at Agra, Benares, Bareilly and other cities, where candidates are prepared for the Calcutta University. There are upwards of six thousand indigenous schools, with sixty-five thousand boys, maintained and managed by the Natives, who "in many instances have shown a remarkable willingness to combine for the purpose of securing to their children the means of learning English." *

In the PUNJAB, as in other parts of India, the people seldom bestir themselves even for objects which they desire without an impulse being first given by the Government. When this is done they will exert themselves for the accomplishment of the measures designed. The Director of Public Instruction is now placed in immediate communication with the local authorities. He has under him inspectors for the supervision of normal, Zillah, Tehseeli, and village schools, the pupils of which were, in 1859-60, Hindoos, twenty-four thousand five hundred; Mohammedans, seventeen thousand; others, four thousand; in all above forty-five thousand: with an average daily attendance of forty-two thousand three hundred. The pupils at indigenous schools exempt from Government instruction number sixty-three thousand. In two of the Government schools—one at Delhi, the other at Umritsur—the range of instruction is sufficiently extensive to qualify students for the University examination. The Delhi school, with two hundred and thirty-four students, is supported by a bequest of Nawab Fuzl Ali, and has two scholarships, founded by Native gentlemen. There are eight classes, and in seven English is taught as well as the vernacular; the studies being reading and translation, history, geography, arithmetic, natural philosophy, Euclid, and Algebra. Umritsur school has two hundred and nineteen names on the register, but only forty-three learn English. There is a good missionary school at Umritsur. Many of the chiefs and courtiers connected with the old Seik monarchy re-

* Administration Report, North-West Provinces, 1860-61.

side at and near Lahore, and, notwithstanding their aristocratic exclusiveness, the position of their children has induced them to request the Governor-General to found a college at Lahore. To meet their wishes a first-class institution has been formed, and divided into two departments: into the higher school none but the sons of persons who are eligible for the Governor-General's durbar are admitted; in the lower there is no distinction of rank. This arrangement is extremely agreeable to the upper class; indeed, without it they would not have sent their sons (sixty in number) to the institution, which contains altogether one hundred and forty boys. The change which is taking place in the education of the Seik aristocracy may be understood by remembering that Runjeet Sing in the memory of the present generation kept his royal accounts by cutting notches on a stick.

The total expenditure from all sources on education in the Punjab in 1859-60 was nearly thirty-five thousand pounds; of which sum the State contributed sixteen thousand two hundred and sixty-two pounds. The number of books sold, increased from thirty thousand in 1858-59 to fifty-three thousand in 1859-60.

OUDE.—Schools of a superior order have been established at Seetapoor, Fyzabad, and Pertabghur; and it is intended to make that noble institution the Martinière College available for promoting the education of the families of chiefs and large landed proprietors. A scientific territorial survey is in progress, and a demarcation of village-boundaries nearly completed, which will prevent disputes as to limits, that now occasion frequent affrays and bloodshed. Horticultural gardens are to be established in each district for rearing seedling-trees and plants of the most useful kinds, and to encourage the talookdars in introducing improved staples of agriculture. New Orleans cotton-seed has been, for instance, widely distributed. At several towns a Gunj or grain-market, with shops and a covered square in the centre, has been erected. Serais or caravanserais, for the use of travellers, are in course of construction at all the principal towns throughout the province. Periodical fairs, have been established for the sale of horses, elephants, bullocks, and milch kine.* Dispensaries and hospitals are opened for the poor, and a lunatic asylum and Lock institution have been found useful in Lucknow.

BRITISH BURMAH.—In Eastern India progress is also making in the education of the people. One Government school at Rangoon has sixty-eight Burmese on the rolls who are taught English; an American Baptist high school at Kemmendine, has one hundred and twenty Karen boys, who are instructed in English, geography, arithmetic, and chemistry, and have made satisfactory progress, as shown at a public examination in 1859. There are one hundred and thirty-three village schools throughout the province, with two thousand two hundred pupils, who read the Bible and are taught arithmetic. The mountain tribes are being gradually instructed, especially the Karens, for whom there is a female institution at Tonghoo for the education of teachers, and normal schools at Bassein, Henzada, and other places; the clergy of the Churches of England and Rome and ministers of the Baptist persuasion are the teachers.

In Tenasserim a great desire prevails among the Burmese to learn the English language as the key to general knowledge; numerous schools are maintained there by different missionary societies, and there is a Government school at Moulmein. Every Boodhist monastery is also a school.

Medical Aid.

There is no more effective mode of winning the heart of a people than by relieving their bodily ailments. Forty-

* This and other measures were suggested by Henry Wellesley (afterwards Baron Cowley) when Commissioner in Oude in 1801, to his brother the Governor-General.—See 'Wellesley Papers' in British Museum.

seven dispensaries in Bengal are supported by Government, in which fifty-six thousand patients were treated in 1859-60. Almost the entire number of sick were Natives. The cost is not heavy; the General and Seamen's Hospital at Akyab, for Europeans as well as Natives, being maintained at a charge of less than five shillings per head for two thousand one hundred and seventy-seven out-door patients. A munificent bequest by the late Mr. Mitford—to be employed in various "charitable, beneficial, and public works, for the exclusive benefit of the Native inhabitants of Dacca"—was the means of affording medical aid to more than thirteen thousand patients in that city during the year 1860.

The Medical College Hospital at Calcutta receives about five thousand indoor patients annually, of whom one half are Christians, the remainder Natives. The proportion of deaths to admissions is, thirty-five per cent. of the latter, and twelve per cent. of the former. In cholera cases, about one half the number of patients of both classes perish. Midwifery wards for the delivery of European and Native women are attached to the hospital, which has several out-door dispensaries, with seventeen thousand patients. A nursing establishment has been added by a committee of Calcutta ladies, who maintain several European attendants.

The Police Hospital tends greatly to the mitigation of suffering among the multitudinous poor of Calcutta and its suburbs.

An eye infirmary, attached to the Medical College Hospital at Calcutta, has afforded extensive relief to the Natives, who are much afflicted with cataract and chronic ophthalmia. The in-door patients treated during the year exceeded five hundred; the out-door patients, eighteen thousand six hundred; of whom thirteen thousand were Hindoos, three thousand three hundred Mohammedans and above two thousand two hundred Christians.

There are five public (but no private) lunatic asylums in

Bengal. Two of these are at Calcutta, the others are at Patna, Moorshedabad, and Dacca. The total number of insane treated during the year was—Europeans and Eurasians, one hundred and forty-four; Natives one thousand and twenty-nine. The abuse of spirituous liquors and narcotics appears to be, as in England, the chief cause of insanity; and voluntary employment of various kinds, regular hours, wholesome food, and freedom from threats, coercion or mechanical restraint, afford the best means of restoring sanity. The returns show that the number of cures has increased with the healthful occupation of the patients. Out of one hundred and seventy-one cases in the Patna asylum in 1860 no death occurred among the industrious insane.

Where unusual sickness occurs Government aid is promptly granted. An extraordinary epidemic prevailed in Behar between October 1859 and January 1860, caused, it is supposed, by a heavy and unseasonable fall of rain, which inundated large tracts of country. When evaporation began, fever and ague raged virulently, at first among the rural and poorer classes, but subsequently among all ranks, including the Europeans. In some of the villages the rice-crops remained uncut, and there were no peasants to till the ground. The deaths were numerous. Extra medical officers were sent from Calcutta with large quantities of quinine, the use of which was nearly always successful in arresting the disease.

In the Madras provinces there are thirty-eight civil dispensaries. European medicines and practice are making great progress among the Natives. Throughout the Presidency the number of patients in 1859-60 was—indoor, thirteen thousand; out-door, two hundred and eighty-one thousand. Of the in-patients, the deaths were eight hundred and fifty-eight, or 6·4 per cent.; of the out-door patients four hundred and seventeen died, or 0·1 per cent.

Vaccination is extensively performed; about three hundred and fifty thousand persons are annually inoculated. The failures are in the ratio of eighty to ninety per thousand.

In the Bombay Presidency there are five civil hospitals and several dispensaries supported by Government. The confidence of the Native community in the resources of European medical practice is shown by the great increase of persons applying for relief. In the five civil hospitals more than six thousand patients were admitted in 1859-60: and the out patients in the dispensaries numbered one hundred and eighteen thousand: of whom the Christians were nearly ten thousand; Hindoos, sixty-eight thousand; Mussulmans, twenty-nine thousand; Parsees, eight thousand; other classes, one thousand five hundred. The *Jamsetjee Jeejeebhoy* Hospital, founded by the late Parsee baronet, received four thousand six hundred patients during the year. There is a lunatic asylum, an eye infirmary, a vaccination establishment, and an obstetric institution at Bombay.

At the Government dispensaries in the Punjab the number of patients treated in 1859-60 exceeded one hundred and seventy-two thousand. Of these there were, in-door—males, nine thousand; females, twelve hundred: out-door—males, one hundred and nineteen thousand; females, forty-one thousand. The application of women for medical aid is a favourable symptom of popular feeling towards the British Government. Vaccination is making progress; the number of persons vaccinated in two years, 1858 and 1859, was one hundred and fifty-four thousand, of these one hundred and fifteen thousand cases were successful, twelve thousand were doubtful and about fifteen thousand unsuccessful.

The Press.

At the commencement of the present century one newspaper was published at Calcutta, which for several years continued to be the sole English journal in India. In 1835 the

Government abandoned the censorship of the press and its operations have since rapidly increased. There are no stamp or advertisement duties, and free discussion is permitted on all subjects. No official statistics have been collected on the subject of the periodical publications issued in India; the following summary of journals and newspapers in 1862 is, therefore, given on private authority.*

Bengal, English, 9 daily, 14 weekly and bi-weekly, 13 monthly and bi-monthly, 15 occasional.
" Native, 2 daily, 8 weekly and bi-weekly, 5 monthly.
Mofussil, English, 11 daily, 2 monthly and bi-monthly, 1 annual.
" Native, 4 weekly.
Bombay, English, 2 daily, 7 weekly and bi-weekly, 9 monthly and bi-monthly, 1 quarterly, 1 half-yearly, 5 annual, 5 occasional.
Mofussil, English, 5.
" English and Gujaratti, 1 weekly, 1 monthly.
" English and Marathi, 1 bi-monthly.
" Portuguese, 1.
" Gujaratti, 3 daily, 1 tri-weekly, 2 bi-weekly, 8 weekly, 3 monthly.
" Marathi, 4 weekly and 1 bi-weekly.
" Hindoostani, 2 weekly.
Madras, 9, including one daily, weekly and bi-weekly.
Sinde, 4 weekly and bi-weekly.

The number of Native periodicals is probably very large, but the press being unlicensed, there is no record of its circulation. A measure is under discussion for placing Native editors and proprietors under *surveillance*; the chief argument being that previous to the mutiny in 1857, much mischief was done by their unchecked writings in sowing the seeds of sedition throughout Hindoostan.

There are English and Native printing-presses at each Presidency and in several large towns. Elementary and other books are printed on good paper manufactured in India, and typography and its associate arts are improving.

* Mr. Street, Colonial Newspaper Agent, 20, Cornhill, London; and Bombay Directory for 1862.

CHAPTER VI.

RAILWAYS, ROADS, CANALS, TELEGRAPH AND POST-OFFICE.

UNTIL recently very little attention was paid to public works. Lord Dalhousie, with his energetic and practical mind, laid down the plan of triangulating India with railways, so as to connect the three Presidencies, facilitate the movement of troops and open up internal communication.

Railways.

Although the railway system of India is but in its infancy, many beneficial results have already been produced, and it is surprising that the Court of Directors should have been so long either practically opposed or indifferent to its introduction. In 1845, two Companies were formed (the *East Indian* and the *Great Indian Peninsula*), but their promoters could not obtain the necessary capital without the assistance of Government. Several years were spent in discussing preliminary arrangements; at length Lord Dalhousie induced the Government to encourage British capitalists by sanctioning a plan for the furtherance of such railways as the authorities might deem advisable. This encouragement consisted in granting the land required for an approved line free of cost; and in guaranteeing to private individuals, as shareholders for ninety-nine years, a stipulated interest (usually five per cent.) on the capital raised and expended by the several Companies.

In return for these concessions the State exercises the power of supervision over all capital and outlay; has a veto through a Government Director on all the proceedings of the managers and directors in India and in England; and has a right to purchase the lines, at a period of twenty-five or of fifty years from the date of contract. At the expiration of ninety-nine years the land and the works thereon revert to Government: but the Railway Companies may at any time after a portion of the line has been opened for three months surrender it to Government (giving six months' notice) and receive back the whole sum that has been expended and sanctioned on the undertaking. Mails and post-office servants are to be conveyed free of charge. The British army and its stores, horses, guns, &c., are charged for at the lowest rates. The net receipts of traffic are paid into the Imperial Treasury, and the profits beyond five per cent. are divided between the Companies and the Government; and if at any time the whole of the moneys advanced by the Government for interest shall be repaid, with simple interest thereon, the Companies will become entitled to the whole of the profits. On these general terms, with some minor provisions, the railways described in the annexed table are now in satisfactory progress.

The *East Indian Railway* at the close of the year 1861 traversed about six hundred miles, of which three hundred and sixty are in Bengal, and the remainder in the North-West Provinces. It is expected that passengers will be conveyed the whole way from Calcutta to Delhi at the end of the year 1862. The total expenditure for a single line of rails from Calcutta to Delhi will be twenty million sterling. The working expenses range from thirty-seven to fifty-four per cent. The cost of maintaining the permanent way and works in good order is about ten pence a mile for the half year. The traffic in goods and passengers rapidly increases. The proportion of third to first class passengers is about eighty to one.

The line connecting Allahabad with Bombay (*viâ* Jubbulpoor) is in progress; the estimated cost is two million sterling.

The *Madras Railway Company* has been successful from its commencement as regards traffic and the absence of any casualty entailing loss of life or limb. The main line from Madras to Beypoor, four hundred miles long, is expected to

Designation of Railway Companies.		Termini.	Number of Miles. Whole length of Line.	Under construction.	Open for Traffic on 30th June, 1860.	Number of Passengers carried, Year ended 30th June, 1860. 1st Class.	2nd Class.	3rd Class.	Total.	Receipts from Passenger Traffic.	Merchandise carried, Year ended 30th June, 1860. Tons.	Receipts.	Capital Authorised. In Shares.	By Debentures.	Total.	Capital Paid up to 31st January, 1862.	Amount Expended to latest date received.	Date of Incorporation.	Date when Traffic commenced.
										£.		£.	£.	£.	£.	£.	£.		
East Indian	Main Line	Calcutta to Delhi	1310	1302	289	20,313	77,126	1,637,084	1,734,523	118,647	362,911	174,676	14,328,616	6,421,384	20,750,000	16,916,804	17,233,260	1 Aug. 1849	15 Aug. 1854
	Branches	Burdwan to Raneegunge	54			The works in progress.													
		Allahabad to Jubbulpoor	227	27	..						..	..	2,000,000	..	2,000,000	1,059,770	192,660	..	..
		Total	1591										16,328,616	6,421,384	22,750,000	18,876,574	17,425,920		
Madras	Main Line	Madras to Beypore	405½	..	..	..	..	..	..	..	..	..							
	Branches	Bangalore Branch	84½	..	..	..	..	..	..	..	..	..	3,000,000	2,000,000	5,000,000	4,895,187	4,840,217		
		Coimbatoor to Neilgherries	30	..	..	..	..	..	..	..	..	..							
		Arconum to Cuddapah	120	..	..	..	..	..	..	..	..	..							
	Branch Extension	Cuddapah to Bellary	140	713	137	2,346	10,346	795,289	807,981	35,448	55,629	40,513						June, 1853	1 July, 1856
		Bellary to Junction with Great Indian Peninsula Line from Bombay	66	..	..	..	..	..	..	..	..	..	1,000,000	..	1,000,000	961,940	585,576		
		Total	846										4,000,000	2,000,000	6,000,000	5,857,127	5,425,793		
Great Indian Peninsula	Main Line	Bombay to Callian and Jubbulpoor	605	..	..	..	..	..	..	..	..	..	..	..	..	..	..	..	18 Apr. 1853
	Branches	Bombay to Mahim	1¼	..	..	..	..	..	..	..	..	..	..	..	..	..	..	..	
		Bhosawul to Nagpore	263	..	..	..	..	..	..	..	..	..	..	..	..	..	..	..	
		Callian to Moodgul, the Junction with the Madras Line from Bellary	380	968	297	11,183	166,740	1,116,947	1,294,820	72,747	154,758	81,267	9,000,000	2,000,000	11,000,000	8,933,677	7,585,279	Aug. 1849	12 May, 1856
		Padusthurree to Campoolee, near Poona	7¼	..	..	..	..	..	..	..	..	..	..	..	..	..	..	..	
		Total	1266																
Great Southern of India	Main Line	Negapatam to Trichinopoly	80	..	80	..	..	No returns of traffic yet received.			..	..	418,720	140,000	558,720	558,720	571,539	..	May, 1861
	Branches	Trichinopoly to a Junction with Madras Line; Trichinopoly to Madura and Tuticorin	220	220	..	..	..	Sanctioned, but not yet surveyed.					..	..	..	..	..	1858	
		Total	300																
Bombay, Baroda, and Central India	Main Line	Bombay to Baroda	245	281	29	312	1,045	49,263	50,620	2,619	No goods carried.		2,450,000	550,000	3,000,000	2,395,178	2,069,816	July, 1855	Feb. 1860
	Branch	Baroda to Ahmedabad	64																
		Total	309																
Sinde	Main Line	Kurrachee to Kotree, including Branch to Ghizree Bunder	114	..	114			No returns of traffic yet published.					1,169,300	330,700	1,500,000	1,439,683	1,486,128	July, 1855	May, 1861
Indus Flotilla	By Steamers	Kotree to Mooltan	575	..	575			No returns of traffic yet published.					417,000	83,000	500,000	332,735	265,623	June, 1857	May, 1861
Punjab	Main Line	Mooltan to Lahore and Umritsur	252	252	32	..	..	Opened for traffic, 1 March, 1862.			..	..	1,500,000	..	1,500,000	1,251,143	991,412	1859 ..	Opened, 1 Mar. 1862.
	Extension	Umritsur to Delhi	280	..	..	..	..	Line surveyed.			..	..	..	..	..	..	..		
		Total	1,221	490	914								3,086,300	413,700	3,500,000	3,023,581	2,741,163		
Eastern Bengal	Main Line	Calcutta to Kooshtee, on the Ganges, opposite to Pubna, eventually to proceed to Dacca	110	110	..			Expected to be opened for traffic in 1862.					1,000,000	400,000	1,400,000	1,301,127	936,291	Aug. 1857	
South-Eastern	Main Line	Calcutta to Mutlah	29	29	..			Expected to be opened for traffic in 1862.					250,000	90,000	340,000	337,468	324,737	1856	
		Grand Total	5,859	4,113	1,746	34,104	255,257	3,598,583	3,887,944	229,461	573,298	296,656	36,361,536	12,015,184	48,376,720	41,160,452	37,928,538		

be completed in the present year. The number of passengers increased in six months thirty per cent.; nine-tenths of them used the third-class carriages.

The Bellary or North-West line, three hundred and thirty miles in length, is now in course of construction.

The *Great Indian Peninsula* Railway Company had about four hundred and fifty miles of rail open in December 1861, but there are still gaps at the Bhore and Thull ghats which render the line incomplete. The great works for the ascent of the sea-coast mountain-barriers are fast approaching completion. The entire line to Jubbulpoor is in progress. The total cost of the works of the Great Indian Peninsula Company is calculated at about twelve million sterling. The contractor, Jamsetsee Dorabjee, a Parsee, employs eighteen hundred men on the embankment and tunnel-arches across the Goolbun ravine—a fact which affords some idea of the energy with which the undertaking is prosecuted. As on the other lines, the passenger-traffic, especially by third-class carriages, increases largely every succeeding half-year.

The *Great Southern of India* Railway Company has been opened from Negapatam to Trichinopoly, a distance of nearly eighty miles. So far as has yet been ascertained, the traffic receipts have been forty-six pence, the expenditure twenty-two pence, and the net profits twenty-four pence per mile.

The *Bombay, Baroda and Central India* Railway Company have furnished the following tabular view of their operations:—

For the weeks ending	No. of Miles	Passengers and Goods Conveyed.		Proportion to Mileage.		Increase per cent. from the time of opening to Baroda.		
		Passengers.	Goods.	Of Passengers.	Of Goods.	In Miles.	In Passengers.	In Goods.
1861.		No.	Tons.					
February 10	81	28,994	1,304	357·95	16·10	..	..	..
June 23 ..	109	52,303	2,491	479·84	22·85	34·57	80·39	91·02
October 20	132	87,466	4,803	662·62	36·38	62·96	201·67	268·32

The *South-Eastern Railway* from Calcutta to the Mutlah River has rendered the "Sea Island" cotton district of the Sunderbunds available for public enterprise, and by affording means of easy transit facilitates the supply of food and fuel required by the citizens of Calcutta.

The *Sinde Railway* was opened on the 13th of May, 1861; the cost of construction was estimated at eleven thousand pounds per mile. From the sea terminus at the port of Kurrachee to the river terminus at Kotree the line is in working order, with ample stations and accommodation for the transhipment of goods between the Indus and the Indian Ocean. The importance of this line will be developed when the river-navigation between the Punjab and Kurrachee comes into full operation.

The *Indus Steam Flotilla Company*, connected with the Sinde railway, has several vessels on the river and in course of construction, besides four steam-boats with ship-yards workshops and stores on the Indus, recently transferred by Government. Steamers employed in towing barges ply between Kurrachee and Mooltan; the upward voyage occupies eighteen days. Arrangements are in progress for extending steam-navigation from Mooltan up the Sutlej to Ferozepoor; also for the carriage of goods from Mooltan up to the Indus and to Kalabagh, from whence a road is planned by Government to facilitate communication with Peshawur.

The *Punjab Railway** was opened for traffic on 1st March, 1862. The distance between Lahore and Umritsur, thirty-two miles, was performed in less than an hour and a half, including a stoppage at Meean Meer. Thus the political and commercial capital of the Punjab, containing one hundred and twenty thousand citizens, is connected by cheap and rapid communication with the sacred city of Umritsur, which has a

* For information regarding the Sinde and Punjab railways and for the Map of the Euphrates Valley and Persian Gulf route, I am indebted to W. P. Andrew, Esq., Chairman of the Sinde and Lahore Railways.

fixed population of ninety thousand. The road runs through a densely peopled, fertile Seik country, whose resources will be increased by the opening of the Baree Doab Canal to Lahore, in the present year. The line from Lahore to Mooltan is in rapid progress. A line from Umritsur to Delhi, two hundred and eighty miles in length, has been sanctioned by Government, and the capital, two million five hundred thousand pounds, is to bear a guaranteed interest at the rate of five per cent. per annum. No works of any magnitude are required; the average height of embankment for the whole of the railway is only four feet, and ballast is easily procurable along the line. The total cost, including rolling stock, is estimated at less than eleven thousand pounds per mile. The city of Delhi is still depressed by the effects of the recent siege, yet its trade in 1860 was valued at four million pounds sterling. More than half a million travellers annually pass between Umritsur and Delhi through the Jullundur Doab. Kurrachee and Calcutta will now therefore be brought into direct communication by railway and steamboat, *viâ* Delhi, Umritsur, Lahore, Mooltan, and Hydrabad. It has been strongly urged on economical grounds, that the Indus ought to be made the highway from Europe, not only to Northern but to Central and Eastern India. But doubts have arisen as to the expediency of this scheme. The enormous outlay necessary for blasting the rocks, and performing other operations necessary to render the navigation of the river possible to large vessels by night as well as day, is not the only obstacle urged by practical men; the strength of the current and the occasional shallowness of the stream, with other drawbacks,* render it doubtful whether capital might not be

* The obstacles to the navigation of the Indus are clearly stated in the following memorandum, drawn up by Mr. Arthur Ormsby, late civil engineer in the Punjab:—

"The river Indus is navigable from its mouth, in the Gulf of Cutch, up to Attock, between Rawul Pindee and Peshawur, and the distance is upwards of 1000 miles. During the inundation the navigation is difficult, from the vast better expended in forming a cheap tram-line from Mooltan to Hydrabad, a distance of about six hundred miles, through

extent of country covered by the floods, so that the channel is quite uncertain and cannot be depended on even for a day. In dry weather the water is so low and so widely spread over the shallows that it is equally difficult to find the channel; and it is therefore a work of extreme labour—in fact, an impossibility—to come down the Indus without grounding, and at times sticking on the banks for hours, and sometimes days, together. The channel in the low season is both shallow and winding, so that when a vessel strikes the bank on one side, the recoil and force of the current brings her up head to stream, and in turning to go down stream she strikes the opposite bank so forcibly that anchors have to be got out to 'heave off' by. I have known this to happen five times during the day; and it took twelve days to go from the anchorage, fifteen miles below Mooltan, to Kotree; and as this is 600 miles, it appears that the rate of steaming on the Indus (going down stream in the low season, December, 1861) is only fifty miles per day, or about four miles per hour, while even this rate cannot be depended on, as vessels are sometimes hard and fast aground for days together. In the event of an injury happening to their machinery on the voyage up or down, there is no dépôt for repairing them, except at Kotree; and I met one of the steamers with her engines disabled, moored to the bank above Mittenkote, where she was obliged to remain until aid arrived from Kotree. The Indus is the most erratic of rivers; for its course one season may be eight to ten miles away from that of the preceding one; and the soil is of such a light sandy nature that the grounding of a vessel for an hour or so is sufficient to change and deepen one shoal while forming another. It may therefore be reasonably concluded that it would be much more advisable, in a commercial point of view, to make a light railway or tramway from Hyderabad to Mooltan than to expend any more money either upon the Indus or its 'flotilla.' The navigation never can be profitable until steamers can go ahead full speed, night and day, from Kotree to Mooltan, and *vice versâ*. So that it would take three days, or, say seventy-two hours, to make the trip both ways, at the rate of only ten miles an hour; while it could be done in a day and a half, if steamers that could go twenty miles an hour were placed upon the river, and that the river were so improved and preserved as would allow of their navigating it with equal confidence at night as in the day. The works required to make the Indus navigable, and to confine its course and preserve its depth, would be expensive and difficult; and even if that were done it would not insure punctuality, as the steamers are occasionally obliged to wait for hours until the fog that at times covers the surface of the river clears away.

"These observations are the result of remarks made during a trip down the river in the month of December 1861, on the steamer 'Lawrence;' and while I admit that it was a wise step to place such vessels upon the Indus, as a temporary measure, I am decidedly opposed to any further outlay on that account.

"With a clear navigation, where steamers can go twenty miles an hour with a large cargo, water-communication may be able to compete with rail-a flat region, along the margin of the Great Desert, with no engineering difficulty. The cost is estimated at less than four thousand pounds a mile. The land route would be used for passengers; and merchandize be conveyed by the river. It is not easy to exaggerate the national importance of being able to despatch troops from England, *viâ* the Euphrates and the Persian Gulf, to Kurrachee in one month, and thence by rail to most parts of India in twenty-four hours. "The Guards" might be placed at Delhi almost in as short a period as in Canada. With such rapid means of transit, the number of British troops in India might be reduced from eighty to fifty thousand men,—a number more than sufficient to garrison the great strongholds and large cities. While England maintains maritime supremacy, troops can be at all times landed in the East, at Kurrachee, with extraordinary rapidity, to repel invasion or quell insurrection. No European Power would dare to attack India *viâ* Persia, Afghanistan, or the Oxus, if the Indus and Euphrates valleys formed a connected military route for a British army.

Weekly intercourse between England and India is maintained on the Overland route, *viâ* Egypt and the Red Sea, by the Peninsular and Oriental Steam Navigation Company. This long established and successful corporation has a capital of two million five hundred thousand pounds sterling, by which a magnificent steam fleet of about fifty vessels, registering nearly seventy thousand tons, with ten thousand horse-power, is maintained. The organisation is admirable; the vessels are adapted for the navigation of the Atlantic and Mediterranean on one side of the Isthmus of Suez, and for the

ways; but as this is absolutely impossible on the Indus and its tributaries, I believe that the sooner a twenty-miles-an-hour railroad is made between Mooltan and Hyderabad the sooner will the surplus produce of the rich and fertile districts of the Punjab, Central Asia and Sinde be brought to a favourable market, and the sooner will the Punjab and Sinde Railway shareholders realise those dividends in the expectation of obtaining which they invested their money in that undertaking."

temperature and monsoons of the Red Sea and Indian Ocean. The service is performed with regularity, at a contract speed of ten knots an hour, the time being kept to the day. A railway from Alexandria to Suez facilitates the transit through Egypt. The time occupied in the journey between England and Bombay is as follows: Southampton to Gibraltar, five days, including three hours for coaling; thence along the Algerine coast to Malta, five days. Here the packet is joined by the Marseilles mail, which leaves London six days later than the Southampton mail, and crosses France. After six hours spent at Malta, three days bring the packet to Alexandria; from thence passengers and mails are conveyed by railway to Cairo, one hundred and sixty-two miles, in five hours; and from Cairo to Suez, ninety miles, in four hours; from Suez to Aden by steamboat in six days, allowing twelve hours for coaling; and eight days more bring them to Bombay. The distance traversed is five thousand nine hundred and two miles by land and sea, from Southampton to Alexandria; and five thousand nine hundred and forty-four miles, from Suez to Bombay: in all, eleven thousand eight hundred and forty-six miles by sea, and two hundred and fifty-two by land. Thus, a journey of twelve thousand and ninety-eight miles is accomplished in twenty-nine to thirty days.

During twenty years the Peninsular and Oriental Service has lost only one life by shipwreck. A fleet of five hundred colliers is employed in supplying coals for the different stations, and about ten thousand persons are employed in various departments.

Notwithstanding the merits and success of this powerful association, it is desirable that a communication by rail and steam-boat should be established between England and India, *viâ* the Euphrates valley and the Persian Gulf. The Red Sea route is now occupied, not only with the Indian traffic, but with that of China, Australasia, and the Mauritius. This traffic is yearly augmenting; and commercial considerations, as well as political circumstances, necessitate the opening of a new and shorter route than that by Aden. The proposed line runs from the port of Seleucia in the Mediterranean to Jaibar Castle on the Euphrates, by rail, one hundred and fifty miles; thence by river or rail to Bussorah, at the head of the Persian Gulf. From Bussorah to Kurrachee there would be a sea voyage of one thousand miles, unless a railway were made through Beloochistan.

It is calculated that the journey from England to Kurrachee, at the mouth of the Indus, *viâ* Trieste, may be performed in fifteen days; that is, in half the time occupied by the present Red Sea route. Merchandise and passengers are now conveyed by caravans and camels along the Euphrates valley; but if assisted by a moderate subsidy a rail might be constructed at a cost of six million sterling, which would materially promote the commerce of Europe and Asia.

The formation of railways in India is tedious and costly, owing to the numerous bridges and viaducts required. On the *East Indian* railway, the construction of the bridges formed a great engineering difficulty; that over the Sone consists of twenty-eight spans of one hundred and fifty feet each, and is formed like the others with a brick or stone foundation, and a wrought-iron superstructure; the rails are laid upon the top of the girders, leaving the space beneath available for an ordinary carriage road, eleven feet wide. The *Jumna* bridge has fifteen spans of two hundred feet each. These bridges from two of the finest structures in the world. On eight other rivers the spans vary from fifty to one hundred and fifty feet each; and an idea of their extent may be formed from the fact that the water-way of the Jumna, Tonse, Keeul, and Hullohur bridges is nine thousand one hundred and fifty feet, while that of the London, Southwark, Blackfriars, Waterloo, Hungerford, and New Westminster bridges over the Thames, is only six thousand six hundred and nine feet.

On the western side of India, the chief obstacle is that of

passing from Bombay over the barrier range of mountains which separate the low sea-coast from the high table land of the Deccan. These mountains are crossed by the *Great Indian Peninsula* at two points. The Bhore Ghaut is more than two thousand feet above the sea; the incline is fifteen miles in length; the average gradient one in forty-eight, the steepest, one in thirty-seven; the length of the tunnelling one mile and forty-four chains: the estimated cost per mile is forty-eight thousand pounds. The Thull Ghaut, above nineteen hundred feet high, has an incline nine miles long, with gradients as above, and two thousand yards of tunnelling: the estimated cost is fifty thousand pounds per mile. A viaduct over the estuary of the Tannah River comprises twenty-three masonry arches of thirty feet span, and an iron girder opening in the centre, of eighty-four feet span. The Nerbudda, Taptee, Beema and five other large rivers are bridged.

In the south and in the east of India the country generally speaking is favourable to railway operations, excepting that there are numerous rivers to be crossed, which is also the case on the Sinde line. The bridge over the Bahrun is six hundred yards in span, built of hard, white, durable stone; that over the Mulleer, five hundred and sixty yards long, is composed of iron girders of sixty feet span, resting on stone piers. Expensive embankments are required to prevent inundations. The contractors in Sinde are principally natives of Cutch. There is only one tunnel in lower Bengal, extending nine hundred feet through a quartz rock in the neighbourhood of Monghyr. The average cost of the lines is estimated at sixteen thousand pounds per mile; probably it will reach twenty thousand pounds. Passenger fares range from $2\frac{1}{4}$*d.* to $\frac{3}{8}$ths of a penny, and goods from $3\frac{3}{4}$*d.* to $1\frac{1}{8}$*d.* per ton, per mile.

The number of Europeans employed is large; in October 1860, there were in India, on six hundred and eighty-six miles of open rail, above eleven hundred Europeans, and seventeen thousand five hundred Native officials engaged in the secretariat, locomotive, engineer, traffic and general store departments, exclusive of the artisans and labourers on the respective lines. Natives are superseding Europeans as station-masters and in various departments. The pay of station-masters is from five pounds to fifteen pounds per month; guards, seven pounds ten shillings to fifteen pounds, according to length of service and merit. Engine-drivers from England earn sixteen to twenty pounds, those trained in India, twelve to fifteen pounds per month. Skilled Native labourers, carpenters, masons, and blacksmiths, tenpence to a shilling, and ordinary labourers, twopence-halfpenny to fourpence per day.*

The conveyance of railway materials from England to India, consisting of iron rails, sleepers, girders for bridges, locomotives and other rolling stock, turn-tables and various machinery, has been very large and given much employment to shipping; thus, for the East India railway alone, vessels carrying three hundred and fifty thousand tons have been employed in ten years. During the year 1860-61, the raw materials despatched from England for nine Indian lines amounted to two hundred and thirty-five thousand tons, valued at considerably more than two millions sterling. The average weight of the rails is seventy-five pounds a yard; so that one mile of single line requires for its conveyance one hundred and twenty tons of shipping. From the commencement of the exportation to the close of the year 1860, above nine hundred thousand tons of shipping have been sent to India.

Tonnage of Vessels carrying railway materials.

	Tons.
Up to 1854	77,200
1855	111,642
1856	126,835
1857	123,103
1858	147,844
1859	208,280
1860	234,710
Total	929,614

* 'Railway Report,' by Juland Danvers, Esq., p. 9.

The proprietors of shares in Indian railways number seventeen thousand, of whom only six hundred and seventy-nine are registered in India; of these, three hundred and thirty-six are natives.

Roads.

Hitherto, except on the great military highways, roads have been culpably neglected, and there is now much to be done.

There are eleven Imperial trunk roads existing, or under construction in Bengal, whose aggregate length is two thousand miles; there are eleven hundred miles of Imperial branch roads, and above six hundred miles of "feeder" roads projected; the latter will bring the most important towns and marts in communication with the railways. It is intended to make several tramways in connection with rail and river transit, at a cost of about two thousand eight hundred pounds per mile, to be worked by animal or by steam power. A Company is being established in London, with one million sterling capital, to construct these tramways.

A grand trunk road extending from Peshawur, the North-West outpost of India, to Calcutta, a distance of fourteen hundred miles, cost about one thousand pounds per mile, and requires fifty thousand pounds a year to keep it in repair.

A purely military road runs along the whole line of frontier posts from the Peyzoo Pass on the north of the Dehra Ismael Khan frontier to the Sinde boundary, a distance of three hundred and eighty miles. This road is kept by the frontier field officers, is passable in all weathers for cavalry and guns, and is very valuable for political purposes. A line of road, partly military, partly civil, proceeds from the Peyzoo Pass, *viâ* Bunnoo, and thence *viâ* Buhadoor Kheyl to Kohat, distance one hundred and twenty miles. From Kohat to Peshawur, there is a made road except through the Pass, which is traversible for troops. There are one hundred and fifty-two miles of lesser military roads connecting Head Quarters in the Punjab with district posts.

Soon after the annexation of the Punjab, a great trunk road was commenced to connect Lahore and Peshawur, the route lying through a region where wheel carriage is almost unknown. The estimated cost of the work is upwards of a million sterling. It is difficult to convey an idea of the obstacles to be overcome in the construction of a highway forty feet wide, with sharp slopes and steep gradients, with cuttings and embankments sixty feet in height or in depth; and in carrying the line across valleys filled by distorted and half indurated strata worn by the action of water into fantastic gullies and pinnacles,—over the uplying plains and undulating country of the central region between the Jhelum and the Indus, interrupted by sudden and deep ravines, and many rivers of formidable volume and velocity. The construction of an embankment across a ravine of sixty feet in width necessitates a culvert of two hundred, and if oblique of three hundred feet in length, in order to afford a waterway of ten, twenty or thirty feet for the sudden discharge of rain from a mountain region. The Governor-General declared that no engineering work in India had impressed him so strongly with its grandeur and utility and with the difficulties to be overcome; and he considered its prosecution "one at least of the elements which impressed the most manly race in India with the vigour and beneficence of British rule, and, under Providence, tended, through the maintenance of order and active loyalty in the Punjab, to the recovery of Hindoostan." The work done or doing in a country almost devoid of skilled labour is surprising.* There are required—bridges of twenty to forty feet span, fifteen; of forty to eighty feet, twenty-six; of eighty to one hundred feet, seven; of one hundred to two hundred feet, ten; of two hundred to four hundred feet, eight; of four hundred to five hundred feet, two. Seventy-one tunnels are needed, in length from

* 'General Report on the Administration of British India in 1859-60' (printed at Calcutta in 1861), pp. xxxvi.-xl.

one hundred to two hundred and fifty feet; and three hundred and eighty-nine drains with ten to twenty feet water way. The masonry is of the most solid and durable character.

In 1850, Lord Dalhousie sanctioned the formation of a road practicable for beasts of burden (sixteen feet wide in some places) from the plains of Hindoostan (Kalka, thirty-six miles from Umballah) to Simla, with branch lines to the hilly stations and sanitaria of Dugshai, Kussowlie, and Subathoo. From Simla the road traverses the salubrious valley of the Sutlej; crossing the river, it ascends to the village of Chini, in the healthy and beautiful district of Kunawar, then onwards by Thibet to the Chinese frontier, which is reached at a point where practicable roads stretch eastwards and northwards towards the emporia of Garoo and Yarkund, passing through the shawl-wool and borax producing districts of Changtong and Rudok, and affording means of communication with Central Asia. Bungalows have been constructed along the line, a distance of about two hundred miles, for the accommodation of travellers at each stage of ten miles, thus obviating the necessity for their being burdened with camp equipage.

The highest elevation of this extraordinary road over the Himalaya is at Kundoolah, where it is nearly ten thousand feet above the sea. The engineering triumphs include a tunnel, five hundred and sixty feet long, in which ten thousand convicts and eight thousand four hundred and fifty free labourers were employed; several strong and handsome viaducts, one two hundred and twelve feet long; and ranges of cliffs cut down to a depth of one hundred and thirty feet. Work can be carried on here only during a part of the year, owing to the severity of the Alpine climate.

The mode of facilitating the passage of the Indus river at Attock, the great outpost on the Western frontier of the British dominions, has been much discussed. The Indus at its low level in February discharges forty-five thousand cubic feet of water each second through a channel of four hundred and forty feet in width; the surface velocity at the centre is then nine miles an hour. The extraordinary swiftness of the stream, and its liability at uncertain periods to great floods, render the passage at present very precarious. During eight months of the year, the transit is effected over a bridge of thirty boats, which cost five hundred pounds each; for the other four months, twenty-eight ferry boats, which cost eighty pounds each, are used; but they afford a tedious and dangerous passage. A steam ferry has failed; suspension and other bridges have been suggested, and now it is proposed to make a tunnel under the Indus, where the breadth is fifteen hundred feet. Government has sanctioned the experiment of a shaft being carried beneath the bed of the river to ascertain whether there is any copious influx of water from springs, or from filtration through fissures in the rocky bed of the stream. Considerable progress has been made in sinking perpendicular shafts at each side of the river, of one hundred and one hundred and seventy feet depth each. From the shaft-bottom two galleries proceed under the river-bed, and at the level of the Lahore and Peshawur road a gallery has been driven in to meet the perpendicular shaft, by which the drainage-water and rock excavated are removed. The work is carried on night and day by European and Native soldiers, under military engineer officers; and the Natives "think far more of the tunnel than of the railway works or telegraph lines; many come from distant places to visit it, especially from beyond the Khyber." * If the shafts now commenced at each side prove successful, it is estimated that a tunnel may be constructed for fifty thousand pounds. The military command of the transit is essential, and the tunnel entrances could be easily and effectually secured.

Many of the Indian rivers are bridged with boats, which

* Memorandum by Sir R. Montgomery, dated 6th May, 1861.

serve as ferries when the water is low and the stream not rapid. In the Punjab, the Chenab and Jhelum are crossed by one hundred boats, the Ravee by seventy, and the Indus by fifty. On these boat-bridges there is a double roadway of twenty-four feet wide, which will support the most ponderous artillery.

The North-West Provinces and Central India are deficient in means of transit and intercourse. In Oude, the Lucknow and Cawnpoor road, forty-eight miles in length, is in good order; several streets, one hundred and fifty feet broad, have been formed through the city of Lucknow; two of these wide thoroughfares radiate from the stone bridge fort. The fortifications commanding the city are complete. The internal communications between different districts are in rapid progress: eight hundred and eighty-three miles of new road have been finished, four hundred and fifty miles of old road repaired, three hundred and twenty-seven miles of road aligned; and one hundred and fourteen bridges, some of large span, have been built. These works have been principally executed from the Road Fund, aided by the grant of a lakh of rupees. A railway is projected from Cawnpoor to Lucknow, and thence to Fyzabad. There are some good highways in the Madras Presidency and a few in Bombay; that from Bombay to Poona is equal to an English turnpike road.

Canals and Irrigation.

Public skill and capital have for some time been directed to a system for rendering rivers available for both transit and irrigation. The upper waters of the rivers Ganges and Jumna have been turned into canals; the Ganges affords above eight hundred miles of watercourse; the West Jumna, four hundred and twenty-five, and the East Jumna, one hundred and fifty-five miles.

In the Dehra Doon, the sole provision of water for man and beast is made by canals, owing to the great depth at which water is found, which renders well-sinking impracticable. Until the lesser canals were made in this district, large tracts of fertile land were covered with jungle and wild grass; now they are gradually being occupied by a thriving population.

The Ganges, the Western Jumna, the Eastern Jumna, and the Rohilcund canals, all yield a profit on the outlay; in 1859-60 the Eastern Jumna afforded a clear revenue of ten thousand pounds. The Western Jumna and other canals yielded for 1859-60 a revenue of thirty-six thousand pounds, against sixteen thousand pounds current expenses and establishments, independent of the indirect revenue obtained by increased land-rents throughout the Paniput, Delhi, Rohtuck, and Hissar districts, which, in a season of drought, entirely depend on the canal water. An injury has arisen from some of the canals being in parts above the level of the adjacent country; and, owing to an unscientific construction of their beds, the drainage has been checked, and swamps formed. Moreover, by excess of water a coating of salts is brought to the surface, which deteriorates the productive power of the soil, and impairs the physical condition of the people. A system of permanent drainage is now being devised to remedy the evil.

In no province has so much been done by Government for irrigation as in the Punjab. The soil is a desert without water, but with it the whole may be made one garden, or, in the words of Arnold, the Lombardy of India.* Sloping gently to the southward, watered by fine rivers and several smaller streams which flow on two sides from hills and mountains that "drink the clouds," † it is exactly the region suited for canals, and the Mogul emperors gave much attention to their formation, as is attested by existing watercourses and the traces of others. In 1663 the Mogul emperor Shah Jehan brought the water of the Ravee one hundred and ten miles

* 'Marquis Dalhousie's Administration of British India,' by E. Arnold, M.A., vol. i., Punjaub, p. 368. † Ibid.

to supply the fountains of his palace gardens at Lahore, and the Seiks now use the canal to fill the sacred tank at Umritsur. Lord Dalhousie, always particularly zealous for the success of his favourite annexation, followed the example of the Moslem rulers and of Runjeet Singh by adopting liberal plans for the maintenance and improvement of the canals which existed on his assumption of the Punjab, for the repair of such as were defective, and for the construction of new sources of irrigation. The most important of these works is the Baree Doab (between the Sutlej and the Ravee), which taps the waters of the last named stream where it bursts from the rocky ledge of the sub-Himalaya. The canal then passes on to Umritsur and Lahore, has several branches, and discharges its waters into the Ravee and its confluents at Mooltan. When completed, the main channel will be two hundred and forty-seven miles long, and the Lahore, Kussoor and Sobraon branches two hundred and nineteen miles long: in all, four hundred and sixty-six miles in length. The channels are navigable throughout, the depth varying from two to five feet, and the width from sixteen to one hundred and twenty feet. Two hundred and fifty thousand trees are flourishing on the banks, and about one hundred and fifty thousand have been planted in nurseries. More than fifty miles of the work are complete. The cost of the whole canal, with its distributing channels, is estimated at one million five hundred thousand pounds. There are seven hundred and fifty-four miles of canal roads and fences.

Several canals for agricultural irrigation are in course of construction; one at Mitra, in the Hyderabad collectorate (Sinde), of ninety miles long and twenty feet deep, is in great part accomplished, and land in its vicinity is much sought by farmers.

In the Madras Presidency, large sums of money have been expended on anicuts and embankments for the rivers

Godavery, Kistna and Cauvery, and in the making and improving of channels in connexion with a general system of irrigation and canal navigation.

The *Madras Irrigation and Canal Company* was sanctioned by the Council of India in January 1859; and in October 1859, a report of the Government engineer was made on its first projected work, viz., the diversion of the waters of the Toombuddra into the rivers Kundar and Pennar, to provide irrigation to the Kundar valley and to the Nellore district; and, by connexion with the Eastern Coast Canal, afford water communication from Madras to Kurnoul. On this important work five thousand people find daily employment, under a staff of eight civil engineers, sent from England.

The capital of the Company is one million pounds, on which the Indian Government guarantees an interest of five per cent. per annum; all surplus profits beyond that rate are divisible between Government and the Company; such arrangement to be determined only by Government purchasing the works of the Company within six months after the expiration of periods of twenty-five years, at a sum equal to the market value of the shares of the Company, on an average of the three preceding years.

Owing to the skill and unwearying exertion of Colonel (now Sir Arthur) Cotton, the Godavery river is navigable for a considerable distance, and a highway to the ocean is thus being opened for the rich districts of Berar.

The profits on works of public utility are very large. The late Colonel Baird Smith stated that the irrigation canals in Northern India would pay at the rate of fifty per cent. Mr. John Dickinson, who has done so much for India, says, "The dividends of the Ganges Navigation Company have been from fifty to eighty per cent.; those of the Rajahmundry Transit Company have been fifty-five per cent.; those of the Ganges Canal Company have been thirty per cent.; those of the East India Railway Company's steamboats have been one hundred per cent."*

The canals in the Punjab are now beginning to yield a revenue to the State, by the letting out of their waters for irrigation. The Huslee, an old Native canal, affords an income of nearly ten thousand pounds, while three thousand pounds cover the charges for its maintenance. The banks of the Huslee are adorned by seventy-three thousand flourishing trees, with several nurseries.

Telegraphs.

Telegraphic communication was commenced during the administration of the Marquis of Dalhousie, under the superintendence of Sir W. B. O'Shaughnessy. The system now extends over eleven thousand miles of territory, and there are one hundred and fifty offices open for public correspondence. A large part of the wires have been placed on durable iron posts, of which forty thousand with stone-ware insulators have been laid down. As the mean duration of timber supports is but five years, and the cost of replacing them is at least four thousand pounds per annum, measures are being adopted for the substitution of iron standards throughout India. Multiple wires are used in several localities, and powerful screw-clamps, which grasp each wire tightly at the posts, and prevent its slipping off or coming in actual contact with another wire. The heavy tropical rains cause little or no diversion of currents from wire to wire. Rain or distilled water is, in fact, an excellent insulator of voltaic currents of low tension, which are used for signalling. During the years 1859-60, the line was frequently worked direct from Calcutta to Bombay, *viâ* Benares, Agra and Indoor, a distance of sixteen hundred miles; also from

* 'Cotton Crisis and Public Works in India,' by John Dickinson, Chairman of the India Reform Society (London, 1862, p. 23).

Kurrachee to Bangalore, a distance of eighteen hundred miles; and mail messages have been sent from Bombay to Agra, eight hundred miles apart, in five minutes; and a service message has been sent from Simla to Coonoor in the Neilgherries, a distance of two thousand miles, and an answer received in four hours and a half.

The "Morse" system of signalling is being generally adopted, by means of seventy assistants from England; and in nearly all the offices the signallers receive perfectly by ear; reading from the paper-tape, with its clockwork and roller mechanism, is now discarded. Complete sets of a very simple, cheap instrument, equal in finish and solidity to the best Prussian manufacture, are made in the Bangalore workshop. A school of signallers at Coonoor has proved successful, and supplied fifty-eight well-trained officials in eleven months, at an expense of two hundred rupees each; while the youths brought from England cost Government sixteen hundred rupees each by the time they are landed in India. Local signal-schools are in process of formation.

The staff employed consists of a superintendent in India and Ceylon, at a salary of three thousand six hundred pounds per annum; three deputy-superintendents for east, west, and south divisions, at six hundred pounds each; ten deputy-superintendents of circles at a monthly salary of four hundred to five hundred rupees; five assistant deputy-superintendents of circles (three hundred to three hundred and fifty rupees monthly); seventeen first-class inspectors (two hundred and fifty rupees); thirty-two second-class inspectors (one hundred and fifty to two hundred rupees); thirty-six third-class inspectors (one hundred rupees); one hundred and seventeen assistants in charge of offices, not inspectors; twenty-two head signallers; three hundred and sixty-nine signallers; one hundred and two probationers; two sub-inspectors; five overseers; eighty-five artificers; thirty-five assistant-artificers; one hundred and sixty-one accountants, clerks and writers;

sixty-one mounted line-guards; and a variety of other line-guards, artificers and messengers.

Special telegraph-stamps are on sale at the Treasuries and stamp-offices all over India, by which persons residing at places where there are no stations may send their telegrams prepaid by post, to the nearest office.

Perfect success has attended the arrangements for the protection of the telegraph buildings, instruments and signallers from the effects of lightning. The signallers do not now heed the worst thunder-storms. Of two hundred Morse instruments in use, only two suffered injury during the years 1859-60; but the teeth of the brass lightning-plates and the safety coils are melted in great numbers by lightning.

TELEGRAMS SENT THROUGHOUT INDIA.

Years.	Service.	Private.	Total.
1858–59	56,670	101,164	157,834
1859–60	31,868	170,566	202,434

The diminution in the number of messages on Government service in 1859-60 was caused by requiring cash payments for them, and by abolishing the right of precedence, except in urgent cases. The increase in private messages was mainly occasioned by reductions in the tariff, "amounting to seventy-five per cent. on the mass of transactions."

The total expenditure in 1859-60 was one hundred and seventy-two thousand pounds, chiefly employed in the construction of new lines. The receipts were: private messages, forty-two thousand four hundred pounds; service messages, twelve thousand pounds; total, fifty-four thousand pounds. Native merchants and Native correspondents sent seventy-one thousand five hundred and fifty-four messages. Their communications are increasing so that they generally give as much work as the lines can perform. The business from the European community is comparatively small. One-half the private messages contained from one to sixteen words. There are ten circles, and the following statement shows the amount of business done in each.

	Number of Messages.	Miles of Line.
Bengal and North-West Provinces to Agra ..	39,315	1700
Bombay ..	43,228	1499
Madras ..	31,030	1038
Central India ..	6,366	1267
Indoor ..	5,491	708
East Coast ..	9,871	1027
Ceylon and South-East Coast ..	10,760	597
Pegu ..	6,513	404
Punjab, Rohilcund, and Oude ..	12,356	1500
Sinde ..	5,660	766

The head-quarters are at Bangalore. It is proposed to establish telegraphic and commercial communication between Rangoon and the western inland half of China through Eastern Pegu and Burmah, aided by the rivers Maka and Kiang-Hung, which are navigable for a long distance by deeply-laden boats. The telegraph wires now stretch from Calcutta to Rangoon; and they may be extended to Hong-Kong and the British consular ports in northern China. Russia is forming telegraph lines from St. Petersburg to the settlements on the Amoor, along the Northern Pacific, and the newly acquired port of Novogorod and its arsenal in the Sea of Japan.*

A Company was formed in 1858 for the establishment of telegraphic communication between Egypt and India, *viâ* the Red Sea. Her Majesty's Government guaranteed an interest of four-and-a-half per cent. on a capital of £800,000 for a term of fifty years. The line was successfully laid between Suez and Aden under water; but a failure occurred in the cable between Aden and India, which put a stop to further operations, the whole of the capital having been expended.

In 1861, another Company was formed, for the purpose of

* Aërial Telegraph to and Commerce with China, with an excellent Map, by Captain Sprye, and R. H. F. Sprye, 1862.

purchasing the "plant" of the old Company, and laying down a new cable. This Association has fulfilled the terms of its engagement with Government; subscribed two-thirds of the stipulated capital, despatched a steamer with two hundred miles of cable on board, and applied for transfer of line from former Company, whose guarantee is to be converted into an annuity at the rate of four and a half per cent. on the capital, for the unexpired residue of the term during which the guarantee was granted. As few practical difficulties are believed to exist either by the Red Sea or the Persian Gulf, it may be expected that in a short period there will be daily communication between London and Calcutta.

Post-Office.

The state of this Department affords a good indication of the progress of the country. There is one General Post-office for all India, and about one thousand Post-offices and agencies,* which distribute in the course of the year, from house to house, fifty million letters and covers, at a lower rate of postage for a single letter than in any other country in the world.

The increase of correspondence in India is remarkable. Prior to 1854-55, the rate of postage was high; in that year the charge for a single letter was reduced to half an anna (less than one penny). The number of letters passing through the post, at the high rate, was under twenty million. Since then they have yearly augmented, and in 1860-61 amounted to forty-eight million.

The number of chargeable newspapers increased from one million five hundred thousand in 1854-55, to six million in 1858-59. The diminution of European troops has lessened the number of newspapers. The stamped covers for books and pamphlets have increased from one hundred and thirty-three

* Post-offices, 848; receiving-houses, 66, exclusive of British Burmah.

thousand in 1854-55 to above three hundred thousand in 1860-61. The Indian Post-office may ultimately rival in magnitude that of Britain.*

The Post-office officials comprise a Director-General, five Postmasters-General, forty-six inspecting Postmasters, eight hundred and thirty-eight Postmasters, and Deputy Postmasters; above eleven hundred Clerks, of whom five hundred and thirty-nine are English; two thousand two hundred Postmen and other servants of the Post-office; twenty thousand persons employed in the Road establishment, consisting of superintendents, overseers, runners, bearers, coachmen, ostlers, boatmen, and others; seven hundred bullock-train guard; making a total of about twenty-five thousand—of whom five thousand one hundred and forty-eight are in Bengal; four thousand nine hundred, in Madras; four thousand one hundred and ninety-seven, in Bombay; and ten thousand three hundred and twenty-seven in the North-West Provinces, Punjab and elsewhere.

The Mails are conveyed through India by railway ten thousand and forty-six miles; by mail cart and on horseback five thousand seven hundred and forty miles; by runners and boats thirty-six thousand seven hundred and eighty-four miles;—total, forty-three thousand five hundred and seventy

* The number of post-offices in the United Kingdom is 11,441, of which 818 are head, and 10,623 sub-post-offices; in addition to which there are 2473 road letter boxes; through all these there passed during the year 1860 no less than 564,000,000 letters, and 82,000,000 newspapers and book packets, giving employment to 25,282 officials—of whom 11,428 were postmasters, 11,889 letter-carriers, 1634 clerks, and 195 mail-guards. In England and Wales the deliveries were 462,000,000, or 22 to each individual; in Scotland, 54,000,000, or 18; and in Ireland, 48,000,000, or 8 per annum. On an average, each person in London annually receives 43 letters; in Edinburgh, 36; in Dublin, 34; in Manchester and Birmingham, 28; and in Liverpool, 26. The mails travel daily 39,047 miles by rail, 32,297 by coach or cart, and 69,994 by walking messengers. 2,390,000 covers were not delivered, chiefly on account of insufficient directions, and of these 10,000 letters were not even directed. The average charge for mail service by rail was 7¾*d.*, by coach 2½*d.*, and by pedestrian 1½*d.* per mile. The gross revenue was 3,524,710*l.*, the net expenditure, exclusive of packet service, 2,422,231*l.*

miles. The value of the postage labels sold in 1860-61 was one hundred and sixty thousand pounds. Total receipts of the Indian Post Office, four hundred and twenty thousand pounds.

Public Works.

This Department is every year expanding in each Presidency, and supervises a great variety of labour on military and civil buildings, roads, bridges, rivers, canals, tanks, and irrigation. The work to be done throughout India is enormous, and Government is endeavouring to educate a class of civil engineers,* both European and Native, fitted to direct public undertakings, and enable leading citizens and wealthy landed proprietors to originate and execute required improvements.

A certain number of appointments in the Civil Engineer establishment and in the subordinate offices of the Department of Public Works are open to public competition in the United Kingdom. Of the successful competitors, one-half in each class, with the designation of Probationers of the first and second classes respectively, are sent to Bengal; the other half, in equal proportions, to Madras and Bombay. From the date of embarkation, or as may be arranged in their covenants, and while studying in India, they receive a salary of seventeen pounds and of eight pounds five shillings a month respectively. When they are pronounced by the Principal of the Thomason College at Roorkee sufficiently qualified, and have acquired a colloquial knowledge of one of the Native languages, they are transferred to the effective Establishment of the Public Works Department, with the grade to which their attainments entitle them. The plan appears to be good, but it is understood to be undergoing some alteration.

A trigonometrical survey of India has been in progress

* General Report on the Administration of British India, 1859-61, Public Works Department, p. 13.

since the commencement of the present century. The meridional arc for the survey is the largest measurement of the kind that has been made. The arc extends from Cape Comorin, in 8° 5", to Dehra, in 30° 19" N. lat.—a distance of one thousand three hundred and thirty-four geographical miles, with a breadth varying from fifteen to twenty miles. About two-thirds of India have been surveyed, and a large number of the maps engraved on a scale of four miles to an inch. Local surveys for revenue purposes are in progress; they include village boundaries and other demarcations, and are nearly complete for Bengal and the North-West Provinces. Those of Madras and Bombay are in progress.

CLASSIFIED EXPENDITURE OF GOVERNMENT ON PUBLIC WORKS

CLASSIFICATION OF WORKS.	Bengal.	North-West Provinces.	Punjab.	Oude.	Madras.
	£.	£.	£.	£.	£.
Military; Barracks, Forts, &c. ..	48,147	138,523	75,891	368,123	174,630
Marine; Harbours	..	..	..	..	..
Naval; Dockyards, &c.	..	..	..	..	..
Judicial { Buildings	2,266	1,000	..	..	8,000
Judicial { Gaols	6,700	..	..	..	..
Revenue; Buildings, &c.	14,507	..	..	..	..
Industrial; Mines, &c.	..	..	7,998	..	..
Ecclesiastical; Churches, &c. ..	..	920	..	2,335	..
Educational; Schools, &c.	900	1,700	..	..	..
Agricultural { Irrigation	..	..	..	..	5,765
Agricultural { Canals	..	1,679,283	1,023,712	..	20,478
Agricultural { Embankments ..	4,700	..	..	..	..
Agricultural { Other works	4,000	..	..	..	..
Communications { Roads	24,400	20,911	746,414	..	34,298
Communications { Bridges	51,662	..	..	..	27,725
Miscellaneous Civil Buildings ..	..	6,450	..	..	..
Minor works not enumerated	31,736	4,916	2,905	400	14,257
Totals	189,018	1,853,703	1,856,920	370,858	285,153
Electric Telegraph	73,707	..	16,617		43,627
Railways	3,467,548		282,925	..	1,117,530
Total Expenditure	5,583,976		2,527,320		1,446,310
Total Expenditure sanctioned for 1860-61	515,000	610,000	510,000	250,000	620,000
Original work and repairs, exclusive of railways or private undertakings, 1860-61	510,000	630,000	520,000	190,000	640,000

*. About 70,000*l.* was reserved by Government for future appropriation at the time these data

IN INDIA FOR 1859-60 AND TOTAL EXPENDITURE FOR 1860-61.

Bombay.	Sinde.	Tenasserim and Martaban.	Hyderabad.	Hyderabad Assigned Districts.	Coorg.	Mysoor.	Nagpoor.	Pegu.	Total India.
£.	£.	£.	£.	£.	£.	£.	£.	£.	£.
96,451	..	1,000	6,157	..	..	..	Amount not given.	Amount not given.	908,922
..	4,000	..	..	..	..	..			4,000
6,649	..	..	..	..	..	..			6,649
..	..	1,250	..	..	..	..			12,516
1,002	..	..	..	..	..	..			7,702
..	..	..	..	11,992	..	500			20,999
..	..	..	..	..	..	..			7,998
..	..	..	..	..	..	..			3,255
..	..	..	..	..	..	..			2,600
..	..	..	..	..	..	600			6,365
2,542	..	..	..	..	..	..			2,726,015
..	..	..	..	..	..	..			4,700
..	..	..	..	..	..	..			4,000
64,761	3,267	..	2,502	..	..	..			896,553
..	..	..	..	..	..	..			79,387
16,381	..	..	..	..	..	..			22,831
4,744	..	642	386	..	100	..			60,086
192,530	7,267	2,892	9,045	11,992	100	1,100	..	..	4,780,578
20,851	12,123	..	..	..	..	..	..	5,118	172,043
1,791,123	547,873	..	..	..	..	..	..	..	7,206,999
2,004,504	567,263	2,892	9,045	11,992	100	1,100	..	5,118	12,159,620
505,000		20,000	55,000		5,000	..	60,000	110,000	2,740,000
500,000		40,000	42,500		2,500	..	75,000	100,000	3,257,000

were furnished. Since then a further sum of 120,000*l.* has been employed in public works.

CHAPTER VII.

COMMERCE, SHIPPING AND PRODUCTS OF INDIA.

THE maritime trade of India is everywhere rapidly increasing. When the East India Company possessed a monopoly of its commerce, evidence was repeatedly tendered to Parliament to show the impossibility of extending the consumption of British manufactures; but since then the value of the exports from the United Kingdom has been augmented more than fivefold and is still susceptible of indefinite expansion. The trade of India was thrown open in 1814, that of China in 1834. In the latter year the total imports of India were in value:—

	£.
Merchandise	4,261,106
Treasure	1,893,023
	£5,154,129

The total exports for the same year were in value:—

	£.
Merchandise	7,993,420
Treasure	194,740
	£8,088,160

These figures contrast strongly with the following returns for the years 1855-56, 1859-60. (See next page.)

The twenty-four millions' worth of imports and the twenty-eight millions' worth of exports returned for 1859-60 as the declared value is much within the actual amount of the trade. Estimating the population of all India at two hundred millions, it seems reasonable to suppose that the import of British manufactures might be raised to twenty shillings per head, which is less than the consumption of the coloured population

COMPARATIVE STATEMENT SHOWING THE TRADE OF THE SEVERAL PRESIDENCIES OR PROVINCES OF BRITISH INDIA WITH FOREIGN OR EXTERNAL PORTS FOR THE YEARS 1855–56 AND 1859–60.

PRESIDENCIES OR PROVINCES.	IMPORTS.						EXPORTS.					
	1855-56.*		1859-60.		1860-61.†		1855-56.*		1859-60.		1860-61.†	
	Merchandise.	Treasure.	Merchandise.	Treasure.	Merchandise.	Treasure.	Merchandise.	Treasure.	Merchandise.	Treasure.	Merchandise.	Treasure.
At and from Ports in—	£.	£.	£.	£.	£.	£.	£.	£.	£.	£.	£.	£.
Bengal . .	7,505,538	5,457,287	12,557,209	7,694,168			12,528,798	83,299	12,125,501	390,928		
Pegu . .	235,946	15,127	330,837	65,099			236,861	8,100	114,147	4,242		
Tenasserim and Martaban . .	117,212	7,440	59,073	11,212	No	Returns.	171,141	21,137	268,842	120	No	Returns.
Madras. .	1,349,386	852,487	1,938,682	1,062,164			1,964,500	70,730	2,312,735	179,421		
Bombay .	4,585,523	4,965,856	9,016,449	7,518,332			8,111,529	417,810	13,034,928	353,085		
Sinde . .	149,889	3,091	362,890	5,988			25,430	100	104,050	1,211		
Total India	13,943,494	11,301,288	24,265,140	16,356,963			23,038,259	601,176	27,960,203	929,007		
Total Merchandise and Treasure for each Year	25,244,782		40,622,103				23,639,435		28,889,210			

* Earliest date for which separate Returns for each Presidency or Province have been received.
† The Returns for 1860-61 have not arrived in England.

population in our West Indian colonies. This enhancement would produce an export of manufactured goods from the United Kingdom to India to the value of two hundred million sterling; whereas according to the annexed table, the present value is within eighteen million, which is small in comparison to what it may become shortly if this increase continues in the ratio shown in the returns on the opposite page.

The rapidity with which the British cotton-goods trade augments, is evidenced in a recent Parliamentary return.* Thus the exports from the United Kingdom to the "British territories in India, continental and insular," of cotton piece-goods, were in the—

Years.	Yards.	Value.	Value of Cotton Goods and Yarn.
		£.	£.
1855-1856	945,343,529	10,549,424	13,142,921
1859-1860	1,793,285,596	22,661,648	27,139 548

The years 1857, 1858 were those of the mutiny, when trade was suspended in many places, especially at the largest marts for Manchester goods, viz., Delhi, Agra, Cawnpoor, and Futtehghur; but in the two subsequent years the exports were double the amount of the two years previous to 1857. In the year 1860-61 the grievous famine in the North-West Provinces, which spread over districts containing thirteen million people, materially diminished the consumption of cottons. It is therefore not surprising that the import of these goods was not, during 1861, as great as that of the previous year. Neither could the Lancashire weavers expect to augment largely their export of twist and yarn, when the demand for woven fabrics was nearly doubled. The Hindoos require less twist and yarn in proportion as they increase their import of cloth; so that a lessened traffic in twist might have been anticipated.

About one-third in value of the merchandise exported from India goes to Britain; the same amount to China; and

* Parliamentary Paper, (Commons), March 7th, 1862.

the

MANUFACTURES AND PRODUCE OF THE UNITED KINGDOM EXPORTED TO INDIA (INCLUDING SINGAPORE AND CEYLON).

Specification.*		1827.*	1836.*	1846.*	1856.*	1860.†	1861.
Cotton Manufactures, declared value	£.	1,396,146	2,020,343	3,254,141	5,509,050	10,615,424	10,103,109
Cotton Yarn, quantity	lbs.	3,063,556	6,592,310	24,193,923	25,244,086	30,723,214	24,650,748
„ Declared value ..	£.	273,990	561,878	1,087,744	1,175,785	1,810,312	1,515,227
Woollen and Worsted Stuffs, quantity	pieces	13,742	23,809	27,676	45,765	45,671	34,951
Woollen and Worsted Stuffs, declared value	£.	28,304	57,200	67,177	82,297	83,433	70,884
Woollen Manufactures, exclusive of Stuffs, declared value ..	£.	282,719	267,471	170,769	238,218	290,845	322,335
All other Articles, declared value	£.	1,680,853	1,378,937	1,854,625	4,802,089	6,507,589	5,912,212
Aggregate of British Produce and Manufactures Exported, declared value	£.	3,662,012	4,825,829	6,434,456	11,807,439	19,307,603	17,923,767

* From Parl. Paper. (Commons), xxxviii., 21 June, 1859. The year 1827 is the first year for which returns in this form have been rendered.
† From Annual Statement of Trade and Navigation of United Kingdom, prepared by Board of Trade.

the remainder to our various colonies and to foreign States. To France, the value is about one million five hundred thousand pounds; the same to North and South America and to the Persian Gulf. Two-thirds of the treasure imported is in silver, and nearly half the amount comes from China. Of the treasure exported, about one-half goes to Ceylon.

With the exception of the United States of America, India is the largest consumer of exported British goods and manufactures.*

Products.

From remote ages cotton has been a staple Indian product. It forms a description of clothing, suitable for the greater part of the population, and is applied to numerous purposes for which flax and hemp are used in Europe. Sails, bags, ropes, bedding, household napery, wadded dresses, quilted tunics, coverlets and various other articles are made of cotton. Allowing ten pounds' weight as an average annual consumption for each of the two hundred million inhabitants, twenty million acres of land, each yielding one hundred pounds of cotton per acre, are required to furnish two thousand million pounds' weight, which is about twice the produce of the United States in its best year.

The progressive demand for cotton in Britain is worth noting; it has increased from five million pounds' weight in 1781 to a thousand million pounds' weight in 1861.

Year		Quantity	Year		Quantity
1781	.. ..	5 Million lbs.	1831	.. ..	288 Million lbs.
1791	.. ..	28 ,,	1841	.. ..	487 ,,
1801	.. ..	56 ,,	1851	.. ..	757 ,,
1811	.. ..	91 ,,	1856 } 1861 }	annual average	1000 ,,
1821	.. ..	132 ,,			

* The annual value of British cotton goods consumed in India is not one shilling per head; in the United Kingdom it is estimated (Mr. Ellison's 'Handbook of the Cotton Trade') at 15*s*. per head; in the British West Indies at 8*s*. 4*d*. per head; in Australia 7*s*. 8*d*. per head; in the United States of America 3*s*. 1*d*. per head. If our West Indian emancipated colonists consume to the amount of 8*s*. 4*d*. per head, it is not unreasonable to suppose that the 200,000,000 inhabitants of India might consume 5*s*. worth per head, which would be equal to a trade of 50,000,000*l*. per annum in one article only.

The computed value of the importations for the last six years was one hundred and ninety-four million pounds sterling, or on an average thirty-two millions sterling per annum.

The sources of supply are the United States, the Brazils, the East and West Indies, Egypt and Africa. In 1818, the East Indies supplied a larger quantity and at a lower price than the United States. But improved machinery for cleaning, the culture of longer and stronger fibre, attention to picking and packing, cheap transit to the coast, and low freights, enabled the slave-owners of the Southern American States to beat Eastern free labour almost out of the market. The Indian cultivator had to contend against an oppressive fiscal system, which not only levied the highest possible tax on cotton lands, but subjected him to capricious exactions; no means of irrigation were provided, no roads or river communications were formed; and his poverty was aggravated by the usurious rate of interest for money (frequently two per cent. a month), consequent on the scarcity of capital and the drain of specie caused by constant remittance to England. The result was that the export of Indian cotton to Britain was reduced in 1822 to four million lbs. at 6⅞*d.* per lb., while that from the United States rose to one hundred million lbs. at 8¼*d.* per lb. Spasmodic efforts were made in India to increase the exportable quantity; and the authorities, after the abolition of the trading monopoly of the East India Company, were roused to temporary exertion. Instead, however, of lowering and fixing the Government taxation on land, granting or selling wastes in fee-simple, making roads to ports of shipment, establishing, or permitting associations to establish, banks of circulation, no means, of these or any other description, were taken for the relief or encouragement of the peasant-farmers. All that was done was to endeavour to teach the American system of culture by sending planters to India from the country which had the most direct interest in impeding the growth of long-fibre cotton in another locality.

The Lancashire manufacturers were as supine as the Directors in Leadenhall Street; the fractional part of a penny in the pound of cotton was sufficient to outweigh all prudential considerations in reference to relying on one source of supply, to silence any scruples of conscience as regarded slave labour, and to stifle any patriotic or just feeling in favour of a section of the Empire whose beautiful hand-loom cotton manufactures and Dacca muslins had been destroyed by the imposition of prohibitory rates of duty on their attempted introduction into England, while at the same time the Anglo-Indian Government had favoured the manufactures of Manchester and Glasgow by admitting steam-wrought fabrics at almost nominal rates of duty into Hindoostan. It is not surprising that in such an unequal contest, and under such an unjust course of procedure as was steadily and stealthily maintained for years, both the planter for export and the manufacturer of delicate muslins and embroideries were ruined. When this was accomplished, and there remained no longer any dread of competition, and when free-trade principles were in the ascendant, the high prohibitory duties on Indian cottons were removed. It was too late to resuscitate an almost extinct manufacture; but there is a Nemesis in trade as in other human transactions; several steam-spinning and power-loom weaving establishments have been formed in different parts of India; and the cotton is wrought near the place of its growth, instead of being sent to Europe and returned as cloth, after traversing a distance of twenty to twenty-five thousand miles. The demand for the produce of these Anglo-Indian mills is increasing; cheapness of labour (twopence a day), warmth of climate, cotton from contiguous fields grown at a rate varying from five to six farthings per lb., abundance of coal, to which may now be added increasing means of irrigation, facilities of transit, and available capital, all tend to promote economical production, and to enhance profits; so that even the present generation may witness the Lancashire manufacturer beaten by his Hindoo competitor.

Within the last few years India has been steadily increasing its export of cotton to England and to China. In 1851, the total export was two hundred and twenty-six million lbs.; and in 1857, three hundred and nineteen million lbs. The quantity sent to the United Kingdom in the latter year was two hundred and fifty-three million lbs.; and in 1861 it increased to three hundred and sixty-nine million lbs.*

Whether the Secession war in America terminate in the separation of the Northern from the Southern States, or in their reunion, the American cotton monopoly is at an end; and the free labour of India, if persistently supported by British wealth, skill, enterprise and good government, will produce at a low price all the cotton that England requires. The Indian article is of a superior description, for it possesses the essential quality of a pure white colour, can be dyed with true shades, is soft to the touch and wears longer than the American or any other cotton; for these reasons it has already obtained a preference in Continental mills, where the machinery is adapted for its use; in Switzerland, Germany and France, Indian cotton is largely used. This year (1862), the estimated import of Indian cotton to the value of about twelve millions sterling will render us most material aid in supplying the American deficit. Even should the American blockade terminate, it is expected that in 1863 the production of cotton for export, instead of being limited to Guzerat and a few small places, will be attempted in almost every part of India.†

Wool next deserves notice, for it promises to be a great Indian staple. The English importation has been increasing

* See a valuable work on flax, cotton and other fibre-yielding plants of India, by Dr. Forbes Watson, the Government reporter on Indian products.

† There is a useful article on cotton in 'The Exchange' for April 1862, a magazine well adapted for a commercial epoch.

for the last half-century. In 1820, the quantity imported was under 10,000,000 lbs., it is now upwards of 100,000,000 lbs., valued at ten million sterling. Of the total amount, India furnished 8000 lbs. in 1820; about 20,000,000 lbs. in 1861. Northern India, the Himalaya districts, the famous Shawl plateau and the adjacent Afghan regions, are capable of yielding increasing supplies of the finest carpet and other wool.

Hemp is also becoming a valuable export; in ten years the quantity has risen from two to ten million lbs. *Flax* is still a very small item, but efforts are making to extend the growth of the product in the Punjab, with every prospect of success. It is raised in the Goojranwalla district at eight rupees per maund, or about twenty pounds per ton, and was purchased at Dundee at the rate of from thirty-five to forty-five pounds sterling per ton. The cost of transit from Lahore to Kurrachee, the port of shipment, was about eight pounds per ton. Allowing five pounds per ton freight and charges to Europe, a moderate profit would remain. With extended cultivation and reduced cost of inland transit, a valuable flax-trade may arise. Some flax produced in the Punjab has been valued in England at fifty-five to sixty pounds per ton. A fine species of Himalayan hemp, by some considered identical with the Rheea grass of Assam, or China grass of commerce, would yield thirty pounds per ton in England.

Silk.—England requires about 13,000,000 lbs. per annum of the raw material, valued at ten millions sterling, of which India contributes only 1,500,000 lbs. This export has not recently risen in quantity or in quality. Bengal and the lowlands are too hot for the worm, but the strong silk produced in the highlands is much valued in Europe.

Coffee has increased from 140,000 lbs. exported in 1836, to 4,500,000 lbs. in 1860.

Linseed exhibits rapid progress. A few years since the East India Company sent out linseed oil in large quantities, for painting, being ignorant that the seed was sold in every Native bazaar. At the time of the Crimean war, the Russian supply being cut off, a stimulus was given to the cultivation of linseed in India, and in consequence, out of the 250,000 tons imported into the United Kingdom in 1861, India yielded 100,000 tons.

A fair remuneration for one or more articles will encourage rivalry in the cultivation of other crops, and in time Hindoostan may supplant Virginia in supplying *tobacco* for the English market. The plant is extensively grown throughout India, and is of good quality, but hitherto little care has been given to its curing and preparation for export. It is impossible to say to what extent profitable returns may stimulate the export of tropical products, for which there is a large and increasing demand throughout the civilised world, and for the supply of which, Bengal, Bombay and Madras possess every variety of climate and soil, with abundance of skilled labour. Such mutations of commerce every age has more or less witnessed; and they are on the whole beneficial to mankind by preventing monopoly, averting stagnation of trade, calling into existence not only fresh markets, but new and improved classes of producers, and thus giving a healthy stimulus to numerous branches of mercantile and scientific pursuits. Europe, and even America, may derive great advantage from the re-awakening life of Eastern commerce; while England secures in India a widely expanding mart for her numerous manufactures beyond the reach of foreign tariffs or hostile armaments.*

European skill and capital have created an extensive and

* Two large volumes on the 'Mineral, Vegetable, and Animal Kingdoms, Useful Arts and Manufactures of India,' were printed and published at Madras in 1857, by Edward Balfour, surgeon in the Madras army. The work is a commercial, industrial and scientific Cyclopædia not only of India, but of Eastern and Southern Asia; it must have required enormous reading and research, and is, in the words of the Preface, "a useful and opportune addition to Asiatic literature."

lucrative traffic in indigo. In Bengal and in the North-West Provinces there are three hundred and forty "indigo concerns," comprising upwards of one thousand factories, scattered over the face of the country.

The indigo exported from Calcutta in 1858-59 amounted to one hundred and six thousand and eighty-seven maunds, of which Bengal yielded forty thousand seven hundred and sixty-three; Behar, thirty-two thousand six hundred and sixty-nine; North-West Provinces, twenty-one thousand six hundred and forty-three; and Native cultivation, from all parts, ten thousand nine hundred and eighty-two maunds. There are also factories recently established in the Madras Presidency which yielded, between 1851 and 1859, about twenty-five million pounds.

Disputes between the European indigo-planters and the ryots, or small cultivators of Bengal, are of long standing. They arise chiefly from the system practised throughout India, of advancing money for any special cultivation, which tempts the farmers to avail themselves of the defective state of the law of contracts, and the difficulty of enforcing agreements by evading the supply of an article partly paid for beforehand. The planters on their side are tempted to resort to violence to enforce the fulfilment of the stipulation which provided for a certain supply of the indigo-plant at a given time; the ryot resists sometimes by force, sometimes by selling and delivering to B. that which A. had previously bought. To put a stop to these proceedings, the Government have at length nominated Special Commissioners to inquire into the subject, by whom voluminous reports have been issued. It is to be noted that, during the rebellion of 1857-58, the European indigo-planters with some exceptions held their ground, remained in their commodious homesteads, and carried on their industrial pursuits, unprotected by European troops, in the midst of thousands of the ryots whom they are said to oppress and maltreat. Doubtless there have been instances of individual injustice; but as a body, the indigo-planters of India are an intelligent, enterprising and humane class, who have conferred great benefit on the districts in which they reside.

Tea has been for several years carefully cultivated in Upper Assam, through the agency of a London Joint-Stock Company. Nearly eight thousand acres of land are occupied with the tea-plant; and the produce for 1859-60 was above twelve hundred thousand pounds. The Company have effected much good: the price of labour in their vicinity has risen from two and a half to four and a half rupees per month; and extensive wastes have been reclaimed.

Government has tea-plantations and a factory at Hatta, where the culture is increasing; and seed and seedlings are supplied to other districts. The Native cultivators and manipulators rival their Chinese instructors: the produce of 1859-60 was above twenty-nine thousand pounds, of which five thousand was green tea. The bulk of the yield is taken by the commissariat for the troops. Two independent tea companies have establishments in the Kangra-Kohistan. About one hundred Englishmen are converting the wastes and jungles of Assam, Sylhet and Cachar into prosperous tea-gardens, cultivated by the Indo-Chinese population; and in Gurhwal, Kumaon, Darjeeling and along the slopes of the Himalaya, numerous plantations are being formed by a few associated individuals subscribing one thousand pounds each, or by joint-stock companies; the Government granting the land to the enterprising capitalists in fee-simple. During the season of 1859 one hundred tons of tea-seeds and two and a half million seedling tea-plants were distributed from the Government plantations.

Upwards of two hundred specimens of tea have been sent to the International Exhibition from fifty distinct tea plantations. Twenty-five samples, which I have received, include varieties of Gunpowder, Pekoe, Hyson, Souchong and Congou, raised over a tract of country extending for a thousand miles between the parallels of 23° and 31° N. lat. In the specimens generally, the "theine" principle is very marked, the odour strong, the flavour delicate, and the leaf well dried without being highly fired. The varieties are quite distinct; suited for different palates and different occasions like the diverse fruit of the vine.

The consumption by all classes of Natives is rapidly on the increase. The profit to the cultivators is encouraging; and Government report that "the time is not far distant when tea will become one of the chief Indian staples."

Wheat will ultimately be a large article of trade; and barley is now raised for the breweries on the Neilgherries.*

Rice is extensively grown in Southern India; and there is a very large export of this grain from the rich alluvial tracts of British Burmah and the eastern shores of the Bay of Bengal. From eighty to one hundred thousand tons are annually shipped from Akyab and Pegu.

In every direction there are indications of progress: twelve silk-filature establishments are at work in Bengal; six sugar manufactories in Behar; iron furnaces are blazing in Beerbhoom, in Kumaon and on the banks of the Nerbudda.

Martaban, Tenasserim, Malabar and other regions, furnish valuable teak and ship-timber. In the neighbourhood of the Hindoostan and Thibet road, beyond Simla, on the northern slopes of the Himalaya, there are vast and almost inexhaustible forests of the finest timber. The trees include the Deo-

* Malt liquor (porter and ale) is sent to India by Government for the use of the European troops: the quantity required in 1859 was, porter, seventy-two thousand five hundred and seventy-two hogsheads; ale, forty thousand three hundred and fifty-four. The total value was more than half a million sterling. The beer is supplied at a low fixed price to the troops; and the loss, about fifty thousand pounds a-year, is borne by Government. The attempt to brew beer in the Neilgherries has not been entirely successful as yet; but the liquor made was on the whole good and strong; and there is little doubt that European skill will eventually succeed in the manufacture in the elevated cool districts.

dar, Gerrardiana, Neoza (edible pine), two oaks (*Quercus incana* and *semicuspifolia*), walnut, maple, hazel, horse-chesnut, *Pinus excelsa* and *longifolia*, and many others. There are two forests at Nachar; one of these contains nine hundred trees, averaging in girth nine and a half feet, and in height one hundred and fifteen feet; maximum girth, twenty-four feet; minimum, four feet: some trees attain the enormous girth of thirty-seven feet. The other forest comprises twenty thousand sound trees, averaging in girth eight feet, and in height one hundred and ten feet. Lord William Hay has proved the possibility of forwarding timber from this locality on slides to the Sutlej river, and thence in rafts to the Punjab.

British Burmah, on the eastern side of the Bay of Bengal, is one of the most promising portions of India.

In Martaban there are not eleven persons to each square mile; and of its six million four hundred thousand acres not one hundred thousand acres are cultivated. The boundaries of this province are still undefined on the north-east in the vicinity of the large river Saluen or Salween.

Amherst, Tavoy and Mergui contain nearly sixteen million acres of rich land, with two hundred and fifty miles of sea-coast and three excellent harbours; yet there are only nine persons to each square mile, and but three hundred thousand acres under cultivation.

The Government Commissioner of British Burmah reports, in 1859-60, that the "soil of these provinces is of surpassing fertility; copious and never-failing periodical rains render resort to artificial irrigation wholly unnecessary: excellent water-communication exists between the chief producing districts and the markets, which are also seaports;" but there is a crying "want of men to cultivate." The highlands on the eastern as well as on the western side of the Bay of Bengal yield every variety of cereals.

A COMPARATIVE STATEMENT OF THE PRINCIPAL ARTICLES EXPORTED FROM BRITISH INDIA TO THE UNITED KINGDOM DURING THE YEARS 1836, 1846, 1856, AND 1860.

PRINCIPAL ARTICLES.	1836.*	1846.*	1856.	1860.	1861.
Coffee	lbs. 140,206	.. ..	lbs. 4,760,838	lbs. 4,645,104	No Returns.
Cotton wool	,, 75,430,234	lbs. 43,177,397	,, 170,771,510	,, 258,079,335	
Cotton goods	pieces 361,580	pieces 300,306	£. 37,138	£. 29,004	
Drugs of all kinds	cwts. 10,035	cwts. 4,193	,, 31,971	,, 30,507	
Dyes { Indigo	lbs. 7,218,901	lbs. 7,583,744	lbs. 8,423,659	lbs. 7,907,857	
Dyes { Other kinds	cwts. 14,208	cwts. 7,714	cwts. 33,268	cwts. 75,548	
Grain { Rice	qrs. 24,700	qrs. 118,447	qrs. 14,050,704	qrs. 557,299	
Grain { Wheat	,, 1,224	,, 683	,, 1,427,119	,, 1,775	
Grain { Other kinds	.. ..	,, 17	,, 233,922	,, 2,834	
Gums of all sorts	cwts. 31,163	cwts. 29,088	cwts. 23,512	cwts. 9,878	
Gunnies and gunny bags	.. ..	.. ..	£. 3,160	Nos. 42,504	
Hides and skins	cwts. 36,223	{ cwts. 97,767 Nos. 156,499 }	,, 271,521	£. 328,750	
Ivory and ivory ware	,, 1,730	cwts. 2,670	,, 79,777	,, 86,022	
Jewellery and precious stones	.. ..	.. ..	,, 7,738	,, 11,939	
Jute, hemp, &c.	cwts. 17,955	cwts. 190,669	cwts. 766,467	cwts. 682,304	
Lac	.. ..	.. ..	,, 26,425	,, 27,787	
Molasses	.. ..	cwts. 50,268	,, 2,750	,, 64,686	
Oils	cwts. 8,683	,, 13,173	galls. 1,637,511	galls. 2,510,558	
Saltpetre	,, 177,938	,, 244,777	cwts. 397,250	cwts. 416,333	
Linseed and seeds of all kinds	.. ..	qrs. 30,852	£. 819,087	qrs. 772,918	
Shawls (Cashmere)	.. ..	.. ..	,, 152,167	£. 201,098	
Silk (raw)	lbs. 1,395,549	lbs. 1,415,353	lbs. 1,344,422	lbs. 1,460,949	
Silk goods	pieces 332,358	pieces 612,736	£. 317,742	£. 146,338	
Spices of all kinds	lbs. 6,344,042	lbs. 7,227,139	lbs. 5,419,576	lbs. 3,833,816	
Sugar	cwts. 152,163	cwts. 1,470,663	cwts. 1,066,125	cwts. 687,490	
Tea	.. ..	lbs. 184,890	£. 22,531	£. 111,106	
Timber and woods	tons 538	loads 8,703	,, 95,247	,, 185,279	
Wool (raw)	lbs. 1,084,479	lbs. 4,570,581	lbs. 15,953,942	lbs. 18,688,328	

* The information for 1836 and 1846 is derived from a statement of Imports from India into the United Kingdom, abstracted from Parliamentary Papers. The other two columns represent Exports from India according to returns received in England. Blanks indicate no returns.

N.B.—Where quantities could not be ascertained, the values of the articles exported have been taken.

The shipping employed in the Indian trade has augmented largely. Its condition, according to the latest returns in England, is shown in the general table on "the State of British India." At Bengal the tonnage inwards has been doubled during the past ten years. The "country" maritime trade is very extensive. At Madras the entries in the several sub-ports for 1859-60 were:—

Districts.	Ports.	Number of Vessels.	Tonnage.
Ganjam	6	430	111,858
Vizagapatam	5	259	88,476
Godavery	3	318	90,769
Kistna	1	355	32,625
Guntoor	4	No returns.	
South Arcot	3	403	31,042
Tanjore	6	335	181,814
Madura	4	No returns.	
Tinnevelly	4	255	26,064
Malabar	10	10,091	337,809
South Canara	4	3,165	91,176
North Canara	5	No returns.	

This will afford some idea of the extent of the coasting-craft on the long sea-line from Sinde to Penang. About two thousand vessels varying from fifty to one hundred tons each, with an aggregate measurement of one hundred and fifty thousand tons, pass through the Gulf of Manaar annually.

The commercial progress of Kurrachee, the sea-port of the river Indus, has been rapid. A few years ago (1843) the trade was very small. In 1859-60 there were eighty-three arrivals of square-rigged vessels and steamers, with an aggregate of about fifty-three thousand tons; of which thirty-four thousand tons were from England, fifteen thousand five hundred from Bombay, and three thousand six hundred from other ports. The entries of country coasting-craft exceeded eighty-one thousand tons. The annual value of the imports and exports at Kurrachee is estimated at two and three quarter million sterling; the sea-custom revenues at about fifty thousand pounds a year.

INVESTMENT OF CAPITAL IN INDIAN UNDERTAKINGS.

The following figures are offered as an attempted approximation to the amount of money invested chiefly by British capitalists in Indian associations:—

	£.
Railroads, about..	50,000,000
Ocean and River Steam Navigation and Irrigation and Canal Companies	6,000,000
Banks	10,000,000
Tea and Coffee Associations	1,000,000
Coal and Mining Companies	500,000
Cotton Companies	1,000,000
Gas and sundry other Co-partneries	1,500,000

Thus, about seventy million sterling are now actively employed under British agency for public purposes. This sum will probably be very largely increased. The income of the wealthy classes in the United Kingdom beyond their ordinary expenditure is estimated at thirty million sterling per annum: investment is sought for this surplus, and in no country can it find such profitable and at the same time safe returns as in British India. Certainly nowhere is the investment likely to be more doubly blessed than in a region where capital and enterprise are essential to stimulate the immense population to bestir themselves and cultivate their fertile soil with skill and energy. Modern science will, through English agency, place in the hands of the Hindoos machinery and manures which may render their agriculture far more remunerative than heretofore; and while cultivation is improved on the already occupied area, it may be extended almost indefinitely throughout India. Sir Charles Trevelyan states that "less than half the cultivable lands in the Madras Presidency are cultivated," * although there are one hundred and seventy-six

* 'Minute' by Sir C. Trevelyan, when Governor of Madras, June 23rd, 1859. (Parl. Paper, Commons), published by command, No. 37, 1860, p. iv.

persons to each square mile of area; and Mr. Bourdillon, secretary to the Government, declares that of one million one hundred thousand leases granted by the Madras authorities, nine hundred thousand were for amounts under sixty shillings each, the average being less than nineteen shillings and sixpence each per annum. Among the forty million inhabitants of the Bengal Presidency, the great mass of the people are (as has been stated) just raised above starvation, and are miserably fed, clothed, and lodged.*

In a country where the wages of free labour are two pence per day, and the farmers are devoid of the most ordinary comforts, there must be great and general poverty. Lord Canning observed in 1856: "I am thoroughly convinced that the condition of the people of Bengal cries out loudly for amendment, and that this amendment is in a great degree in the hands of the Government."† This statement was corroborated by the opinions of the members of Council: and yet Bengal, the garden of India, was tranquilly possessed by the East India Company for a century.

The recent famine in the North-West Provinces revealed rather than created an immense extent of destitution in the districts watered by the Ganges and Jumna. In those provinces there are thirteen million acres of unassessed and waste lands, and two hundred and fifty-seven persons to each square mile.

The Punjab, with one hundred and fifty-seven mouths to the square mile, has eight million acres at the disposal of Government, of which more than five million are cultivable.

In the Bombay Presidency there are large tracts uninhabited, covered with jungle and tenanted by wild beasts. Official reports show that half of Western Berar, and considerably more than half of Eastern Berar (one of the finest

* See 'Eastern India,' or Dr. Buchanan's survey of Bengal and Behar.

† 'Minute,' by Governor-General, October 6th, 1856, on Bengal Missionaries' Memorial depicting the condition of the people.

cotton regions in the world), are unemployed. In fact, there are millions of acres ready to be brought under the plough: so also in Assam, in Pegu, and in Tenasserim, where not one-fifth, and in some places not one-tenth, of the available soil is occupied, and the tillage where practised is but a scratching of the earth. If the waste lands of India were cultivated under the "vivifying influences of British energy and British capital," * India might sustain in comfort four hundred million people,† and become one of the wealthiest regions of the earth.

* Vide Earl of Elgin's Speech to the English Merchants at Calcutta, April, 1862.

† An official estimate has been roughly made of the cultivable waste lands in India, in conformity with the requirement made by Lord Stanley in a Despatch dated 22nd December, 1858, and from that estimate the following statements are derived.

The CULTIVABLE HILL WASTES are as follows:—

Bengal.—The Cossya Hills—Chittagong, Mymensing; the Garrow Hills—Sylhet, Bhaugulpoor, Chota Nagpoor, and North Cachar, afford a "very large area." Cachar has 200,000, and Darjeeling 250,000 acres; Assam (Kamroop), 179,560; Nowgong, 1,205,609; Sibsagur, 1,612,636; Luckimpoor, 1,471,728; and Akyab, 3,152,000—acres.

Madras.—Coimbatoor, in the Neilgherries, has 1,385,845; Salem, in the Sheveroys, 409,046; and Madura in the Pulni Hills, 651,921—acres.

North-West Provinces.—Kumaon has a limited extent suited for tea. Dehra Doon has 204,526 acres; Jubbulpoor, 25,180 square miles.

Central Province.—Gondwana, Mahadeo Hills, has "thousands of square miles" unoccupied.

British Burmah.—Tenasserim has 17,920,000; Martaban, 5,760,000 acres; Pegu has 40,000 square miles of waste land.

Punjab.—Simla, 32,995; Kangra, 16,136; Dehra Ghazi Khan, 24,349; Sealkote, 67,083; Jhelum, 3,279; Dehra Ismael Khan, 474,880; Kohat, 16,479; and Hoshiarpoor, 15,000—acres.

Mysoor.—Astagram has 816,619; Bangalore, 547,139; Chittledroog, 1,365,000; and Nuggur, 188,597—acres.

CULTIVABLE WASTES IN THE PLAINS:—

Bengal.—Baraset, 5,289; Soonderbunds, 809,643; Bulloah, 2,500; Ramree, 1,200,000; Sandoway, 8,000; Burdwan, 680; Hooghly, 139; Midnapoor, 3,247; Dinajpoor, 25,681; Moorshedabad, 1,189 acres; Bagra has a large unused tract.

Madras.—Ganjam, 12,461; Vizagapatam, 3,100; Rajahmundry, 172,259; Masulipatam, 2419; Guntoor, 479,774; Nellore, 417,221; Cuddapah, 2,536,747; Bellary, 3,458,820; Kurnoul, 379,434; Chingleput, 499,075; Arcot, N., 426,128; Arcot, S., 949,215; Tanjore, 145,316; Trichinopoly, 620,847; and Tinnivelly, 785,933—acres.

It can scarcely be supposed that such a country will remain for a long period an appanage to a small island in Europe. British statesmen are bound by principles of justice —by the dictates of humanity—by sound, ay, even by selfish policy—to prepare the people of India for independence, and avert, if possible, their becoming subject to any other European State, or being desolated by internal anarchy and internecine wars.

Many years must necessarily elapse before the millions of heterogeneous race in Hindoostan can be fused into national unity; but prejudices of caste, of creed and custom may ultimately yield to the humanizing influences of a higher civilization than has yet been experienced in the East; and the extension of the English language, laws and institutions, may prepare all classes for rational freedom and self-government, either under one or several monarchies, or under federal commonwealths. But, whatever the Supreme Ruler of Nations may decree—whatever be the future condition of Britain or of Hindoostan—whatever be the relation in which they may stand to each other in this or in subsequent centuries—the present responsibility of England is great, and the policy adopted towards India must be fraught with momentous consequences to both countries. It is believed that

Bombay.—Sholapoor has 414,433; Rutnagherry, 5,902; Dharwar, 178,847; Poona, 141,192; Belgaum, 218,542; Sattara, 331,315; Ahmedabad, 218,415; Kaira, 73,846; Broach, 8,000; Surat, 95,410; Tanna, 8,552; and Candeish, 1,635,666—acres.

Sinde.—The whole of the frontier districts are cultivable waste, except 2,028 square miles.

Punjab.—Umballa, 13,917; Jullundur, 1,136; Lahore, 225,057; Goojranwallah, 174,357; Ferozepoor, 399,414; Umritsur, 16,505; Goojerat, 64,196; Shahpoor, 574,309; Mooltan, 1,510,388; Jhung, 1,737,571; Googaira, 1,636,242; Moozufferghur, 17,134; Leiah, 1,750,000; Hissar, 1902; Jhujjur, 11,925; Sirsa, 467; Rhotuck, 2,375—acres.

Oude.—Seetapoor, 8,500; Duriabad, 5,731; Hurdui, 29,327; Baraitch, 98,300; Gondah, 98,340; and Mahomdee, 188,045—acres.

Hydrabad and Nagpoor.—Berar, W., 544,475; Berar, E., 565,741; Nagpoor, unknown; Raepoor, 493,384; Chanda, 32,707; Chindwarrah, 2,000 acres.—'*Madras Almanac*,' 1862, pp. 120-121.

the new and juster Anglo-Indian policy, inaugurated with the actual supremacy assumed by the Crown, is already producing useful results; and it is hoped that this change is intended to prelude still greater reforms than those already initiated, and to lead to the gradual extension of municipal rights and the concession of electoral privileges to the wealthy and educated classes of society; so that European and Hindoo may, in Representative and Hereditary Assemblies, vie with each other in improving the condition of the great bulk of the people.

There is now no distinction between the white and coloured man—both stand equal before the law. They sit side by side in Legislative Councils; they administer justice from the same Bench; they co-operate in the affairs of Government, and there is a similarity of feelings, of duties, privileges and rights, such as has not heretofore existed, and which no "Morganatic" alliances of the early days of Clive could engender. It is true that this assimilation is as yet restricted in its sphere. Time is necessary for its full accomplishment; but when the wise principle which has admitted Hindoo, Seik, Mohammedan and Parsee to seats in Council, shall be carried through the gradations of public offices, and permeate the habits of social life, its beneficial working will be more and more extensively manifested among all classes. And let it be remembered that the dominancy of a caste, whether distinguished by race, colour, creed or political status, operates injuriously for the oppressors as well as for the oppressed. Hitherto the English officials, civil and military (with some noble exceptions) have treated the people of India as an inferior race. This pernicious and demoralizing feeling is passing away. The new European functionaries are men of high education, taken from every grade of society in Britain, with no privileges except those inseparable from official position; and they are brought into association with intelligent and gentlemanly Hindoos from the very outset of their career. On the other hand the spread of education throughout the

Indian community, the emulation created by the contest for University honours, and the instruction imparted in medicine, in surgery, in engineering, and in the highest branches of human knowledge, will year by year raise the tone of Native society, and enable the upper classes of both races to meet on a more equal footing, divested of the jealousies and prejudices which have heretofore hindered their friendly intercourse. The rapidly extending use of the English language indicates the progress of an intellectual civilization which, if established in India, must exercise a material influence throughout the neighbouring countries; over Persia, to the very borders of the Caspian sea on the north-west; over Khorassan, Afghanistan and Bokhara onwards to the fine regions watered by the Oxus and thence to the sea of Aral and its tributaries on the north; over Budeshaon and Kokan to the steppes of the Kirghis in Central Asia; over Nepaul and Thibet, to the almost unknown districts of the Upper Yang-tze-kiang and the regions contiguous to China, Russia, and Independent Tartary; and over Burmah, Siam, and Cochin-China to the east. With the Ganges and Indus traversing India, from opposite quarters each for a thousand miles from the ocean to the Himalaya; with a caravan-road from Simla to Chini across the Snowy mountains; with the Bamian and other passes rendered easily available; and with the Irrawaddy and the Saluen rivers navigable by steamboats for many hundred miles, British commerce may find new and profitable outlets; and Manchester, Leeds, Glasgow, Belfast, Birmingham, Sheffield, and other manufacturing communities discover a latent value in the possession of Hindoostan second only to that which its internal resources afford. Every year of tranquillity and good government in India, by giving scope to unfettered enterprise and capital, will promote commercial intercourse with regions as yet scarcely known to us by name; and Asia, where high civilisation flourished during the early history of the human race, but where ignorance and despotism now prevail, may be restored to more than its former greatness. The present generation cannot expect to witness this consummation; but events are concurring to extend the civilisation of Europe over Asia through its southern promontory, and to diffuse the English language and influence from Syria to Japan. The work is even now being done silently, slowly, almost imperceptibly, by British enterprize seeking its own objects, but overruled by Omnipotence for the attainment of higher ends than short-sighted, selfish humanity is capable of conceiving. Of the thousand million people on this globe, nearly seven hundred million inhabit the continent and islands of Asia; of these, two hundred million dwell in India, and three hundred million in China: over both of these countries Britain exercises a paramount influence—in the one by direct government and military control, in the other by commercial and political relations.

England has reason to be proud of the noble career before her in the East, and to rejoice at the opportunity of accomplishing a vast amount of good; and—earnestly endeavouring to fulfil her arduous duty, may well confide to Him whose Providence is over all, that future which, though hidden from mortal ken, is certain, soon or late, to manifest results in accordance with the universal law, that what men or nations sow, that and that only shall they reap.

NOTE.—Since the preceding pages were printed, EARL CANNING died in London on the 17th June, two months after his arrival in England, and seven months after the decease of his lamented wife.

THE END.

INDEX.